Economic Analysis of Production Price Indexes

This long-awaited work on index-number construction focuses on production indexes, including the deflators that can be used for constructing real output and real input. Fisher and Shell treat separately the different production units: the firm, the industry, and the economy, as well as the different forms of industrial organization: monopoly, monopsony, and competition. Only in the simplest cases is the appropriate theory fully isomorphic to that of the cost-of-living index because of the interlinkages among the various production units. A firm cannot always assume that the behavior of its competitors, suppliers, and customers will be unaffected by price changes and only in special cases can an industry take supply and demand conditions as given.

This contrasts with the cost-of-living index in which the representative consumer is assumed to face fixed prices and no quantity constraints. The approach taken by Fisher and Shell in this book is ripe for extension to the consumer side for analyses that dispense with the single representative consumer in order to measure the living costs of various groups and subgroups of consumers.

Economic Analysis of Production Price Indexes

FRANKLIN M. FISHER
MIT

KARL SHELL
Cornell University

PUBLISHED BY THE PRESS SYNDICATE OF THE UNIVERSITY OF CAMBRIDGE
The Pitt Building, Trumpington Street, Cambridge, CB2 1RP, United Kingdom

CAMBRIDGE UNIVERSITY PRESS
The Edinburgh Building, Cambridge CB2 2RU, United Kingdom
40 West 20th Street, New York, NY 10011-4211, USA
10 Stamford Road, Oakleigh, Melbourne 3166, Australia

First published 1998

Printed in the United States of America

Typeset in Times Roman

Library of Congress Cataloging-in-Publication Data

Fisher, Franklin M.
Economic analysis of production price indexes / Karl Shell.
p.   cm.
Includes bibliographical references and index.
ISBN 0-521-55416-0 (hb). — ISBN 0-521-55623-6 (pbk.)
1.Input-output analysis. 2. Prices. I. Shell, Karl.
II. Title.
HB142.F57   1997
339.2'3—dc21   97-6564
                                                 CIP

*A catalog record for this book is available from
the British Library*

ISBN 0 521 55416 0   hardback
ISBN 0 521 55623 6   paperback

To Ellen and Susan

Contents

Preface

Our subject is the theory of production-price indexes, encompassing both output-price and input-price indexes. These indexes serve as the appropriate deflators for calculating the corresponding quantity indexes, namely real output and real input.

A price index, or index number, is a scalar representation of a list of prices relative to some base value. Why would one ever think about representing a vector by a scalar? Isn't this always a losing assignment? Why not work solely in terms of the most disaggregated model? There are several answers to these questions. First, there is no "most disaggregated model." For every breakdown of apples into their various types, sizes, qualities, etc., there is always a finer breakdown. Second, at highly disaggregated levels, price and quantity measurements are likely to be of lower quality. Hence one might choose to work with more aggregated data while being mindful of the relationship between these data and less aggregated data. Third, the most appropriate economic model might be at a reasonably high level of aggregation. To use such a model requires the use of aggregated data, but it also requires an understanding of the relationship of these data to less aggregated data.

We adopt the *economic* approach to index-number construction, which is based on the theory of the relevant economic unit such as the consumer, the firm, the industry, or the economy. This is in contrast to the axiomatic approach, which posits reasonable properties that an index should satisfy and then finds the class of index numbers (if any) that satisfy the "reasonableness" axioms.

In our first work on index numbers,[1] we analyzed the problems inherent in applying the theory of the true cost-of-living index to a changing environment. Our application was new, but the analysis was based on the well-known theoretical index put forward by Alexander Alexandrovich Konüs in 1924. In our second work on index numbers,[2] we proposed a price index for deflation of gross domestic product. For the fully closed economy, the theory of this index is isomorphic to that of the Konüs index.

In the present monograph, we put forward a more general theory of price indexes for inputs and outputs. We treat separately the cases where the economic unit being analyzed is the firm, the industry, or the economy. We also treat separately different forms of industrial organization – in particular monopoly, monopsony, and competition. Only in the simplest cases is the appropriate theory isomorphic to that of the true cost-of-living index. The theory is typically more complicated because more general production environments naturally arise. For example, only in special cases can an industry take supply and demand conditions as given. Furthermore, a firm cannot always assume that the behavior of its competitors, its suppliers, and its customers will be unaffected by price changes.

This is in sharp contrast to the theory for the cost-of-living index, in which the *representative consumer* faces fixed prices and no quantity constraints. The basic approach taken in this monograph does have possible extensions on the consumer side to the theories of consumer-welfare measures such as the social cost-of-living and the group cost-of-living indexes, where the assumption of representative consumers might not be appropriate. We have not explored the consequences of applying the logic of our present approach to the consumer side.

We began work on this project in the early 1970s. We are grateful to Jack Triplett and the Bureau of Labor Statistics for their encouragement and support of this project until its near completion in the early 1980s. We also thank the National Science Foundation and the National Bureau of Economic Research for research support. Erwin Diewert, Zvi Griliches, and six anonymous referees provided patient and detailed criticisms of earlier drafts. Our colleagues and students at MIT, Penn, and Cornell provided serious criticism, some amounting to "Why do index numbers, anyway?" These guys kept us honest. Tuba Geredelioglu did the technical typing and Xuelin Yang assisted with the technical drawing. Huberto Ennis assisted with the final manuscript.

1. Fisher and Shell (1972, Essay I).
2. Fisher and Shell (1972, Essay II).

We thank our (respective) wives – Ellen and Susan – for their patience over this long period. We are especially grateful to Todd Keister of Cornell for very thoughtful and patient research assistance. Of course, we are solely responsible for the remaining errors.

November, 1996

Franklin M. Fisher
Cambridge, Massachusetts

Karl Shell
Ithaca, New York

1 Introduction

1.1. Index Numbers and Economic Theory

The representation of prices and quantities by index numbers is an indispensable tool of applied economic analysis. The Consumer Price Index (CPI), the Gross Domestic Product (GDP) and its associated deflator, the Producer Price Index (PPI), and the Telecommunications Price Index (TPI) are examples of important economic index numbers. The values of these and other familiar aggregates are publicly announced and debated. Empirical and theoretical studies rest on treating them as well-defined concepts that measure, or at least approximate, magnitudes of economic interest.

The question of what is really being measured by such indexes is important. What are we really doing when we calculate GDP or use the GDP deflator as a measure of inflation? How should we interpret such indexes and statements about them?

At a simplistic level, of course, such questions answer themselves. GDP, for example, is calculated as a Laspeyres quantity index in which the value of current domestic output is valued at base-year prices. GDP is customarily defined in this way, and statements about GDP could be interpreted as being merely statements about this particular Laspeyres index, no more and no less. Correspondingly, the GDP deflator is customarily defined as the corresponding Paasche price index, and statements about the GDP deflator could be interpreted as being merely statements about this particular Paasche index.[1]

---

1. Denote prices and quantities in the "current" period by $p^A = (p_1^A, \ldots, p_i^A, \ldots, p_n^A)$ and $x^A = (x_1^A, \ldots, x_i^A, \ldots, x_n^A)$, respectively. Denote prices and quantities in the "base" period

But such an appeal to custom and definition provides little guidance for the usefulness of these indexes in economic analysis. If one defines GDP as the value of current output in base-year prices, then one needs to ask why this is an interesting number. Why does this index number tell us anything we want to know? There are (at least) two different approaches to this problem. The first – the "axiomatic approach"[2] – begins with a list of appealing consistency properties that must be satisfied by the proposed index or indexes. Examples of frequently encountered axioms are the requirements: that price indexes be homogeneous of degree one in the underlying prices, that the product of a change in the price index and the corresponding change in the associated quantity index be equal to the observed change in total value, and that the relative change in an index from year one to year three be the product of the relative changes from year one to year two and year two to year three. There exists a large literature[3] on such matters going back more than a generation.

The axiomatic approach, however, cannot provide a fully satisfactory answer to the underlying question of what it is that we are trying to measure when we use index numbers. At its basic level, this approach amounts to axiomatizing the intuition behind the construction of aggregates and requiring the resulting aggregates to have reasonable-appearing properties. It does not really address the more fundamental question of the economic theory underlying index number construction. Moreover, the fruit of the axiomatic approach is often merely an impossibility theorem: No index number meets all the reasonable tests.[4] This is not surprising. An index number is meant to summarize in a scalar the information that is typically given by a vector. For example, GDP is a scalar measure of domestic "output" summarizing a vector of the various consumption, investment, and government goods produced by the domestic economy. Hence, any scalar index is unlikely to

---

by $p^B = (p_1^B, \ldots, p_i^B, \ldots, p_n^B)$ and $x^B = (x_1^B, \ldots, x_i^B, \ldots, x_n^B)$, respectively. Some computed price indexes for comparing the current period to the base period can be written as $(\sum_{i=1}^n \xi_i p_i^A / \sum_{i=1}^n \xi_i p_i^B) = (\xi \cdot p^A / \xi \cdot p^B)$, where $\xi = (\xi_1, \ldots, \xi_i, \ldots, \xi_n)$ is a vector of weights. Some computed quantity indexes for comparing the current period to the base period can be written as $(\sum_{i=1}^n \zeta_i x_i^A / \sum_{i=1}^n \zeta_i x_i^B) = (\zeta \cdot x^A / \zeta \cdot x^B)$ where $\zeta = (\zeta_1, \ldots, \zeta_i, \ldots, \zeta_n)$ is a vector of weights. Laspeyres indexes employ base-period weights. Paasche indexes employ current-period weights. Hence, by definition, we have: for the Laspeyres price index $\xi = p^B$, for the Paasche price index $\xi = p^A$, for the Laspeyres quantity index $\zeta = x^B$, and for the Paasche quantity index $\zeta = x^A$.

2. The "axiomatic approach" is also referred to as the arithmetic approach or test approach.
3. See, for example, Eichhorn (1978), Diewert (1992a), Balk (1995), and the references cited therein.
4. For a recent reference, see Theorems 1 and 2 in Balk (1995), but there is a long tradition of impossibility results in this literature.

have all the properties one would like because it cannot perfectly summarize the information provided by the vector of disaggregates.

By contrast, the "economic approach" to index number construction attempts to get at the problem in terms of what economic theory suggests we would really like to measure. In consumer theory, this approach is well established. Konüs (1924) defines the true cost-of-living index – a price index based on the theory of consumer demand that one would ideally construct in a world of complete information. The CPI as actually constructed by the Bureau of Labor Statistics is a Laspeyres price index that gives the costs of purchasing the base-year market basket of goods at current prices relative to purchasing the same basket at base-year prices. The CPI can be taken as an *approximation* to the Konüs *true* cost-of-living index – the relative costs of attaining a given indifference curve (the one tangent to the base-year budget constraint) in the two different price regimes.[5]

The economic approach to the construction of the corresponding consumer quantity index has developed along two distinct lines. The first method notes that if we require the product of the change in the price index and the change in the quantity index to equal the change in total value, then any price index implicitly defines a corresponding quantity index. Thus, if we use the Konüs cost-of-living index, applying this multiplication property[6] gives us an implicit Konüs quantity index. The second method starts by looking directly at quantities instead of prices. Debreu (1951) introduced a coefficient of resource utilization that can easily be recast as a quantity index. Malmquist (1953) developed essentially the same quantity index for consumption aggregation by exploiting a dual interpretation of the true cost-of-living index.[7] This Debreu–Malmquist quantity index is only in special cases equal to the implicit Konüs quantity index; see Diewert (1981a, pp. 174–179) for details.[8]

Just as the economic approach to consumer indexes is grounded in the theory of consumption, the economic approach to production indexes ought to be grounded in the theory of production. Production indexes are abundant

5. Later developments in the economic approach to the construction of consumer price indexes include those of Fisher and Shell (1968, 1972, Essay I) and Pollak (1971, 1981). See Pollak (1989) for an extensive review and analysis of the various issues arising in the theory and application of the cost-of-living index.
6. This property is referred to in the axiomatic literature as the product test, or the weak factor-reversal test. See, e.g., Diewert (1993b, pp. 40–41).
7. For Malmquist, the primal cost-of-living problem is based on the indirect utility function of the consumer.
8. Other contributions to the economic approach to the construction of consumer quantity indexes include those by Pigou (1920), Hicks (1939, 1940, 1975, 1981), and Samuelson (1950).

and important. They are used in the measurement of real output – and its associated price deflator – and in the measurement of real-input usage – and its associated price deflator. However, the economic approach to the construction of production indexes is not nearly as established as it is in the case of the construction of consumer indexes. Indeed, in calculating production aggregates, practice has come before theory, and practice has dominated. Our goal in writing this book is to set forth an economic approach to the construction of production indexes that will illuminate and perhaps guide the construction and interpretation of actual indexes.

This book focuses largely on the construction of price indexes; the implications for the construction of the associated quantity indexes are often left implicit. The economic approach for production quantity indexes was developed by Hicks (1940, 1975, 1981), Samuelson (1950, 1961), Debreu (1951), and Moorsteen (1961). Our earlier book (Fisher and Shell, 1972, Essay II) introduced the economic approach for production-price indexes. This approach has been extended by us and by others.[9] The relationship of the present monograph to the previous literature is as follows: In Fisher and Shell (1972, Essay II), we provided an economic approach to the price indexes used in GDP deflation, and therefore to the measurement of real GDP, built on an isomorphism with the true cost-of-living index. We took the view then – as we do now – that satisfaction of the multiplication property is essential for mutually consistent quantity and price aggregation. For example, we assume that "real output" multiplied by the appropriate "price deflator" equals "money output." Hence, by defining the price deflator we also define real output.

That is, any choice of a price index is also in general a choice of a quantity index. (We discuss the rationale for this later in this chapter.) We considered the case of an entire closed economy, with the production possibility frontier (PPF) defined by fixed factor inputs. In our 1972 essay, we examined neither the possibility of international trade nor the question of deflating output for a production subunit such as a firm or an industry.

Following our work, John Muellbauer (1972) pointed out that a theory isomorphic to ours could be built for the case of input deflation, and he proceeded to do so. However, as we shall later discuss in more detail, the applicability of Muellbauer's work to actual deflation problems is somewhat

---

9. See Muellbauer (1972), Samuelson and Swamy (1974), Archibald (1977), Shell (1975), Fisher and Shell (1979, 1981), Diewert (1981a, 1983b), Caves, Christensen, and Diewert (1982a), and Fisher (1988, 1995).

limited. Note that the characterization of a PPF by fixed factor supplies has as its parallel the characterization of an isoquant in terms of the production of a fixed vector of outputs. Since Muellbauer's (isomorphic) theory uses isoquants in the way our earlier work uses PPFs, this means that his proposed index number is designed to answer the question: What is the relative input usage required to produce a fixed output vector under two different regimes? Since firms and industries (and economy-wide production systems) usually do not face fixed demand vectors, this treatment is too narrow. (An exception is the special case of the single-output, competitive firm. In fact, our first example below is based on this special case.)

To find a more applicable input deflator, we must consider wider (and more realistic) constraints on the production unit than that of a fixed vector of outputs. Consider – for concreteness – the important and relatively simple case of the competitive firm. The demand conditions that the competitive firm faces are described not by a vector of fixed output quantities but by a vector of fixed output prices. Hence the input deflation and input-usage problems for competitive firms ought to be analyzed based on the assumption of fixed output prices. (If the firm sells its output in a noncompetitive market, then it is constrained by the demand conditions in that market. Generalizations of the analysis to noncompetitive cases are discussed in succeeding chapters.)

These remarks immediately suggest a necessary generalization of the closed economy, output-deflation analysis of Fisher and Shell (1972, Essay II). A single competitive firm does not face a fixed vector of inputs, but instead a fixed vector of input prices. Hence, for a single firm or small group of firms, output deflation should be isomorphic to the simple input deflation case above. Of course, the same analysis also applies for a small, open economy with factors purchased in international trade.

Moreover, even a large economy may buy some inputs at fixed prices yet face fixed supplies of other inputs. More generally, when analyzing output deflation, one should allow for the fact that inputs may be available to the production unit according to flat, vertical, or rising supply curves. Similarly, when analyzing input deflation, one should allow for the fact that outputs may be sold according to flat, vertical, or falling demand curves. Index number construction and interpretation should be sensitive to the type of economic unit being analyzed (e.g., a firm, an industry, a group of industries, or the economy as a whole) and to the market conditions involved (e.g., competition, monopoly, or monopsony).

Our analysis of price and quantity index numbers for inputs and outputs will also enable us to analyze issues of aggregation over vertically related sectors of the economy. What sort of statement can be made, for example, concerning the extent to which a given industry itself contributes to inflation rather than merely reflecting price changes in its own inputs? Other aggregation questions can be asked and answered as well.

In going beyond the Fisher and Shell (1972, Essay II) and Muellbauer (1972) studies of production price indexes, we dispense with the restrictive assumption of a representative producer facing fixed input prices or fixed output prices.

On the demand side, dropping the assumption of the representative consumer would make possible a theory of group and social cost-of-living indexes parallel to that developed here on the supply side for (say) industries and the economy. Consumer groupings that would be interesting include income groups, age groups, urban versus rural, family-status groups, and so on. Some of these groupings could be theoretically similar to the production groupings we analyze, but others appear to be quite different. Hence, even though our general methods are likely to be helpful on the consumer side, the precise applications are not likely to be immediate analogies of the results in the present monograph.

In the remainder of this chapter, we introduce general principles for constructing price and quantity indexes for both inputs and outputs. We also relate these production indexes to efficiency indexes and productivity measures. In Chapter 2, we focus on the theory of output deflation and the measurement of real output. We examine both the closed economy case of Fisher and Shell (1972, Essay II) and the more general cases indicated above. Only the principles of index construction are discussed in this chapter; comparative-statics analysis is postponed until Chapter 3. The parallel analysis of input and input-price measurement is introduced in Chapter 4. Chapter 5 is devoted to the corresponding comparative-statics theorems. We analyze aggregation in Chapter 6.

1.2. Actions or Reactions? Quantity Versus Price Effects

The index number problems that we shall address have the following structure in common. Some "dollar" (or "money") magnitude changes. It is desired to separate the change into its price component and its real component. Thus, for example, the money value of output is observed to increase.

How much of that change is the change in real output and how much is the inflationary (or deflationary) effect? Similarly, when money expenditures on inputs rise, we may wish to speak of the extent to which this is simply due to changes in factor prices and the extent to which it represents a real increase (or decrease) in the use of resources. In the case of the consumer indexes (not considered explicitly in this monograph), a change in money income is to be separated into its price-level component and its real-income component. Note that the very nature of these questions suggests that the price and quantity indexes we choose should satisfy the multiplication property.

In all such examples, it is natural to think of the price effect as coming from changes on the side of the market being studied as faced by the production unit under analysis – for example, supply prices for factors in the case of input deflation, demand prices for goods in the case of output deflation, and supply prices for goods in the case of the consumer price index. Any change in real magnitudes must involve an action on the part of the production unit which is different from that which would have been observed had the unit, with other circumstances unchanging, been faced with the price changes.

An example will make this clear. Consider a competitive firm producing a single output. A change in costs is to be apportioned between the *factor-price effect* and the *real change in input usage*. If we consider factor-price changes as coming from outside the firm, then it is natural to ask what would have happened to costs had the other circumstances of the firm remained constant. Clearly, this amounts to asking what effect the changes in factor prices would have had if the firm had remained on the same production isoquant as in the base period. This change is the price effect. The remaining change in costs represents the real change.

There is no reason, however, that we must restrict ourselves in the above analysis to focusing on the firm's actual base-period isoquant. We could choose any conceivable isoquant through the base-period input vector as our reference. We would then say that the change in costs associated with a move along this isoquant is the pure price effect. The proper choice of the reference isoquant is a very important issue. It is discussed in detail in the following chapters.

There is another way to think about this. Any solution to the problem of measuring real aggregate input use must begin with an answer to the question: Since we shall be reducing input vectors to index-number scalars, and since we wish to obtain a complete ordering for the resulting scalars and the input vectors they correspond to, how must we choose a set of equivalence classes for input vectors such that all vectors in the same equivalent class will be said to involve the same aggregate input?

The above reasoning suggests starting with the reference isoquant as one equivalence class. We can then construct the equivalence class for any given point by scaling this isoquant up or down, keeping it parallel along rays from the origin, until it passes through the point. We will then say that another input vector involves greater or lesser aggregate input use as it is above or below the scaled isoquant. If factor prices change and the firm remains on the reference isoquant, then any change in money input costs will be considered as a pure price phenomenon.

The case of output deflation and measurement is similar. Here the prices that are to be taken as given from outside the production unit are those for output. The situation of the production unit itself is represented by a reference production possibility frontier, or PPF. It is natural to take the response to the new prices that would have occurred with this PPF as the money (or price) effect and any other change in the value of output as the real output effect. Thus, the given PPF defines an equivalence class: All output combinations on it are real output equivalent.

Obviously, this theory is isomorphic to the theory of the consumer price index, in which the consumer faces prices as given from outside and for which the equivalence classes are based on indifference surfaces: All consumption bundles on an indifference surface are utility-equivalent, or consumption-equivalent.

Returning to production, it should be remarked that matters are not always so simple. For one thing, the production unit might have monopoly or monopsony power, so that prices cannot be taken as given from outside. We analyze the role of market power in production index-number construction in succeeding chapters. The expanded theory generalizes the theory based on competitive markets. For example, in the case of output deflation and a firm with monopoly power, output prices cannot be taken as given, but demand conditions can. A change in the value of output can then be separated into the change that would have taken place had the production unit merely responded to altered demand conditions and the remaining effect – the real change in output.

In each of these situations, we separate the aggregate dollar change into its price effect – those caused by the other side of the market being studied – and its real effect – the remaining actions of the productive unit being studied. However, the case of monopoly or monopsony points out the somewhat artificial nature of such a division. After all, when we study a unit as large as the entire productive system, the prices at which outputs can be sold will not be independent of the actions of the production system itself, even if no monopoly power is involved.

The underlying cause of this problem is simple. The division of a change in money value into a single measurement of price change and a single measurement of quantity change is necessarily arbitrary. In the true world of general equilibrium effects, no such division is truly possible. Instead, all we can do is to ask "what if" questions. In particular, if we wish to examine the production sector, we can ask what would have happened if the production sector characterized by the reference isoquant had faced different prices (or demand conditions). Answering such questions provides insight into whether the capacity of the production sector has increased or decreased. Similarly, we can analyze the same change in money output in terms of the consumption sector. We can ask what would have happened had the consumption sector faced different prices (or, more generally, different supply conditions). Answering such questions provides insight into whether real income has increased or decreased. But, despite the fact that money income equals money output, the two sets of questions are not the same, they do not have the same answers, and each of them involves a different set of hypothetical worlds. (We return to these issues in Chapter 6 when considering aggregation over vertically related sectors.)

1.3. Simple Input Deflation in More Detail

For the remainder of this chapter, we shall focus on a simple illustrative case: the competitive firm that produces a single output and uses two factors. We take the firm's actual base-period isoquant as our reference. This case is instructive: It is more than a mere example, since the concepts that follow generalize to more complicated situations.

The base-period iso-output locus, or simply the base-period isoquant, is drawn in Figure 1.3.1. Let $\hat{w} = (\hat{w}_1, \hat{w}_2)$ be the vector of base-period factor prices. The slope of the solid line is $-\hat{w}_1/\hat{w}_2$. The factor combination $\hat{v} = (\hat{v}_1, \hat{v}_2)$ is the cost minimizing plan for producing the base-period output at factor prices $\hat{w}$, that is, $\hat{v} = (\hat{v}_1, \hat{v}_2)$ minimizes the cost,

$$C = \hat{w} \cdot v = \hat{w}_1 v_1 + \hat{w}_2 v_2,$$

subject to the constraint that v be on the isoquant. The minimum cost is denoted by $\hat{C}$.

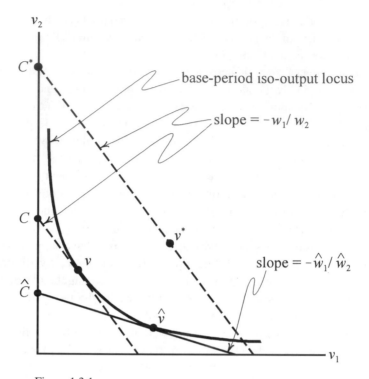

Figure 1.3.1

In the current period, factor prices are $w = (w_1, w_2)$. Each of the dashed lines has slope $-w_1/w_2$. Actual factor usage in the current period is $v^* = (v_1^*, v_2^*)$ and actual factor cost is $C^* = w_1 v_1^* + w_2 v_2^*$. For simplicity in using simple diagrams, assume that the second factor is the *numéraire*,[10] so we can set

$$w_2 = \hat{w}_2 = 1.$$

This implies that the intersection of each cost line with the vertical axis gives the factor two (or "dollar") value of input bundles along that line.

This polar case is easily handled. Had factor prices been w instead of $\hat{w}$ in the base period, the output corresponding to the base-period isoquant would have been efficiently produced with inputs v rather than with inputs $\hat{v}$ and money costs would have been C rather than $\hat{C}$. Consider the following

---

10. Actually, the second factor can be interpreted in these diagrams as "commodity money." This interpretation does not generalize.

identity:

$$(C^*/\hat{C}) = (C^*/C)(C/\hat{C}). \tag{1.3.1}$$

The term on the left is the ratio of current-period dollar factor cost to base-period dollar factor cost. The view of input deflation that we are taking here is that the first term on the right (C^*/C) represents relative real factor usage between the current period and the base period, while the second term on the right $(C/\hat{C})$ represents the ratio of factor prices. The term (C^*/C) is the real effect and the term $(C/\hat{C})$ is the money effect.

Let the firm's cost function be $C(w, x)$, where x is output. The construction just given uses base-period output, $\hat{x}$, and calculates the deflator for money input costs as $(C(w, \hat{x})/C(\hat{w}, \hat{x}))$. This deflator is divided into the relative change in money input costs to give the measure of real aggregate input usage relative to the base period.

Obviously, this approach will lead to a theory largely isomorphic to that of the Konüs cost-of-living index (and also to the Fisher–Shell theory of output deflation). In fact, in this case the price index we propose reduces to what Diewert (1981a, p. 168) calls the Laspeyres–Konüs price index. In considering possible objections to the theory being advanced, therefore, it is well to consider what those same objections imply about the relatively well-established theory of the cost-of-living index. Consideration of such objections leads to insight as to what is involved in the present analysis.

The first objection is conceptual. The procedure just described treats input vectors as identical if they are on the same (constructed) isoquant and treats a movement to a higher-numbered isoquant as an input increase. But we are trying to build a theory of input aggregation and measurement. Is it not odd that levels of outputs become central to the theory? Moreover, different firms with different technologies facing the same set of input prices will have different factor-price deflators constructed for them.

The answer lies in consideration of the object of the exercise. We are treating the firm as the entity of interest, with factor prices given from outside. Any production-theoretic view of input deflation must involve the production function of the firm. Just as the cost-of-living index describes price changes from the point of view of the individual consumer, so the production-theoretic input-price index describes factor-price changes from the point of view of the individual firm. The fact that different firms have different points of view, so to speak, is not a valid objection. The aggregation problem it points to cannot be solved by choosing a firm-independent measure of input prices. To do that is merely to impose on all firms a measure not relevant to any of them.

We make two more comments on this before proceeding. First, from the point of view of the input-producing sector (which could also be made up of firms if inputs are intermediate products), the construction of an index of prices for its *outputs* ought not to depend on the production functions of its customers. However, that enterprise is a different one, with price changes taken as originating in the purchasing sector. Here, in the case of input deflation, price changes are taken as originating in the selling sector. This is consonant with the general view of price and quantity indexation taken above. The relation between the two different questions and their answers is considered in Chapter 6.

Second, the fact that the production-theoretic input-price index will be different for firms with different production functions does not imply that nothing can be said about the nature of such dependence. On the contrary, interest certainly attaches to the way in which such indexes change as the production function varies over firms or over time. Such matters are treated in our comparative-statics analysis in Chapter 5.

1.4. Homogeneity and Related Properties[11]

The second objection to the approach we have taken is somewhat more troublesome – at least at first glance (and here the axiomatic and economic approaches to index-number construction may appear to collide). Suppose that input prices change but that the usage of every factor changes in the same proportion, so that the actual input vector in the current period is on the ray through $\hat{v} = (\hat{v}_1, \hat{v}_2)$ in Figure 1.4.1. Suppose, for example, that the usage of every input exactly doubles to $v^* = (v_1^*, v_2^*) = 2\hat{v} = (2\hat{v}_1, 2\hat{v}_2)$. It is evident that our production-theoretic view taken here does not lead to a doubling of the measure of real-input usage. As the isoquants are drawn in Figure 1.4.1, "real-input usage" increases by more than a factor of two, since we have

$$(C^*/C) > 2.$$

It is easy to see that this inequality is no accident. The Paasche quantity index bounds the production-theoretic input-quantity index from below.

11. This section and the following one draw heavily on the work of Fisher (1988). Note, however, that some improvements have been made in Theorem 1.5.1.

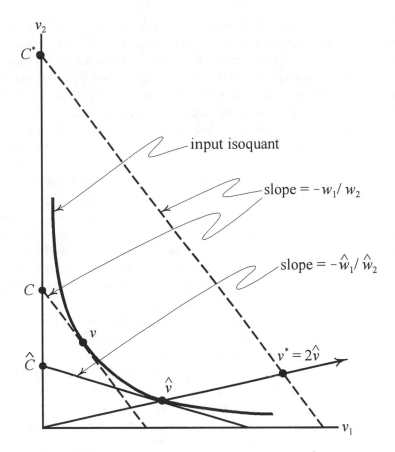

Figure 1.4.1

Moreover, if relative prices have changed from one period to the next and the reference isoquant is smooth and strictly convex to the origin, this bound is strict. Here, the Paasche quantity index $(C^*/(C^*/2))$ is obviously equal to 2. Hence the production-theoretic index of aggregate input usage is not homogeneous of degree one in the inputs being aggregated.

This objection was made by Diewert (1983b, pp. 1,063–1,071) to our (parallel) theory for the measurement of real output. At first glance, it seems to be a telling criticism. Careful consideration, however, reveals that its force is less than it appears.

Suppose first that the technology is one of constant returns-to-scale and that there has been no technological change between the base period and the current period. Then the isoquant through the point $2\hat{v}$ must be parallel along rays to that through $\hat{v}$. In this case, however, the situation pictured in Figure 1.4.1 cannot occur. In such circumstances, $2\hat{v}$ can be the input point for the current period only if relative input prices do not change. But if relative input prices do not change, then it is easy to see that the production-theoretic approach (like every other sensible approach in such circumstances) will lead to an input-usage index equal to 2.

Now suppose (still with no technical change) that the technology does not exhibit constant returns-to-scale. If the isoquant map is homothetic,[12] the situation pictured in Figure 1.4.1 still cannot occur; in more general circumstances, however, it can. Once one leaves constant returns-to-scale, however, it ceases to be obvious why one would desire an index of aggregate input usage to be homogenous of degree one in the individual inputs. Inputs are important because they are employed in production. Hence the measurement of aggregate input usage ought also to be from the point of view of input employment in production. Without homotheticity in the underlying technology, it is not clear why movements along a ray should play any special role in aggregate input measurement.

If this view that "doubling does not mean doubling" seems hard to swallow, consider the parallel issue that arises in the theory of the cost-of-living index. There is nothing about Figure 1.4.1 that could not apply to that theory with isoquants and costs being replaced by indifference curves and expenditures, respectively. Indeed, in the case of the cost-of-living index, there is relatively little interest in homothetic maps and none at all in constant returns-to-scale, so situations such as Figure 1.4.1 are the rule rather than the exception. In such a context, one surely hesitates to insist that a doubling of the consumption of every commodity *must* mean a doubling of real income. Yet the apparent appeal of the homogeneity property is every bit as strong in the consumer context as in the production one – precisely because that appeal does not rest on any consideration of the particular context or the question being asked.

This is, of course, not to say that the homogeneity property may not be an interesting one. The Debreu–Malmquist quantity index in effect asks by what factor the current-period input vector must be multiplied to place it on

---

12. In this simple case, homotheticity means that the production function is a monotonic transformation of a constant returns-to-scale production function so that the only difference between homotheticity and constant returns-to-scale is in the numbering of the isoquants. A more detailed discussion of homotheticity, necessary for more complicated cases, is given in later chapters.

the base-period isoquant.[13] Such a construction guarantees the homogeneity property but concentrates on movements along a ray. Once one leaves homothetic isoquant maps, it is not clear why such movements should be of special interest.

One can think of such a ray-centered construction in a different way. Instead of asking by what scalar the current-period input must be multiplied in order to place it on the base-period isoquant, ask the equivalent question: By what factor must the base-period isoquant be expanded (or contracted) parallel along rays to pass through the current-period input point? Clearly, this amounts to the same thing.

This clarifies the difference between such an approach and the one taken here. The aggregate real-input index constructed in the theory that we are espousing answers the question: By what factor must the base-period isoquant be expanded (or contracted) parallel along rays to become tangent to the iso-cost line at the new prices through the new input point? (See Figure 1.4.2.) Where the isoquant map is homothetic (and unchanging), this construction gives the same answer as does the ray-centered one. Where homotheticity is lacking (or the isoquant map changes), the answers are different.

This difference can be seen in another way. The ray-centered construction takes as its reference vector the point at which the ray through the current-period input point crosses the base-period isoquant. In effect, it begins by asking the question: What would inputs have been in the base period had the firm been restricted to current-period input proportions? By contrast, the production-theoretic index takes as its reference vector the point on the base-period isoquant that is tangent to an iso-cost line, the slope of which corresponds to current-period input prices. In effect, it begins by asking the question: What would inputs have been in the base period had the firm faced current-period prices? Both ways of looking at the problem are interesting, but we believe the approach taken here is more natural for the economic analyst. Certainly it lends itself readily (as the ray-centered approach does not) to an accompanying theory of input-price deflation in which the multiplication property is satisfied. The following section goes more deeply into this matter.

13. In the case of real output measurement this is what Diewert (1983b, p. 1,064) terms the "Malmquist–Bergson–Moorsteen" approach. That paper and Diewert (1981a) discuss these matters and provide extensive bibliographies.

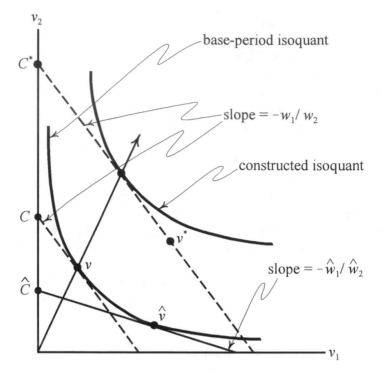

Figure 1.4.2

1.5. A Uniqueness and Impossibility Theorem

As mentioned above, we take the view that every way of constructing a real-input-usage index implies the construction of a corresponding input-price deflator and vice versa. Hence, in considering the properties of any approach to the problem, one must consider the properties of both the price indexes and the quantity indexes, rather than focusing solely on one of the indexes.

Implicit in the idea that homogeneity of degree one in the input vector is a desirable property for a real-input index is the view that a weaker property is even more naturally desirable: The measure of aggregate input should not change if the input vector itself does not change. Parallel to this is a similar statement about the input-price deflator: The input-price deflator should not change if input prices do not change (and, we may add, should be homogeneous of degree one in those prices).

Unfortunately, one cannot have all these desirable properties at the same time, as the following theorem illustrates.

Theorem 1.5.1:

   A. *The production-theoretic input-price deflator and its associated index of real-input use are the only indexes having the following four properties:*

      1. *The relative change in the index of factor prices multiplied by the relative change in the index of real-input usage equals the relative change in expenditures on inputs.*

      2. *With an unchanging technology, a movement along the base-period isoquant leaves the index of real-input usage unchanged.*

      3. *The relative change in the index of factor prices from the base period to the current period is equal to the product of the relative changes from the base period to any other period and from that other period to the current period.*[14]

      4. *The index of factor prices does not change if factor prices remain constant.*[15]

   B. *There is no way to construct a pair of input-price and real-input-usage indexes that satisfy Properties 1–4 and also satisfy:*

      5. *The index of real-input usage does not change if inputs remain constant.*[16]

Proof:

   A. It is obvious that the indexes resulting from the production-theoretic approach have Properties 1–4. Once again consider Figure 1.3.1, now taking the hatted symbols to represent base-period values, the starred symbols to represent current-period values, and the "plain" symbols to represent values for some intervening period. Since v and $\hat{v}$ both lie on the base-period isoquant, Property 2 implies that the index of real-input usage is the same at both points. Hence, by Property 1, the movement in costs from $\hat{C}$ to C is entirely a money effect. Since input prices (as shown by the slopes of the dashed lines) are the same at v as at v^*, Property 4 implies that the price index does not change between those two points. By Property 3, then, the division of the total movement from $\hat{C}$ to C^* into money changes and real changes must be exactly that of the production-theoretic approach. (See Equation (1.3.1).)

---

14. In view of Property 1, Property 3 could equivalently be stated in terms of the index of real-input usage.
15. Property 4, combined with Properties 1 and 3, implies that the production-theoretic input-price deflator is homogeneous of degree one in input prices.
16. Wald (1937) proves that no index number can satisfy Properties 1, 3, 4, and 5.

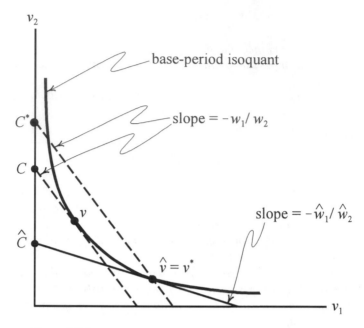

Figure 1.5.1

B. In view of Part A of the theorem, it suffices to show that the production-theoretic approach does not satisfy Property 5. Consider Figure 1.5.1. Here, the technology changes between the base and the current periods, and it just so happens that input usage remains at $\hat{v}$ despite the fact that relative input prices change. (Obviously, this requires a change in the isoquant map.) The production-theoretic input-price deflator, however, will still call the change in money costs from $\hat{C}$ to C a pure price phenomenon and the change from C to C^* an increase in real-input usage. It follows that real-input usage will be said to have changed from $\hat{v}$ to v^*, violating Property 5. ∎

Lest the violation of Property 5 exemplified in the above proof be considered particularly damaging, it is instructive to examine the situation in Figure 1.5.1 again to see the contradiction between Property 5 and Property 4 in the presence of Properties 1, 2, and 3. In Figure 1.5.1, the base-period and current-period input vectors are the same, but prices have changed. Any approach (the ray-centered one, for example) that satisfies Property 5 by having real-input usage unchanged from $\hat{v}$ to v^* must describe the change in costs from $\hat{C}$ to C^* as a pure price-change effect to satisfy Property 1.

Let us again take prices w and inputs v at some other period. By Property 2, real-input usage is the same at v as at $\hat{v}$, so the change in cost from $\hat{C}$ to C must be regarded as a price-change effect. It then follows from Property 4 that the change in costs from C to C^* must also be a pure price-change effect even though no input price changes, thereby contradicting Property 2.

Thus, in the presence of Properties 1, 2, and 3, Properties 4 and 5 are contradictory. One cannot have a situation in which an input-price index depends only on input prices, an input-usage index depends only on input usage, and these indexes multiply in the obvious way while insisting that movements along an isoquant represent no change in input usage. Something has to give. In the case of Paasche or Laspeyres indexes, the missing property is Property 2 – equivalence along an isoquant. In the case of more sophisticated approaches, either Property 4 or Property 5 must be abandoned once we leave homotheticity and an unchanging technology.

Which property should be retained? That depends on what one is trying to do. We take the view that input-price deflation means looking at input prices from the point of view of the input-using unit – the firm, in the simplest case. Those prices are among the givens of this unit's problem, whereas the quantities of input used are functions of those prices. If we wish to form aggregates in this context, it is Property 4 that should be retained. The resulting input-price index should depend only on the input prices; the fact that the corresponding input-usage index will depend both on prices and on quantities merely reflects that input quantities themselves depend on input prices.

We add two points in this connection that may serve to make the argument more convincing. First, we have already seen that the tension between Properties 4 and 5 does not arise until we leave the case of an unchanging, homothetic isoquant map. When we leave homotheticity behind, the case in favor of an input-usage index homogeneous of degree one in the input vector stops being a convincing one. With or without a homogeneous isoquant map, however, the case in favor of an input-price index homogeneous of degree one in the input prices remains convincing. The cost function continues to have that property even when the underlying isoquant map is not homothetic.

Second, consider again the case of the cost-of-living index. For the moment, interpret Figure 1.5.1 as an indifference map. Insistence on Property 5 in this isomorphic context leads to a case in which unchanging consumer prices (shown by the equal slopes of the dashed lines) imply a change in the cost-of-living index. Retention of Property 4, in contrast, does not do this, but it does lead to the proposition that the change from C to C^*

involves an increase in real income despite the fact that v and v^* appear to be on the same base-period indifference curve. Once one realizes that v^* must be on a higher-numbered indifference curve than v according to the current-period indifference map, this property does not seem so odd. Plainly, the same argument must apply to input (or output) deflation and measurement.

Thus, although it might be nice to have both Property 4 and Property 5, this is impossible in the presence of Properties 1, 2, and 3. Given this impossibility result, it seems sensible to us to retain Property 4 and abandon Property 5. Certainly, the implications of an approach that does so are well worth investigating. It is far from a fatal objection that such an approach fails to make the measurement of real-input usage depend only on the input vector and fails to be homogeneous of degree one in the elements of that vector. The reader is reminded that similar analysis and similar results apply to more complicated cases of input measurement and deflation and to output measurement and deflation as well.

Having said all this, we should in fairness point out that much of the comparative-static analysis given in Chapters 3 and 5 is of interest primarily in the case of homothetic technologies. Homotheticity is a leading case for technology, including within it the constant returns-to-scale case. As we have already observed, under homotheticity, if the technology does not change, both the ray-centered approach and the one we propose give the same answers, and the input-usage index we construct does in fact have the homogeneity property. It is only when technology is not homothetic or when technical or other changes act to shift the isoquant map (or the PPFs in the case of output deflation) that the issues we have been discussing apply. Although, as we shall see, such cases are important, they are not universal.

1.6. Efficiency Measurement and Production Quantity Indexes

A *quantity index* is a scalar measure of the "ratio" of quantities in observed situation A to quantities in observed situation B. In efficiency analysis, an *efficiency coefficient* is calculated. It is the "ratio" of quantities in some observed situation to those in an efficient set. Obviously, any method for constructing an efficiency index can also be used for constructing a quantity index and vice versa.

The seminal work on the theory of efficiency measurement is by Debreu (1951). It is no accident that there are many close connections between Debreu's theory and Malmquist's (1953) important work on the theory of the construction of production (and other) quantity indexes. It is a reflection of the close connection between efficiency analysis and production index-number construction.

Just as there are input-quantity indexes and output-quantity indexes, there are also input-based efficiency indexes and output-based efficiency indexes. To be concrete, we will focus on the input case for a competitive firm. Suppose we have an index E_v that measures the efficiency of input vector v relative to a reference isoquant (which we can think of as the efficient isoquant for some given output) and given prices. Then, given two input vectors, $\hat{v}$ and v, we can define a quantity index by $Q = E_{\hat{v}}/E_v$. This says that the index of quantity at v relative to a base of $\hat{v}$ is the inverse of the ratio of v measured relative to the efficient set and $\hat{v}$ measured relative to the efficient set. We take the inverse, of course, because a firm of higher efficiency uses a lower quantity of inputs to produce the given output.

The following two examples show that some well-known efficiency and quantity indexes are indeed related in this fashion. Färe, Grosskopf, and Lovell (1985, p. 53) define the Farrell Input Measure of Technical Efficiency[17] as the factor by which the input vector must be multiplied in order to place it on the efficient isoquant. For the input vector v, this is equal to the ratio of line segments (Ov'/Ov) in Figure 1.6.1.

The quantity index would then be

$$(O\hat{v}'/O\hat{v})/(Ov'/Ov) = (Ov/Ov')/(O\hat{v}/O\hat{v}'),$$

which is exactly the Malmquist quantity index of v relative to $\hat{v}$.[18]

As a second example, we look at the Overall Input Efficiency Measure (p. 64 of Färe et al.), which takes into account input prices. For input vector v in Figure 1.6.2, this index is the ratio of line segments (Ov''/Ov), which is equal to the ratio (C''/C).

The constructed quantity index of v relative to $\hat{v}$ is then

$$(O\hat{v}''/O\hat{v})/(Ov''/Ov) = (C''/\hat{C})/(C''/C) = (C/\hat{C}),$$

which is exactly the production-theoretic quantity index for this example. For the sake of simplicity, we have used the same reference prices for both

---

17. This approach to efficiency measurement originated with Farrell (1957).
18. See Malmquist (1953) for the original exposition and Caves, Christensen, and Diewert (1982a) for further details.

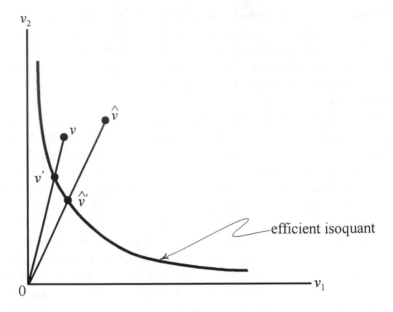

Figure 1.6.1

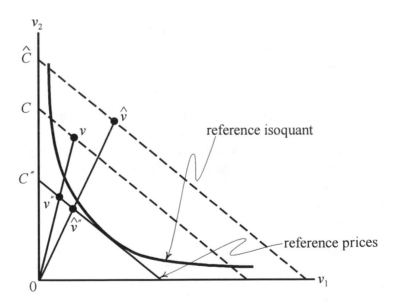

Figure 1.6.2

situations $\hat{v}$ and v, which has made the production-theoretic quantity index somewhat trivial (since the production-theoretic price index is equal to 1). This makes the analysis based on Figure 1.6.2 relatively simple, but this simplification is by no means necessary.

We can also establish a converse relationship. Given any quantity index of an input vector v relative to a base $\hat{v}$, we can construct an efficiency index for v simply by replacing the base vector $\hat{v}$ with the input vector we wish to consider "efficient." Using this procedure with the Malmquist quantity index yields the Farrell Input Measure of Technical Efficiency and using it with the production-theoretic quantity index leads to the Overall Input Efficiency Measure. Thus, there is a one-to-one relationship between input-based efficiency measures and input-quantity indexes. Obviously, a similar one-to-one relationship exists between output-based efficiency measures and output-quantity indexes.[19]

Ray-based indexes are featured in the literature on efficiency measurement, but these are not by any means necessary either for efficiency measurement or for quantity-index construction. What is important is the relationship between efficiency measurement and quantity-index construction. We will show in this monograph how to do quantity-index construction from the production-price index point of view. Using the above relationships, this implies the production-theoretic approach to efficiency measurement. We model particular sources of inefficiency, including monopoly and monopsony, and describe their implications for production-index construction and therefore for efficiency measurement.

1.7. Productivity Measurement

Measurement of economic productivity is important in macroeconomics, growth and development economics, and comparative economic systems. Although there is no single agreed-upon method for measuring productivity, several well-known methods are based directly on quantity indexes. One common measure of the productivity of an economic unit is the ratio of an

---

19. The theory of efficiency measurement was developed by Debreu (1951), Koopmans (1951, 1957), and Farrell (1957). A detailed analysis of Debreu's coefficient of resource utilization and a comparison with other measures of "inefficiency" including those of Hotelling, Allais, and Boiteux can be found in Diewert (1981b). Axioms for the Debreu coefficient are provided by Weinberg (1980). For a complete treatment of efficiency measurement and bibliographies, see Färe, Grosskopf, and Lovell (1985, 1994).

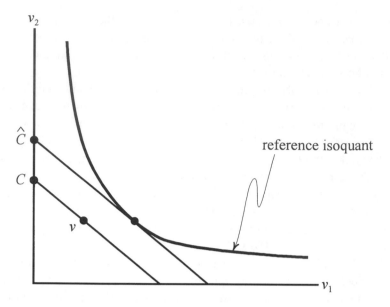

Figure 1.7.1

output-quantity index to an input-quantity index.[20] Measuring productivity change is then simply a matter of measuring the change in this ratio over time.

Another approach is to measure productivity change directly rather than first measuring productivity at a point in time. Solow (1957) and Jorgenson and Griliches (1967) developed measures of productivity change related to Divisia[21] (1926) quantity indexes, which in principle require continuous-time data. Caves, Christensen, and Diewert (1982a) and Diewert (1992b) developed discrete-time productivity change measures based on the Malmquist (1953) quantity index. Using these as our guide, we can construct a production-theoretic index of productivity change as follows.

Like efficiency measures, productivity indexes can be either input based or output based. We will again focus on the input case for a competitive firm. Starting with the production-theoretic quantity index, we make the following substitutions: For the reference isoquant, we now want to use

---

20. See the recent note by Griliches (1996) for references, a history of productivity indexes, and the relation of these indexes to the "residual" from time-series estimation of production functions. Griliches's earliest reference to an "output-over-input" index is Copeland (1937).
21. Divisia indexes were introduced in Divisia (1925) and are examined in detail in Hulten (1973).

the base-period technology and current-period outputs (i.e., the set of input vectors that could have efficiently produced today's output using yesterday's technology). In place of the base-period input vector, we take the point of tangency between this isoquant and the current-period price line; this is the input vector that yesterday's firm would have chosen if it had to produce today's output at today's input prices. See Figure 1.7.1.

We now define the production-theoretic index of productivity change to be $(\hat{C}/C)$; this is the ratio of the cost of producing today's output with today's technology versus yesterday's technology. This approach is similar to that in Caves, Christensen, and Diewert (1982a), with the exception that they use Malmquist quantity indexes rather than an index based on our production-price indexes.

1.8. Other Approaches

As an alternative to estimating or bounding the reference isoquant, the economic analyst may be willing to posit a functional form for the production function (or some other description of technology). One can then explicitly calculate the functional form of the price and quantity indexes that are *exact* for this production function, that is, that give the theoretically correct answer.[22]

Diewert (1976) works with *flexible* functional-form production functions – those that are capable of providing a second-order differential approximation to an "arbitrary" constant returns-to-scale production function. Diewert then defines an index to be *superlative* if it is exact for a flexible functional-form production function. The goal of this approach is to provide approximations to the true index that are better than the standard (i.e., Laspeyres and Paasche) bounds.[23]

The theory of functional forms provides the basis for rather different approaches from ours. When there is confidence in the class of functional forms and there are satisfactory econometric estimates of parameters, the functional-form approach would be attractive. Application of our approach places emphasis on observed input–output combinations and uses these

---

22. The theory of exact index numbers was developed by Konüs and Byushgens (1926), Pollak (1971), and Samuelson and Swamy (1974).
23. See Diewert (1976, 1978b) and Allen and Diewert (1981) for comprehensive treatments. Superlative index number formulas have been widely applied, including in the analysis of regulated monopolies and for incorporating product attributes to handle changes in quality. See, e.g., Fixler and Zieschang (1992) and other articles in *The Journal of Productivity Analysis*.

data to put bounds on unobserved technological situations.[24] Hence, our approach would be attractive for situations in which there have been large changes or in which the local econometric estimates are not very reliable.

If the analyst had a perfect numerical model of technology, there would be no need for bounds. He could always calculate the exact or "true" indexes. It might be agreed further that if the precise numerical model of technology is known with certainty then there would be no need for index numbers. It is precisely when the full model is unknown or uncertain that index numbers and bounds on true index numbers are most appealing.

In principle, there are other circumstances in which index numbers would be unnecessary. These are the rare cases in which perfect aggregation over goods is possible. In this case, one should proceed directly to the aggregated quantities and the corresponding aggregated price.[25] In Chapter 6, we analyze the situation in which aggregate index numbers can be derived solely from the relevant disaggregated index numbers.

Aggregation – perfect or otherwise – is an essential task for realistic economic analysis. It is inconceivable that one would ever choose a model as disaggregated as the data would permit. There would be too much data to comprehend. Furthermore, statistical errors and quirks of definitions could be expected to play a dominant role in overly disaggregated data. This is why some form of index-number construction is desirable and inevitable.

It should be noted that the economy itself performs much imperfect aggregation of commodities and their prices. Not all oranges in any particular supermarket bin are the same. Electricity and other utilities sell their outputs on a time-of-day basis – but typically there are only a few time periods. This means that the electric utility has for pricing purposes lumped together (i.e., aggregated) service over rather long time intervals. The menu-cost approach[26] for explaining the fixed prices observed in macroeconomic analysis is based on the idea that prices do not change too frequently because printing new "menus" or "price lists" is costly. In the terminology of Arrow and Debreu, this amounts to the aggregation by the producer of time-dated goods over (some) neighboring time periods.

---

24. See especially our Chapter 2 on optimistic and pessimistic PPFs.
25. See Appendix A.
26. See, for example, the papers collected in Part I of Mankiw and Romer (1991).

2 Principles of Price and Quantity Measurement: Outputs

2.1. The General Approach

We now consider the application of these general principles to the measurement of real output and the deflation of output prices. The production possibility frontier (PPF), the boundary of the set of technically producible output vectors, plays a basic role in the analysis. At first, we take the PPF as arbitrarily given, but a major part of our discussion is devoted to the questions of how to choose the PPF appropriately and how this choice affects the resulting indexes.

In Figure 2.1.1, the PPF is represented by the outer curve. The region to the southwest of the PPF (shown shaded in Figure 2.1.1) is the corresponding production possibility set (PPS). Production of commodity one is denoted by x_1; production of commodity two is denoted by x_2. Four production vectors are indicated in the figure, namely x^A, x^B, x^C, and x^D. Can these production vectors be ranked? No matter what method of aggregation is employed, the vector x^C clearly represents more output than the vector x^D, because x_1^C is greater than x_1^D *and* x_2^C is greater than x_2^D. No other comparison among the four vectors is so simple. For example, if we compare x^B with x^C, we find that x_1^C is larger than x_1^B but x_2^B is larger than x_2^C.

The technology as summarized by the PPF helps us to sharpen the comparisons of output vectors. Given these technological opportunities, the economic unit that produces x^B could choose to produce x^A and vice versa. The same technology would also permit the production of x^D, but x^D is inefficient in the sense that more of both outputs could be produced by moving northeast from x^D toward the PPF. Since x^C lies to the northeast

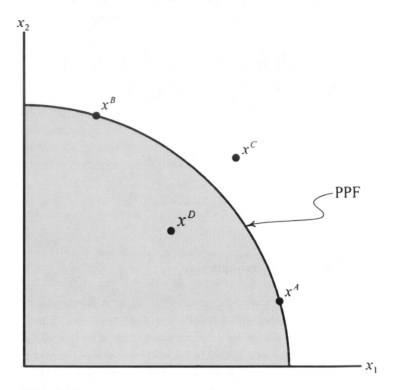

Figure 2.1.1

of the PPF, an economy constrained to the PPF of Figure 2.1.1 would be unable to produce this vector of outputs.

As indicated in Chapter 1, we adopt the position that, *based on the PPF drawn in Figure 2.1.1*, of the four output vectors, x^C represents the greatest "overall" output and x^D represents the least "overall" output. We consider the two output vectors x^A and x^B to be equivalent because each vector lies on the reference PPF, the PPF on which our analysis is based. These output vectors are equivalent in the sense that the economy that produced one could have chosen to produce the other.

We now consider prices and market values. In Figure 2.1.2, we have drawn tangents to the PPF at x^A and x^B. The absolute values of the slopes at x^A and x^B are the efficiency price ratios, (p_1^A/p_2^A) and (p_1^B/p_2^B) respectively, which support the output vectors x^A and x^B. For ease of graphical analysis, we choose the second good as the *numéraire*, so we have $p_2^A = p_2^B = 1$. The intersections of the price lines with the vertical axis then give the respective

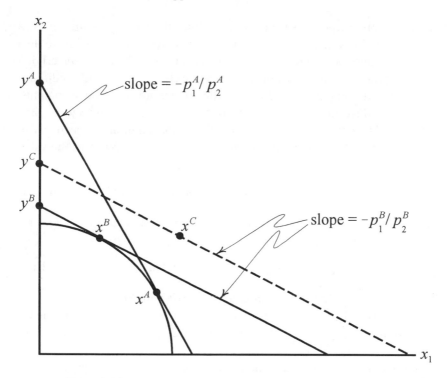

Figure 2.1.2

good-two (or "dollar") values of the outputs, y^A and y^B, at the (normalized) efficiency prices.

Notice that although x^A and x^B lie on the same PPF and therefore represent equivalent overall output, the corresponding "dollar" values of output differ, with $y^A > y^B$. From the point of view of the given PPF, the entire difference between y^A and y^B is a "money" difference. Therefore, if the dollar value of output at x^B, $y^B = p^B \cdot x^B = p_1^B x_1 + p_2^B x_2^B$, is to be compared to the "dollar" value of output at x^A, then the former should be divided by (or deflated by) the scalar (y^B/y^A). Similarly, in comparing the dollar value of the output x^A to the dollar value of output x^B, the deflator should be (y^A/y^B).

As discussed in Chapter 1, this approach to output deflation takes output prices as given from outside the production sector.[1] Output prices are taken to reflect demand conditions; they represent the sales opportunities of the production sector. (This parallels the analysis of the cost-of-living

---

1. We modify this below when dealing with monopoly.

index, where prices reflect supply conditions, the buying opportunities of
the household.) Changes in the value of output along a given PPF are then
treated as pure price effects since they reflect not a change in underlying
resources or technology but only a response to changing demand conditions.

Thus, in the output-price deflation problem, we are *not* given the outputs,
x^A and x^B. Instead we are given two output-price vectors, p^A and p^B, and
the PPF. The output vectors, x^A and x^B, are the solutions respectively to
the problems of choosing the output on the PPF that maximizes the value
of output at each of the given prices. We have

$$y^A = \max_x p^A \cdot x \quad \text{subject to } x \text{ belonging to the PPF.} \tag{2.1.1}$$

Then $x^A = (x_1^A, x_2^A)$ is the maximizing value of x in Problem (2.1.1).
Similarly, we have

$$y^B = \max_x p^B \cdot x \quad \text{subject to } x \text{ belonging to the PPF.} \tag{2.1.2}$$

Then $x^B = (x_1^B, x_2^B)$ is the maximizing value of x in Problem (2.1.2).

Thus, given the PPF, the *production-theoretic price index* appropriate for
comparing the dollar value of output at prices p^A to the dollar value of
output at prices p^B is (y^A/y^B).

For example, suppose that the initial situation is at x^B in Figure 2.1.2,
with prices p^B and money output y^B. Suppose that the situation then shifts to
prices p^A, the output vector x^C, and money output y^C. Then the shift in the
money output from y^A to y^C is broken up into two parts. The first (y^A/y^B)
is the price effect; it is the effect that would be observed if the original
production sector faced the new prices. The second (y^C/y^A) is the change
in real output. It is the latter effect that corresponds to a change in the PPF.[2]

Note that this approach has the following natural property: Suppose that
the two output vectors to be compared lie on the PPF and that in both cases
output is efficient in terms of the PPF (i.e., that p^A and p^B correspond to
the slopes of the PPF at the respective production points). Then the deflated
dollar outputs will be equal, as they should be. Also, any output vector to
the northeast of the PPF will have a larger deflated dollar output than an
(efficient) production point on the PPF. Any output vector to the southwest
of the PPF will have a smaller deflated dollar output than an (efficient) point
on the PPF. Thus, the deflated value of dollar outputs to the northeast of the
PPF will always exceed the deflated dollar value of outputs to the southwest
of PPF, which again is as it should be.

---

2. Of course, this is all based on the initial PPF. A different, but similar decomposition would start
   with the PPF that produced x^C.

2.2. Laspeyres and Paasche Indexes

How does the production-theoretic output-price index relate to the frequently encountered Laspeyres and Paasche output-price indexes? In particular, do the Laspeyres and Paasche indexes provide bounds for the theoretical
output-price index? Do similar properties relate the implied production-
theoretic measure of real output and Paasche and Laspeyres output indexes?
If the PPF is chosen completely arbitrarily, then Laspeyres and Paasche
indexes do not in general provide bounds. However, if the PPF is chosen with care, then bounding properties can be found. We do this in what
follows.

In Figure 2.2.1, the production possibility frontier, PPF^B, is based on
conditions prevailing in situation B. That is, PPF^B is constructed so that
the value line determined by the situation B price vector, p^B, is tangent to
PPF^B at the vector of actual outputs in situations B, x^B. The actual dollar
value of output in this situation is y^B.

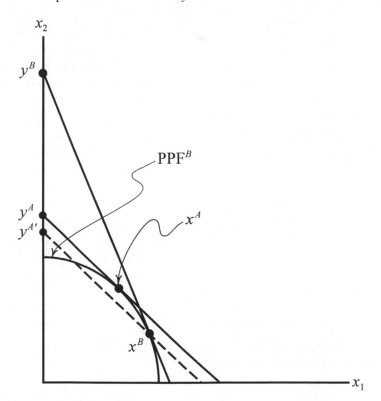

Figure 2.2.1

In situation A, prices are given by the vector p^A. Employing PPF^B, production would be given by the vector x^A (not necessarily equal to actual output in situation A) and money output would be y^A (not necessarily equal to actual money output in situation A). The production-theoretic output-price index based on PPF^B is given by $I^B = (y^A/y^B)$, and the production-theoretic output index is obtained by dividing the relative change in money output by I^B.

If we think of situation B as the base-period situation and situation A as the current-period situation, then the Laspeyres output-price index is $L = (y^{A'}/y^B) = (p^A x^B/p^B x^B)$, since the Laspeyres output-price index is constructed by using base-period output weights. As shown in Figure 2.2.1, $y^{A'} = p^A \cdot x^B \leq p^A \cdot x^A = y^A$, since by definition x^A maximizes the dollar value of output at prices p^A on the PPS formed by PPF^B. Thus, we have $L \leq I^B$, and the inequality is strict if PPF^B is smooth, strictly concave to the origin, and if the prices p^A and p^B are not proportional for all goods produced in at least one of the situations.

Thus, the Laspeyres output-price index understates the production-theoretic output-price index based on the base-period PPF. Because the product of the Laspeyres price index and the Paasche quantity index yields the change in money output,[3] it follows that the Paasche quantity index overstates the production-theoretic index of the change in real output measured on the same basis.

By an essentially identical argument, the Paasche output-price index (i.e., the one based on current-period quantity weights) overstates the production-theoretic output-price index based on the current-period production possibility frontier. The Laspeyres quantity index understates the corresponding production-theoretic index of the change in real output.

Note that the bounding properties of Laspeyres and Paasche indexes are reversed when moving from the case of the relatively well-understood cost-of-living index to that of output-price indexes. In the cost-of-living case, the Paasche price index understates the (consumer-theoretic) true cost-of-living index based on the current-period indifference surface, whereas the Laspeyres price index overstates the true cost-of-living index based on the base-period indifference surface. This reversal of the bounds should be no surprise: In the first case expenditures are being *minimized* subject to an indifference surface; in the second case, money output is being *maximized* subject to a production possibility frontier.

---

3. In symbols, we have $(p^A \cdot x^B/p^B \cdot x^B)(p^A \cdot x^A/p^A \cdot x^B) = (p^A \cdot x^A/p^B \cdot x^B)$. The same property holds for the product of the Laspeyres quantity index and the Paasche price index.

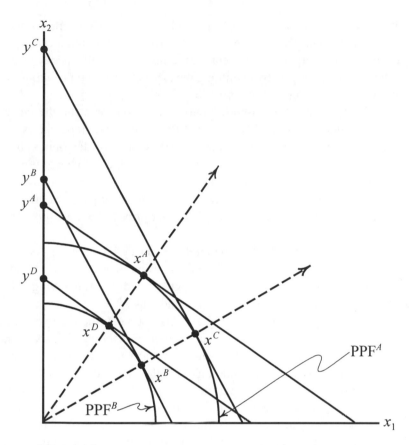

Figure 2.2.2

If the PPF based on the current-period situation is parallel along rays from the origin[4] to the PPF based on the base-period situation, then the production-theoretic output-price index based on the current-period PPF, I^A, is equal to the production-theoretic output-price index based on the base-period PPF, I^B (and the corresponding production-theoretic output indexes will also be equal). In this case, we have $L \leq I^B = I^A \leq P$, where L and P are the Laspeyres and Paasche output-price indexes, respectively.

This situation is shown in Figure 2.2.2. Actual base-period output x^B is the point on the base-period production possibility frontier PPF^B at which the slope corresponds to the base-period price vector p^B. The vector x^D is

4. Hereafter, this is what we mean by "parallel" when speaking of "parallel technologies" or "parallel production possibility frontiers."

determined by the tangency of PPF^B and a line with slope corresponding to p^A, the current-period price vector. Actual base-period money output is y^B, but money output y^D is a theoretical construct; it is the money value of output x^D at prices p^A. By definition, the production-theoretic output-price index corresponding to PPF^B is $I^B = (y^D/y^B)$.

Similarly, actual current-period output x^A is the point on the current-period production possibility frontier PPF^A where the slope corresponds to p^A, the current-period price vector. The vector x^C is determined by the tangency of PPF^A and the line with slope corresponding to the base-period price vector p^B. Actual current-period money output is y^A, but money output y^C is a theoretical construct; it is the money value of output x^C at prices p^B. By definition, the production-theoretic output-price index corresponding to PPF^A is $I^A = (y^A/y^C)$.[5]

Because PPF^A and PPF^B are parallel, x^A and x^D lie on one ray, whereas x^C and x^B lie on another ray. Further, the value lines through y^A and y^D are parallel, as are the value lines through y^B and y^C. Employing similar triangles, we have $(y^D/y^B) = (y^A/y^C)$ and thus $I^B = I^A$.

Although the assumption of parallel PPFs that yields these convenient results is a strong one, it has some basis in production theory. This is because of the important role played by constant returns-to-scale technologies (a special case of homothetic technologies) in the theory of the firm. We provide further discussion of the conditions for parallel PPFs when considering the role of the production possibility maps that generate the relevant PPFs. We do this, not because such conditions are likely to be satisfied in practice when comparing base-period and current-period PPFs, but because our discussion of comparative statics in Chapter 3 builds on such conditions and examines how we can correct for departures from them to restore the double bounding properties of Paasche and Laspeyres indexes when current and base-period PPFs are *not* parallel.

2.3. New Goods and Other Corner Solutions[6]

So far, our analysis has proceeded as though the list of outputs were fixed and the same in all periods. In practice, this is often not the case. New goods appear and old ones disappear. How does our theory suggest that these

5. y^A appears in the numerator because we are comparing current-period prices to base-period prices even though we are using the current-period PPF.
6. This section is based on Fisher and Shell (1972, p. 99–105). The treatment therein carefully distinguishes between goods that fail to be produced for reasons of supply and goods that fail to

changes should be handled? It is easy to see that, provided price quotations exist, there is no difficulty in handling the situation in which the economic unit under consideration does not produce a given good because it is not optimal to do so. That unit will still be maximizing value at the given prices with a given PPF. Nothing in our analysis requires that this imply positive production of all goods.

However, problems do appear to arise when a given good fails to be produced, not because the productive sector being examined decides that it is not worth producing it at given prices, but because there are in fact no price quotations for the good at all. This occurs, in the case of new goods (those produced in the current period but not in the base period), because they had not yet been invented. It also occurs in the case of disappearing goods, which are produced in the base period but are no longer produced in the current period, because they have become obsolete with no price quotations for them available at all. We begin with the case of new goods.

For the production-theoretic output-price index based on the PPF obtained in the base period, the fact that a new good was discovered after the base period presents no difficulties. The question posed when we construct such an index is that of the value of output that the base-period economy would have produced had it been faced with current prices. But the base-period economy could not have produced any of the new good, since the technology for doing so did not exist. Accordingly, one can leave the new good out altogether in constructing the index. To put it another way, the entire increase in the money output that comes from the new good must be considered as an increase in real output; there is no price effect.[7]

Similarly, the nonexistence of a base-period price quotation for the new good is irrelevant for the construction of the Laspeyres price index, which we know bounds from below the production-theoretic output-price index based on the base-period PPF. Since the new good was, by definition, not produced in the base period, its price receives zero weight in a Laspeyres index; it is therefore irrelevant what price is assigned to it. Note that, as

---

be produced for reasons of demand. In the present discussion the first case is taken to be that of new goods and the second that of disappearing goods. The basic distinction lies in whether or not the good was known in the period in which it was not produced.

    The essence of the approach to new goods taken here can be found in Hicks (1940, p. 114). More recent treatments include those by Diewert (1987, p. 779), Diewert (1993b, pp. 59–63), Berndt, Griliches, and Rosett (1993), and Feenstra, Markuscn, and Zeile (1992).

7. Diewert (1980, pp. 500–1) investigates the bias from ignoring the new good in every period in the index relative to the Fisher (1922) ideal price index. The Fisher ideal index is $(LP)^{1/2}$, where L is the Laspeyres Index and P is the Paasche Index.

before, this means that the entire value of the new good's output in the current period will be considered as an increase in real output.

The problem of new goods becomes more complicated (and more interesting) when we consider the production-theoretic output-price index based on the *current*-period PPF and its relation to the corresponding Paasche index, which we know bounds it from above. The productive sector using current-period technology could have produced the new good in the base period. If we had a price quotation for the new good in the base period, then we could proceed as in the rest of our analysis. However, we do not have such a price quotation. Similarly, since the new good is being produced in the current period, a Paasche index will assign the price of the new good a positive weight; hence, it will matter what unobserved (or fictitious) price is assigned to this good in the base period.

We now return to the fundamental idea of the production-theoretic price index. In constructing this index, we take prices as given because they represent the demand conditions – the conditions under which the productive unit being analyzed can sell. We can provide a solution to the new-good problem by observing that one of the demand conditions facing the productive sector in the base period was the fact that consumers did not know that the new good existed (since in fact it did not) and therefore it could not have been sold at any price.[8] In constructing the production-theoretic output-price index based on the current-period PPF, we can therefore consider the maximization problem to be solved when facing base-period prices, given the additional constraint that production of the new good must be kept at zero.

If we proceed in this way, then there is no need (so far as the production-theoretic price index is concerned) to specify a fictitious base-period price quotation for the new good. Nevertheless, one emerges naturally from such a formulation. It is not difficult to see that the shadow price associated with the additional constraint just imposed turns out to be the supply reservation price of the new good given the current technology and the base-period price. That is, the natural price to assign to the new good in the base period is that price at which, given the current technology and the other base-period prices, it would just have been worth producing a very small amount of it.[9]

8. If the good was known but not produced because customers were unwilling to pay for its production cost, the analysis is isomorphic to that given below for disappearing goods.
9. The role of this supply reservation price in the analysis is isomorphic to that of the demand reservation price in the theory of the cost-of-living index. See Fisher and Shell (1972, pp. 22–26).

The same supply reservation price turns up again when we consider the Paasche index problem. The Paasche price index is to bound the production-theoretic price index (based on the current-period PPF) from above. It is easy to see that if we assign to the new good in the base period any price at or below the supply reservation price, then such a bounding property will be maintained. This is because the bounding property comes from the fact that the current output vector is producible with the current-period PPF. Whereas the Paasche index uses in its denominator the value of current output at base-period prices, the production-theoretic output-price index uses the *maximum* value of output that could have been produced at those prices. With the base-period price of the new good at the supply reservation price or below, however, maximizing the value of output at base-period prices would imply not producing the new good. Hence, the value of output at base-period prices when maximized, given such a price quotation for the new good, will be the same as that which is maximized subject to the restriction that the new good will not be produced. This, as we have seen, is the appropriate value to use for the production-theoretic output-price index. Thus, any price at the supply reservation price or below will serve to maintain the bounding property of the Paasche price index.

This does not mean, however, that it is a matter of indifference which price in the indicated range is assigned to the new good in the base period. It is easy to see that the higher the base-period price assigned to the new good, the higher will be the denominator of the corresponding Paasche index and the lower will be the Paasche price index with the appropriate bounding property. Assignment of the supply reservation price itself will produce the Paasche index with the most efficient bound.

The case of a disappearing good is similar to that of a new one but is not entirely identical. A good disappears because consumers are unwilling to buy it at profitable prices. However, it cannot be pretended that consumers do not know the good exists. Indeed, consumers would have been just willing to buy the good at the consuming sector's current *demand* reservation price – the intercept on the consuming sector's demand curve constructed with the prices of other goods fixed at their current period levels. In some cases, this demand reservation price will be zero; in other cases, it will be positive. If we are to take demand conditions facing the production sector as given, then the demand reservation price so constructed seems the appropriate one to use in the case of a disappearing good – both for the production-theoretic output-price index and for the Laspeyres price index that bounds it.

It is not necessary to estimate the demand curve in question, however, to gain some information about that demand reservation price. We know that such a price must lie below the corresponding supply reservation price – the supply reservation price constructed with *current* technology and *current* prices. (Note that this is not the parallel construction to the supply reservation price used in the case of new goods.) Hence, if we know that supply reservation price, we have at least a bound on the demand reservation price in question.

Will such a bound be useful? Possibly not. The problem is that if one uses such a bound in the Laspeyres price index, one will have constructed a numerator for the index that may not be lower than the maximum value of output that the base-period economy could have achieved when maximizing value at current prices including the current demand reservation price for the disappearing good. So the bounding property of the Laspeyres index may be lost.

How can that bounding property be restored? Consider the use of a different supply reservation price: the supply reservation-price using base-period technology and current period prices. (This is the supply reservation price that parallels the construct used in the case of new goods.) At first glance, this change does not appear to help; we do not know whether or not *that* supply reservation price is higher or lower than the demand reservation price that would be appropriate to use.

Such ignorance does not matter. A Laspeyres index constructed with that supply reservation price as a current-period price for the disappearing good will have as a numerator the value of base-period output at such current prices. This will necessarily be less than or equal to the maximum value of base-period output that could be achieved at the same prices, and (as in the case of new goods considered above) optimal output would entail (by the definition of the supply-reservation price) producing a zero amount of the disappearing good. Since it would always have been possible to produce zero of the disappearing good whatever its price, the value of base-period output so produced must have a value no greater than that which could be obtained by maximizing total money output while assigning any other price to the disappearing good. In particular, this means that the Laspeyres index will continue to bound from below the production-theoretic output-price index that assigns the current-period demand reservation price to the disappearing good.

Indeed, we can go further than this. Even if one does not agree that the current-period demand reservation price is, in principle, the right one to use in the production-theoretic output-price index, the argument just given shows that a Laspeyres index using the supply reservation price as described provides a lower bound to the production-theoretic output-price index.

Thus, as in the case of new goods, the case of disappearing goods suggests the use of a supply reservation price – in this case, the supply reservation price using base-period technology and current-period prices. However, whereas we can be sure in the case of new goods that using the supply reservation price not only provides a Paasche index that bounds the production-theoretic output-price index but bounds it efficiently, similar efficiency need not hold in the case of disappearing goods and the Laspeyres index.

2.4. Modeling Production Opportunities: An Overview

The production-theoretic output-price and quantity indexes under consideration are based on a particular production possibility frontier. No matter how the PPF is chosen, a production-theoretic output-price index and associated index of real output can be derived. But not all price and quantity indexes so derived are equally interesting. It is important that the indexes be derived from production conditions relevant to the economic questions being analyzed.

In this regard, there are several issues that confront the would-be index-number maker. First, she must decide which goods are to be labeled as outputs and which are to be labeled as inputs. This may not be a trivial decision in practice. A given economic unit can be a net producer of some good in one situation, whereas in another situation it uses the same good as a factor of production. In yet another situation, the same unit may neither produce this good nor employ it as a factor.[10] We shall generally ignore this issue and take the lists of inputs and outputs as well defined for a particular production unit (although we shall discuss in Chapter 6 the relations between output-price indexes for one unit and input-price indexes for another unit that buys from the first).

A second question the analyst faces is that of which PPF to use. For example, in comparing prices and outputs between the base and current periods, should the production function be the one that prevailed in the base

---

10. The potential arbitrariness of the decision as how to label a given good is stressed in Shell (1975), where we are reminded that a factor of production can be thought of as merely a negative output.

period (before technological change) or should it be the one that prevails in the current period (after technological change)? Similarly, in deriving ouput-price and output-quantity indexes to compare the national economies of France and Japan, should the production function be the one prevailing in France or should it be the one prevailing in Japan?

To understand the choice involved in such situations, one must understand the question that index construction answers. In the France–Japan example, in constructing the production-theoretic price and output index based on the French PPF we start by asking the question: What is the capacity of the French economy to produce money output at Japanese prices? If money output that would have been produced at those prices is less than money output in Japan, then Japanese real output will be said to exceed that of France. In contrast, the construction of the production-theoretic indexes based on the Japanese PPF starts with the question: What is the capacity of the Japanese economy to produce money output at French prices? Prices, however, are taken as representing demand conditions and hence consumer tastes. Thus the index based on the French PPF considers the relative capacity of the two economies to meet the needs of Japanese consumers, whereas that based on the Japanese PPF considers the relative capacity of the two economies to meet the needs of French consumers. These are two different questions, and they will generally have two different answers. In general, there is no reason to suppose that one of them is more interesting than the other.[11]

A similar statement is not true of the comparison of two time periods in a given economy. There are still two different questions, but the questions are not of equal interest. Output and price indexes based on the current-period technology will compare the capacity of the two economies to produce money output valued at base-period prices, whereas indexes based on base-period technology will use current-period prices. Because prices reflect tastes, comparisons using current-period prices and tastes (and hence base-period technology) are likely to be more interesting than comparison using base-period prices and tastes (and hence current-period technology). This is because the ultimate object of production is consumption. It is interesting to ask whether today's consumers would be better or worse off in a world with yesterday's production system than they actually are. It is not

---

11. It must not be thought that these issues only arise for the production-theoretic index. They are endemic in index-number construction. For example, using France as the base observation, the construction of a Laspeyres quantity index values output in French prices; the construction of a Paasche quantity index values output in Japanese prices.

quite so interesting to ask that same question about yesterday's consumers who no longer matter in policy decisions. To put it differently, in planning for the future, one wants to choose policies leading to greater real outputs as valued by the people who will then consume them, not as valued by people now. To quote our earlier discussion of this matter: "It is possible, but not particularly appealing, to say that real output has gone down because suits of armor are no longer produced. Thus the index based on yesterday's capacity to produce items valued today seems the more relevant one."[12]

This is not to say, however, that indexes based on current-period technology are wholly without interest. If nothing else, the Paasche price index and Laspeyres quantity index, which are traditional in the analysis of GDP, only bound the respective production-theoretic indexes based on current technology. If one is to adapt such measurements to bound the more interesting production-theoretic indexes corresponding to base-period technology (or even to see in what direction the errors lie), one must analyze the dependence of the production-theoretic indexes on the PPF. This is true a fortiori of cases such as international comparisons where both sets of indexes are equally interesting. The analysis of such questions is undertaken in the next chapter.

Before coming to problems of comparative statistics, however, a third question must be faced in choosing the PPF: How should factor supply be modeled? The simplest case (treated in Essay II of Fisher and Shell (1972)) is that of a closed national economy with (temporarily) fixed factor supplies. But the fixed-factor-supply point of view is very restrictive. Even national economies face rising domestic factor supply schedules and might possibly be able to obtain factors from abroad at either fixed or rising prices. The assumption of fixed factor supplies is even less appropriate when the economic unit under consideration is smaller than the national economy.

In later sections and the next chapter, we generalize our earlier theory to accommodate different and potentially more realistic factor supply conditions. In so doing, we provide a general theory of output-price deflation and output measurement appropriate to all units of production, from the individual firm, the industry, and the sector, to the national and world economies. We begin with a review of the case of the fully closed economy – the case of fixed factors. After that, we turn to the opposite polar case, the fully open economy, where factors are supplied (perfectly elastically) at fixed factor

---

12. Fisher and Shell (1972, p. 57). The present discussion is based on pp. 56–57.

prices. We then analyze the hybrid case in which some factors are fixed and others are supplied perfectly elastically. It turns out that these cases have much in common. With these analyses in hand, we then proceed to consider more realistic cases in which factor supply curves are neither vertical nor horizontal but are upward-sloping. This introduces a number of new complications including issues of monopoly and monopsony.

2.5. "Optimistic" and "Pessimistic" PPFs

Before analyzing this series of cases, however, it is useful to consider in general how production-theoretic price and output indexes based on different factor supply conditions are likely to be related. We can do this because some of our factor supply conditions are unambiguously less restrictive than others. For example, a PPF based on fixed factor supplies gives a more "pessimistic" assessment of production possibilities than a PPF passing through the same observed point but based on perfectly elastic factor supplies.

Moreover, the analysis of the relation between indexes using relatively "optimistic" and relatively "pessimistic" PPFs is relevant to an issue that we have so far ignored. We have implicitly assumed that the economist is confident in his or her choice of the relevant PPF and has perfect information about that PPF. This may not be true. Generally, econometric (and other) studies of production are most reliable for technological combinations close to recently observed data points; for technological combinations far from the observed data points, the description of technology is likely to be less reliable. For example, estimates of price elasticities of output supply may be dependable for small (or local) price changes but may not be so dependable for large (or global) price changes.[13] (Much of the debate on U.S. energy policy in the 1970s stemmed from differences in beliefs about the value of the price elasticities of supply (and of demand) for relatively large changes in the prices of petroleum and other energy inputs.)

The economist, while uncertain about the global PPF, might nonetheless be able to place some bounds on the PPF. The true PPF might be known to lie between some "pessimistic" PPF and some "optimistic" PPF. In such a situation, the following analysis will be directly applicable.

13. The superlative index-number approach of Diewert (1976) relies heavily on the local specification of the family of technologies and choosing indexes that are exact for this family. Our approach, however, can be helpful even when we do not have reliable local representations of technology or in cases for which the comparisons require a global specification of technologies.

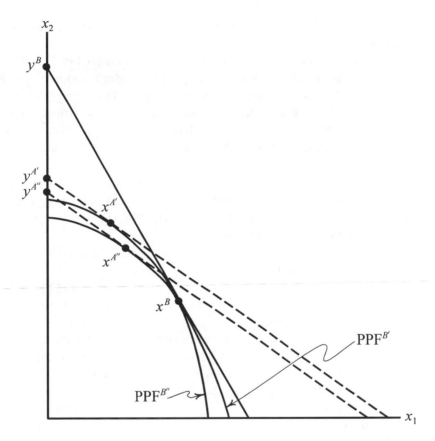

Figure 2.5.1

In Figure 2.5.1, there are two PPFs, $PPF^{B'}$, and $PPF^{B''}$, each based on base-period conditions. The base-period output vector is x^B. Both PPFs pass through x^B and are tangent to each other at that point. Their common slope at x^B is given by the known base-period price vector p^B. The outer curve, $PPF^{B'}$, represents a relatively optimistic assessment of global production possibilities; the inner curve, $PPF^{B''}$, represents a relatively pessimistic one.

The theoretically constructed output vector $x^{A'}$ is determined by the tangency of the price line based on current-period prices p^A and the "optimistic" frontier $PPF^{B'}$. Similarly, the theoretically constructed output vector $x^{A''}$ is determined by the tangency of the price line based on current-period prices p^A and the "pessimistic" frontier $PPF^{B''}$. Actual base-period money output is $y^B = p^B \cdot x^B$. We also define the theoretically constructed money outputs $y^{A'} = p^A \cdot x^{A'}$ and $y^{A''} = p^A \cdot x^{A''}$. Since $\text{PPF}^{B''}$ is more restrictive than $\text{PPF}^{B'}$, we know that $y^{A'} \geq y^{A''}$.

The production-theoretic output-price index based on $\text{PPF}^{B'}$ is $I^{B'} = (y^{A'}/y^B)$. The production-theoretic output-price index based on $\text{PPF}^{B''}$ is $I^{B''} = (y^{A''}/y^B)$. Consequently, we have $I^{B'} \geq I^{B''}$. Thus, the production-theoretic output-price index derived from an optimistic assessment of base-period technology is typically larger than the one derived from a pessimistic assessment of the same technology. Correspondingly, when two such production-theoretic price indexes are used to deflate the same money output to obtain a real-output index, the production-theoretic real-output index derived from an optimistic assessment of base-period technology will be smaller than the production-theoretic real-output index derived from a pessimistic assessment of the same technology.

Consideration of the basic ideas behind production-theoretic index construction shows that this is as it should be. Real output is said to have increased if current-period output lies outside the base-period PPF. If that PPF is assessed optimistically, a given movement will be counted as less of a real-output increase than if the PPF is assessed pessimistically.

Note, however, that the Laspeyres output-price index continues to provide a lower bound to either of the production-theoretic output-price indexes derived from base-period technology; that is, $L = (p^A \cdot x^B/p^B \cdot x^B) = (p^A \cdot x^B/y^B) \leq I^{B''} \leq I^{B'}$, since typically x^B does not maximize money output at prices p^A on either $\text{PPF}^{B'}$ or $\text{PPF}^{B''}$. It follows that the Paasche real-output index continues to provide an upper bound for either of the production-theoretic real-output indexes.

Similar reasoning shows that the Paasche output-price index provides an upper bound for production-theoretic output-price indexes based, respectively, on optimistic and pessimistic assessments of current-period technology, whereas the Laspeyres real-output index provides a lower bound for both of the corresponding production-theoretic real-output indexes. However, the production-theoretic output-price index for an optimistic assessment of current-period technology is typically *smaller* than the production-theoretic output-price index for the pessimistic assessment of the same technology. The corresponding production-theoretic real-output index for the optimistic assessment is *larger* than the corresponding production-theoretic real-output index for the pessimistic assessment.[14]

14. This reflects the fact that current-period values are always in the numerator so that the reciprocal of the real-output index measures how much of a gain in real output has occurred going from the current period to the base period.

2.6. The Fully Closed Economy

We now move away from the diagrammatic exposition that we have used so far; further notation will be required. We assume that the productive unit being studied employs m factors of production, the amounts of which are denoted by the vector $v = (v_1, \ldots, v_m)$, and produces r outputs, the amounts of which are denoted by the vector $x = (x_1, \ldots, x_r)$. Both v and x are nonnegative. Efficient outputs and inputs are described by the solutions to

$$F(x, v) = 0, \tag{2.6.1}$$

where typically F is increasing in the elements of x and decreasing in the elements of v. Technology is assumed to be "convex." When useful, we assume that F is twice continuously differentiable[15] and concave.

The case of the fully closed economy is characterized by fixed factor supplies, that is, by a fixed vector, v. In this case, the PPF is given by

$$\text{PPF}(v) = \{x \mid F(x, v) = 0\}. \tag{2.6.2}$$

As indicated, different choices of v will produce different PPFs and hence different production-theoretic price and output indexes. It will be useful to concentrate on the indexes corresponding to the PPF of the base-period economy, and we shall largely do so henceforward. We adopt the following notation: A hat over a variable denotes its base-period level. An asterisk superscript on a variable denotes its current-period level. A variable with neither a hat nor an asterisk is either at a general level or at some theoretical (optimizing) level. The meaning will be clear in the context.

For convenience, we briefly restate the theory of output deflation and measurement in this context and notation. We are given two output-price vectors, the current-period one, $p^* = (p_1^*, \ldots, p_r^*)$, and the base-period one, $\hat{p} = (\hat{p}_1, \ldots, \hat{p}_r)$. Actual output in the base period was $\hat{x} = (\hat{x}_1, \ldots, \hat{x}_r)$ and dollar base-period output was $\hat{y} = \hat{p} \cdot \hat{x} = \hat{p}_1 \hat{x}_1 + \cdots + \hat{p}_r \hat{x}_r$. Similarly, actual output in the current period is $x^* = (x_1^*, \ldots, x_r^*)$ and dollar current-period output is $y^* = p^* \cdot x^* = p_1^* x_1^* + \cdots + p_r^* x_r^*$.

We continue to assume competition and efficiency, so that $\hat{x}$ solves the problem

$$\max_{x'} \hat{p} \cdot x' \quad \text{subject to } F(x', \hat{v}) = 0, \tag{2.6.3}$$

where $\hat{v}$ is the vector of base-period inputs and $\hat{y} = \hat{p} \cdot \hat{x}$ is base-period

---

15. We shall not need this smoothness assumption until the next chapter.

money output.[16] We define the output vector x to be the solution to the problem

$$\max_{x'} p^* \cdot x' \quad \text{subject to } F(x', \hat{v}) = 0, \tag{2.6.4}$$

where $y = p^* \cdot x$ is the money value the base-period technology would have produced at current prices.

The production-theoretic output-price index for comparing the base period and the current period is then $(y/\hat{y})$ and the production-theoretic output-quantity index is (y^*/y) .

If the base-period technology exhibits constant returns-to-scale (CRS), then the production-theoretic output index has an interesting characterization. Define the *production possibility map* (PPM) as the family of PPF's

$$\text{PPF}(\mu) = \{x, \mu \mid F(x, \mu\hat{v}) = 0 \text{ and } \mu > 0\}, \tag{2.6.5}$$

as μ, the scalar index of factor dosage, varies. Then the base-period PPF implicitly defined in (2.6.2) is a member of this family with dosage μ given by $\mu = 1$. Varying μ corresponds to varying "dosages" of factors in the base-period proportions, and, under constant returns-to-scale, the members of this family of frontiers are parallel along rays.

Consider Figure 2.2.2 once more. Assume that PPF^B is the base-period PPF defined in (2.6.2) and that $x^B = \hat{x}$, so that the line tangent to PPF^B at x^B has slope corresponding to base-period prices and $y^B = \hat{y}$. Take the actual value of current-period output, y^*, to be y^A, and take current-period prices p^* to correspond to the slope of the line through x^A tangent to PPF^A. Then, Problem (2.6.4) above has the solution: $x = x^D$ and $y = y^D$. In other words, y^D is the maximum value that would have been produced by the base-period production sector had it faced current-period prices.

Given this, the production-theoretic output-quantity index is $(y^*/y) = (y^A/y^D)$. This is the amount by which the base-period PPF (PPF^B) must be scaled up parallel along rays to be tangent to the value-of-output line at y^A. Under CRS, this must be the value of μ that generated the frontier PPF^A.

In short, under CRS, the production-theoretic output-quantity index has the property that it represents the increased "dosage" of factor supplies in the proportions of the base period that would be required to generate the current period's value of output quantity at current-period prices given the

---

16. If we were to use an arbitrary PPF or were not to assume efficiency in the base period, we would often start by solving Problem (2.6.3) but typically the solution would not be $\hat{x}$.

base-period technology. That seems a natural property for an output quantity index to have.

Once we leave the leading case of constant returns-to-scale, this interpretation in terms of factor dosages disappears. Nonetheless, it always remains true that the production-theoretic real-output index is the amount by which the base-period PPF would have to be scaled up to produce the current-period's value of output at the current-period prices.

In the case with no technical progress, our output-price index I and our output-quantity index J can be defined through the variable profit function π, which is defined by

$$\pi(p, v) = \max_{x}\{px : F(x, v) = 0\}. \tag{2.6.6}$$

Thus, we have, for example,

$$I(p^A, p^B, v^A) = \pi(p^B, v^A)/\pi(p^A, v^A) \tag{2.6.7}$$

and

$$\begin{aligned} J(v^A, v^B, p^B) \\ &= [\pi(p^B, v^B)/\pi(p^A, v^A)]/[\pi(p^B, v^A)/\pi(p^A, v^A)] \\ &= \pi(p^B, v^B)/\pi(p^B, v^A). \end{aligned} \tag{2.6.8}$$

See, for example, Diewert (1983b, pp. 1063–77) for a discussion of the use of duality in defining these indexes.

2.7. The Fully Open Economy

In the previous section, we analyzed the extreme case in which input proportions are fixed, the case of the fully closed economy. This section treats the opposite polar case in which the inputs to the economic unit are perfectly elastically supplied at given fixed factor prices. We shall call this case "the fully open economy," but the analysis of this section is appropriate in studying, for example, an industry or a firm that is small relative to the overall economy's supplies of those goods that the industry or firm in question employs as inputs.

In this case, the economic unit's efficient production technology is still given by (2.6.1), but the PPF is no longer defined by fixed factor supplies. Rather, we are given a vector of input prices, $w = (w_1, \ldots, w_m)$, and a money value of input cost C. In defining the PPF, the vector of inputs,

$v = (v_1, \ldots, v_m)$, is considered to be a variable chosen so as to yield a vector of outputs, $x = (x_1, \ldots, x_r)$, which is maximal subject to the production function (2.6.1), the fixed input prices w, and the fixed factor cost C. Thus, we define the PPF for the fully open economy by

$$\text{PPF} = \{x \mid x \text{ is maximal subject to } F(x, v) = 0 \text{ and } w \cdot v = C\}.$$

$$(2.7.1)$$

The PPF defined in (2.7.1) can be described in the following way: Choose any input vector v satisfying the cost constraint $w \cdot v = C$. Next consider the set of outputs x corresponding to this v and the production function $F(x, v) = 0$. This defines a production possibility frontier for some given vector v. For each such v satisfying the cost constraint there is a corresponding PPF. Thus, we have defined a family of production possibility frontiers. The PPF defined in (2.7.1) is the upper envelope of this family of frontiers. Each point x belonging to the PPF defined in (2.7.1) also lies on some production possibility frontier defined for v fixed, where the total input cost of that v at input prices w is equal to C.

Given this way of defining the production possibility frontier, the construction of the corresponding theoretical output-price index for the fully open economy is a straightforward application of the general approach already developed. We illustrate this (as usual) using the base-period PPF. The two output-price vectors to be compared are $\hat{p}$ and p. Hats continue to denote base-period values. We are given base-period factor prices $\hat{w}$ and base-period costs $\hat{C}$. For any output-price vector p, define $x(p)$ as the solution to the problem

$$\max_{x'} p \cdot x' \quad \text{subject to } x' \text{ being on the PPF defined in (2.7.1)}$$
$$\text{with } w = \hat{w} \text{ and } C = \hat{C}. \qquad (2.7.2)$$

Define $y(p)$ by $y(p) = p \cdot x(p)$. If we continue to assume competition and efficiency, actual base-period output $\hat{x}$ and base-period money output $\hat{y}$ will satisfy $\hat{x} = x(\hat{p})$ and $\hat{y} = y(\hat{p})$. The production-theoretic output-price index is then $y(p)/y(\hat{p}) = y(p)/\hat{y}$. The function $y(p)$ is closely related to the "balance of trade restricted value added function" of Diewert (1983b, p. 1,086) and the "domestic sales function" S of Deiwert and Morrison (1986, p. 669), where S is defined by

$$S(p, w, C) = \max_{x,v}\{px : F(x, v) = 0 \text{ and } wv \leq C\}. \qquad (2.7.3)$$

Hence, for the case without technical progress, we can describe our price indexes $\tilde{I}$ and our quantity indexes $\tilde{J}$ in the forms

$$\tilde{I}(p, \hat{p}, \hat{w}, \hat{C}) = S(p, \hat{w}, \hat{C})/S(\hat{p}, \hat{w}, \hat{C}) \tag{2.7.4}$$

and

$$\tilde{J}(p, \hat{p}, w, \hat{w}, C, \hat{C})$$
$$= S(p, w, C)/S(p, \hat{w}, \hat{C})$$
$$= [S(p, w, C)/S(\hat{p}, \hat{w}, \hat{C})]/\tilde{I}(p, \hat{p}, \hat{w}, \hat{C}). \tag{2.7.5}$$

Price indexes of the form (2.7.4) are due to Archibald (1977, pp. 60–61). See Diewert (1983b, pp. 1,086–1,090) for bounds on indexes of this type.

As we have already observed, the fully open specification of production conditions is more "optimistic" than the fully closed specification. In the former case, the optimistic assumption is maintained that inputs are perfectly elastically supplied to the economic unit in question. In the latter case, the pessimistic assumption is maintained that input supplies are perfectly inelastic. Suppose that the input vector v used to construct the PPF in the fully closed case costs no more than C at prices w, where C and w are the values used to construct the PPF in the fully open case. (This will certainly be true if base-period values are used throughout.) Then for every output vector from the fully closed production possibility frontier, there is an output vector from the fully open production possibility frontier representing either greater or equal production of *each* commodity. Thus the fully open PPF is a more optimistic representation of production opportunities than the fully closed PPF in the sense of Section 2.5 and Figure 2.5.1.

Continuing to use the base-period PPF, we find that the production-theoretic output-price index for the fully open economy will typically be greater than that for the fully closed economy. Correspondingly, the real-output index in the fully open case will be smaller than in the fully closed case. This corresponds to the fact that the capability of the base-period fully open economy to produce value at current-period prices was greater than that of the base-period fully closed economy. Hence, more of the change in money output is attributed to price change in the fully open economy than in the fully closed one.

As explained in Section 2.5, Laspeyres and Paasche indexes bound both the fully open and fully closed production-theoretic indexes.

Despite the fact that the fully open economy corresponds to a more optimistic description of technology than the fully closed one, there is a useful sense in which the fully open economy can be thought of as a special case of the fully closed one. In the latter case, the PPF is derived from a production function relating r outputs to m inputs, with the vector of inputs fixed. In the fully open case, the PPF is derived from a production function relating r outputs to a single input, money cost C, which is then fixed. In this interpretation, a change in factor prices in the fully open case becomes a shift in the "technology" with which outputs are produced from the given money cost C. (We consider such changes when considering comparative static analysis below.)

Recall from Section 2.1 that if the PPF derived from current-period technology is parallel to the PPF derived from base-period technology, then the production-theoretic output-price indexes are equal, and the Laspeyres and Paasche indexes serve (respectively) as lower and upper bounds. Naturally, a similar statement holds for the production-theoretic real-output indexes. In the case of the fully closed economy (Section 2.6), it is evident that sufficient conditions for parallel PPFs are: (i) constant returns-to-scale and (ii) input proportions unchanging between periods. We next seek conditions under which the PPFs in the fully open economy will be parallel.

In the fully open economy, the PPFs are parameterized by money input expenditures C. Increasing C moves us to the northeast on a new PPF. Thus, if there is a common production function F that exhibits constant returns-to-scale and if the vector of input prices is the same in each situation (or at least proportional to each other), then the PPFs will obviously be parallel. These conditions are clearly far stronger than is needed.

We shall return to a detailed analysis of the fully open economy in Chapter 3. In particular, we analyze the effects on the output-price indexes of changing factor prices and technological change.

2.8. The Hybrid Economy

Both the fully open economy and the fully closed economy represent extreme cases, with the fully closed case giving the most pessimistic and the fully open case the most optimistic assessment of production opportunities. It is obviously important to analyze situations that lie in between; we begin by considering a case that – although still special – generalizes the two cases already considered.

The economic unit we analyze in this section is a hybrid of the fully closed economy and fully open economy. We assume that the economic unit can freely buy some, but not all, of the factors at exogenously given prices. The remaining factors are assumed to be fixed in amount. We shall refer to these as "variable factors" and "fixed factors," respectively. The production possibility frontier to be used in defining the theoretical output-price index for the hybrid economy is the locus of maximal outputs producible at given amounts of the fixed factors and with given cost (at given factor prices) of the variable factors.

The analysis for the hybrid economy reduces to that of the fully closed economy when there are no variable factors and to that of the fully open economy when there are no fixed factors. (Furthermore, by considering the money cost of the variable factors as an additional fixed factor the hybrid case can be thought of as fully closed.) The hybrid economy thus serves as a generalization of the two extreme cases with an assessment of technology more optimistic than that of the fully closed case but more pessimistic than that of the fully open one. Moreover, despite its still special nature, the results of the analysis of the hybrid economy are useful in understanding those for the general case of rising factor-supply schedules. (See Sections 2.9 and 2.11.)

In describing technology in the hybrid case, we must distinguish between fixed factors of production and variable factors of production. Following the notation employed in Section 2.7, we continue to let $v = (v_1, \ldots, v_m)$ denote the vector of variable inputs. (Note that this notation conflicts with that in Fisher and Shell (1972, Essay II) and with that in Section 2.6 above, where v was the entire input vector, assumed to be fixed.) We let $u = (u_1, \ldots, u_s)$ denote the vector of fixed factors. Technologically efficient production plans can be summarized by the relation

$$F(x, v, u) = 0, \tag{2.8.1}$$

where $x = (x_1, \ldots, x_r)$ is the output vector. The production function F is assumed to be increasing in x and decreasing in v and u. Let $w_v = (w_{v_1}, \ldots, w_{v_m})$ be the prices for the variable factors, and let C_v be total expenditure on the variable factors. Then, the PPF for the hybrid economy is given by

$$\text{PPF} = \{\text{maximal } x \mid F(x, v, u) = 0 \text{ and } w_v \cdot v = C_v\}. \tag{2.8.2}$$

In defining the PPF in (2.8.2), we are given fixed inputs u, variable factor prices w_v, total expenditures on variable factors C_v, and the production function F. Given two output-price vectors, one can now form the production-theoretic output-price and real-output indexes for the hybrid economy in a familiar way.

Assume that (2.8.2) is derived from the technological conditions prevailing in the base period. Let PPF_H^B be that production possibility frontier. Hence, we have

$$\mathrm{PPF}_H^B = \{\text{maximal } x \mid F^B(x, v, \hat{u}) = 0 \text{ and } \hat{w}_v \cdot v = \hat{C}_v\}, \qquad (2.8.3)$$

where F^B is the production function that the economic unit faced in the base period, $\hat{u}$ is the vector of fixed factors employed in the base period, $\hat{w}_v$ is the vector of prices for variable factors prevailing during the base period, and $\hat{C}$ is the money expenditure on variable factors in the base period.

Next, we define PPF_{FC}^B and PPF_{FO}^B. These are, respectively, the fully closed and the fully open descriptions of technology to which we can compare PPF_H^B, the description of the hybrid technology derived from base-period conditions. For the fully closed economy, we have

$$\mathrm{PPF}_{FC}^B = \{\text{maximal } x \mid F^B(x, \hat{v}, \hat{u}) = 0\}, \qquad (2.8.4)$$

where $\hat{v}$ is the vector of "variable" factors employed in the base period. For purposes of defining PPF_{FC}^B the vector $\hat{v}$ is held fixed. For the fully open economy, we have

$$\mathrm{PPF}_{FO}^B = \{\text{maximal } x \mid F^B(x, v, u) = 0 \text{ and}$$

$$\hat{w}_v \cdot v + \hat{w}_u \cdot u = \hat{C} + \hat{C}_u\}, \qquad (2.8.5)$$

where $\hat{w}_u$ is the vector of prices of the "fixed" factors during the base period and $\hat{C}$ is money expenditure on "fixed" factors during the base period. (Note that $\hat{w}_u$ can be thought of as the vector of shadow prices associated with the fixed-factor constraints when the value of output is maximized in the base period.) For purposes of defining PPF_{FO}^B, the vector of "fixed" inputs u is allowed to vary. Total money expenditure on factors of production in the base period is given by $\hat{C} = \hat{C}_v + \hat{C}_u$.

Assume that the economy was competitive and efficient in the base period, so that $\hat{x}$, the actual vector of base-period outputs, maximized revenue at prices $\hat{p}$ subject to the input constraint $(v, u) = (\hat{v}, \hat{u})$, the actual full vector of base-period inputs. In this efficient case, it must also be true that actual base-period inputs $(\hat{v}, \hat{u})$ minimized total base-period cost $C = \hat{w}_v \cdot v + \hat{w}_u \cdot u$ subject to the output constraint $x = \hat{x}$. Then the three production possibility frontiers, PPF_{FO}^B, PPF_{FH}^B, and PPF_{FC}^B share a common point, $\hat{x}$, but PPF_{FO}^B dominates PPF_H^B, which in turn dominates PPF_{FC}^B. This is shown in Figure 2.8.1. Thus, in a precise way, the hybrid economy's production possibility frontier, PPF_H^B, as defined in (2.8.3), is a more

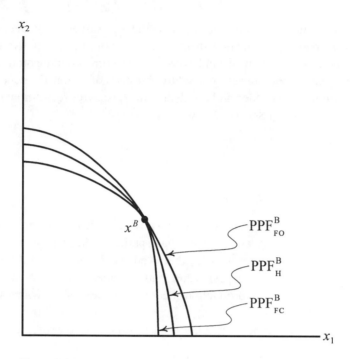

Figure 2.8.1

optimistic assessment of technology than the corresponding PPF derived under the assumption that the economy is fully closed, and it is a less optimistic assessment of technology than the corresponding PPF derived under the assumption that the economy is fully open.

We are now in a position to apply the analysis of Section 2.5, especially that of Figure 2.5.1, to the production-theoretic output-price and real-output indexes derived for the hybrid economy. Let I_H^B, I_{FC}^B, and I_{FO}^B be the production-theoretic output-price indexes derived, respectively, from the production possibility frontiers defined in (2.8.3), (2.8.4), and (2.8.5). Let J_H^B, J_{FC}^B, and J_{FO}^B, respectively, be the corresponding production-theoretic real-output indexes. Let L^P be the Laspeyres output-price index and P^Q be the Paasche real-output index. Then we have

$$L^P \leq I_{FC}^B \leq I_H^B \leq I_{FO}^B \tag{2.8.6}$$

and

$$P^Q \leq J_{FC}^B \leq J_H^B \leq J_{FO}^B. \tag{2.8.7}$$

Now, in a similar notation, let I_H^A, I_{FC}^A, and I_{FO}^A, respectively, denote the three corresponding production-theoretic output-price indexes derived from current-period technological conditions, with the corresponding production-theoretic real-output indexes denoted by J instead of I. Let P^P denote the Paasche output-price index and L^Q-denote the Laspeyres real-output index. Then, as observed in Section 2.5, we have

$$P^P \geq I_{FC}^A \geq I_H^A \geq I_{FO}^A \tag{2.8.8}$$

and

$$L^Q \leq J_{FC}^A \leq J_H^A \leq J_{FO}^A. \tag{2.8.9}$$

Now, if PPF_H^B and PPF_H^A the production possibility frontiers for the hybrid economy derived, respectively, from base-period and current-period technological conditions – are parallel, then we have $I_H^B = I_H^A$ and $J_H^B = J_H^A$. Hence, in this case, the Laspeyres and Paasche indexes provide both upper and lower bounds on the production-theoretic indexes. We now investigate when this will pertain.

Notice that the production relation in (2.8.1) can be expressed in the reduced form

$$G(x, u, C_v) = 0, \tag{2.8.10}$$

where $C_v = w_v \cdot v$ is fixed expenditure on variable factors at the fixed prices w_v. This reduced-form production relation is increasing in x and decreasing in both u and C_v. Thus, the hybrid economy reduces to an economy with $s + 1$ fixed factors, where the $(s + 1)$st fixed factor is money expenditure on variable factors. It also follows that the fully open economy can be interpreted as a fully closed economy with only one factor of production: money expenditure on variable factors. From (2.8.10) we can derive the PPF applicable to the hybrid economy; it is the set of outputs given by

$$\{x \mid G(x, u, C_v) = 0\}, \tag{2.8.11}$$

where u and C_v are fixed.

If F exhibits constant returns-to-scale, then so does G. That is,

$$G(\mu x, \mu u, \mu C_v) = 0 \tag{2.8.12}$$

for any positive scalar μ. We can use the above fact to derive sufficient conditions for the production possibility frontiers derived for the hybrid economy to be parallel to each other. Two hybrid PPFs are parallel if

1. They are based on the same constant returns-to-scale technology and the same factor prices for variable factors and
2. They differ in their factor usage (u, C_v) only by a scalar of proportionality. (Here factor usage is based on both the vector of fixed factors u and the composite factor C_v.)

Note that, if these conditions are met, then the production-theoretic index of real output based on the hybrid economy's base-period PPF can be thought of as the scalar μ by which factor usage would have had to be increased in the base period to allow the economy to produce current-period money output at current-period prices. (We have already seen this result for the fully closed case; since it holds for the hybrid case it holds for the fully open case as well.)

Although the assumption of constant returns-to-scale is quite reasonable in production theory, it can be weakened considerably to the more general case in which the production possibility map is homothetic (i.e., the case in which PPFs are parallel). Of course, if parallel PPFs are to be used to establish the validity of both the Paasche and Laspeyres bounds on the same production-theoretic output-price and real-output indexes (as opposed to the comparative-static purposes discussed in the next chapter), the assumption of homotheticity will not be enough in itself. One must also assume no technological change, unchanging prices of variable factors, and constant-factor proportions, including both the proportions of the different fixed factors and their ratio to the composite factor.

It is instructive to realize that the assumptions that guarantee parallel PPFs for the hybrid economy do not guarantee parallel PPFs for the associated fully closed or fully open economies. Moreover, despite the inequalities (2.8.6) and (2.8.7), such a parallel case for the hybrid economy does not permit the use of Paasche and Laspeyres indexes to provide simultaneous lower and upper bounds on the *same* production-theoretic indexes for the fully closed or fully open cases. This is because neither $I_{FC}^B = I_{FC}^A$ nor $I_{FO}^B = I_{FO}^A$ necessarily follows from the equality $I_H^B = I_H^A$.

Consider first the fully closed case. The fully closed PPF for the base period, PPF_{FC}^B, is defined with fixed-factor usage $\hat{u}$ and variable-factor usage held constant at $\hat{v}$, the actual usage of such factors in the base period. The fully closed PPF for the current period, PPF_{FC}^A, on the other hand, has fixed-factor usage u and variable-factor usage v, the actual usage of such factors in the current period. Even if $u = \mu\hat{u}$ (and $w_v = \hat{w}_v$) as part of the conditions under which PPF_H^B and PPF_H^A are parallel, it will generally not be true that $v = \mu\hat{v}$, since relative usage of variable factors will depend on output prices. Thus, PPF_FC^B and PPF_FC^A will generally not be parallel in such a case, and I_FC^B will not coincide with I_FC^A even though $I_\text{H}^B = I_\text{H}^A$.

Similarly, consider the two PPFs for the fully open case, PPF_FO^B and PPF_FO^A. The first of these, PPF_FO^B is based on a given total cost of all factors at base-period factor prices, $\hat{w}_v$ for variable factors and $\hat{w}$ for fixed factors. The second, PPF_FO^A is similarly based on current-period factor prices, w_v and w_u. Even if $w_v = \hat{w}_v$ (and $u = \mu\hat{u}$) as part of the conditions under which PPF_H^B and PPF_H^C are parallel, it will generally not be true that $w = \hat{w}$ because the relative prices of the fixed factors will depend on output prices. (To put it another way, the shadow prices of the fixed-factor constraints will depend on the objective function.) Hence PPF_FO^B and PPF_FO^A will generally not be parallel in such a case and I_FO^B will not coincide with I_FO^A even though $I_\text{H}^B = I_\text{H}^A$.

Following the formalism of Diewert and Morrison (1986), the corresponding three "sales functions" S_H (for the hybrid case), S_FC (for the fully closed case), and S_FO (for the fully open case) would be defined by

$$S_\text{H}(p, w_v, C_v, u)$$

$$= \max_{x,v}\{p \cdot x : F(x, u, v) = 0 \text{ and } w_v \cdot v = C_v\}, \qquad (2.8.13)$$

$$S_\text{FC}(p, v, u) = \max_x\{p \cdot x : F(x, u, v) = 0\}, \qquad (2.8.14)$$

and

$$S_\text{FO}(p, w_v, w_u, C_v, C_u) = \max_{x,v,u}\{p \cdot x : F(x, v, u)$$

$$= 0, w_v \cdot v + w_u \cdot u \leq C_v + C_u\}. \qquad (2.8.15)$$

Our price indexes can be written in the following form:

$$I_\text{H}(p, \hat{p}, \hat{w}_v, \hat{C}_v, \hat{u}) = S_\text{H}(p, \hat{w}_v, \hat{C}_v, \hat{u})/S_\text{H}(\hat{p}, \hat{w}_v, \hat{C}_v, \hat{u}), \quad (2.8.16)$$

$$I_\text{FC}(p, \hat{p}, \hat{v}, \hat{u}) = S_\text{FC}(p, \hat{v}, \hat{u})/S_\text{FC}(\hat{p}, \hat{v}, \hat{u}), \qquad (2.8.17)$$

and

$$I_\text{FO}(p, \hat{p}, \hat{w}, \hat{C}_v, \hat{w}_u, \hat{C}_u)$$

$$= S_\text{FO}(p, \hat{w}_v, \hat{C}_v, \hat{w}_u, \hat{C}_u)/S_\text{FO}(\hat{p}, \hat{w}_v, \hat{C}_v, \hat{w}_u, \hat{C}_u). \quad (2.8.18)$$

The corresponding quantity indexes J_H, J_FC, and J_FO are defined by

$$J_\text{H}(p, \hat{p}, w_v, \hat{w}_v, C_v, \hat{C}_v, u, \hat{u})$$

$$= S_\text{H}(p, w_v, C_v, u)/S_\text{H}(p, \hat{w}_v, \hat{C}_v, \hat{u})$$

$$= [p \cdot x/\hat{p} \cdot \hat{x}]/I_\text{H}(p, \hat{p}, \hat{w}_v, \hat{C}_v, \hat{u}), \qquad (2.8.19)$$

$$J_{FC}(p, \hat{p}, v, \hat{v}, u, \hat{u}) = S_{FC}(p, v, u)/S_{FC}(p, \hat{v}, \hat{u})$$

$$= [p \cdot x/\hat{p} \cdot \hat{x}]/I_{FC}(p, \hat{p}, \hat{v}, \hat{u}), \qquad (2.8.20)$$

and

$$J_{FO}(p, \hat{p}, w_v, \hat{w}_v, C_v, \hat{C}_v, w_u, \hat{w}_u, C, \hat{C}_u)$$

$$= S_{FO}(p, w_v, C_v, w_u, C_u)/S_{FO}(p, \hat{w}_v, \hat{C}_v, \hat{w}_u, \hat{C}_u)$$

$$= [p \cdot x/\hat{p} \cdot \hat{x}]/I_{FO}(p, \hat{p}, \hat{w}_v, \hat{C}_v, \hat{w}_u, \hat{C}_u). \qquad (2.8.21)$$

The hybrid sales function (2.18.13) and corresponding price index (2.8.16) are defined in Diewert (1983b, pp. 1086–87). Using the Diewert-style formalisms (2.8.16)–(2.8.18) allows one to re-establish the inequalities (2.8.6)–(2.8.9).

2.9. General Factor Supply Conditions: The Monopsony Case

The hybrid economy analyzed in the previous section still represents a very special case, particularly if we are interested in applying the results to single industries or even to a group of industries. Even though it is partly open, the hybrid economy assumes factor supply curves to be either perfectly inelastic or perfectly elastic. Actual firms, industries, sectors, and even national economies face more general supply conditions.

The present section begins the development of the theory of production-theoretic output-price and real-output (or output-quantity) indexes for the general case of an economic unit facing rising factor supply schedules. The special cases previously analyzed retain importance, however, both because comparative-statics results (Chapter 3) are easier to come by in these cases and because they aid in understanding the more general case.

There is no longer any need to distinguish between fixed and variable factors, so we return to the representation of efficient production by

$$F(x, v) = 0, \qquad (2.9.1)$$

where x is an r-vector of outputs and v is an m-vector of inputs (factors). Let w be the corresponding m-vector of input prices; inputs are supplied to the economic unit in question according to the supply schedule v^S, so we have

$$v = v^S(w). \qquad (2.9.2)$$

If, for some factor, the supply is fixed, then the corresponding component of v^S is a constant (independent of w). If some factor is supplied at a constant factor price, then the corresponding component of v^s is zero below that price, infinite above it, and any value in $[0, +\infty)$ at the given critical price.

Suppose that we observe an economic unit employing an input vector v^* at prices w^* so that its total expenditures on factors of production is $C^* = w^* \cdot v^*$. Fixing the level of expenditures C^*, what are the factor combinations the economic unit could have afforded? The answer depends on what is assumed about the factor-supply conditions facing the economic unit. In Figure 2.9.1, the input vector v^* is indicated. For the fully closed economy, factors are supplied inelastically; thus, v^* is the only feasible point for which total expenditures are equal to C^*. All the points to the southwest of the right angle (shown dotted) are feasible for the fully closed economy. The dashed line represents the input combinations consistent with expenditures C^*, that is, $\{v \mid w^* v = C^*\}$. Points to the southwest of the dashed line are feasible for the fully open economy. Finally, the solid curve describes the set

$$\{v \mid v = v^S(w) \text{ and } w \cdot v = C^*\}, \quad \text{where } v^* = v^S(w^*). \qquad (2.9.3)$$

This is the set of the feasible input combinations for the economy facing rising factor-supply schedules and the indicated cost constraint. Each point to the southwest of the solid curve is feasible for this economy.

We now define the production possibility frontier PPF_G based on the general rising factor-supply specification of feasible input combinations. We have

$$\text{PPF}_G = \{\text{maximal } x \mid F(x, v) = 0, v = v^S(w) \text{ and } w \cdot v = C\}.$$

$$(2.9.4)$$

We call this frontier PPF_G because it is based on the *general* case of (non-strictly) rising factor supply schedules. From Figure 2.9.1, we see that PPF_G provides a more optimistic assessment of output opportunities than PPF_{FC}, the corresponding frontier for the fully closed economy, and a more pessimistic assessment of output opportunities than PPF_{FO}, the corresponding frontier for the fully open economy.

This may seem very natural, but a hidden problem has been introduced. In defining PPF_G as in (2.9.3), a very important assumption is implicit: It is assumed that the economic unit "sees" and acts upon its entire supply schedule. It does not take factor prices as given but rather maximizes subject to the constraint $w \cdot v^S(w) = C$. Therefore, in defining PPF_G we have implicitly assumed that the economic unit has perfect monopsony power in all factor markets with truly rising factor-supply schedules. Evidently, matters are not so simple as they appear.

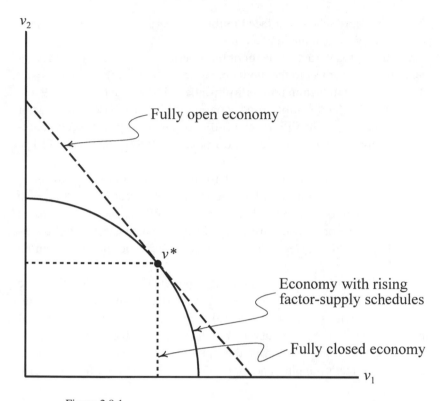

Figure 2.9.1

Since our previous analysis focuses on competition, it might be argued that it would also have been natural to begin with the competitive hypothesis in studying rising factor-supply schedules. We begin, however, with the monopsony case because it is more readily compared to our previous analyses. The rising-factor-supply monopsony case is like those described in the previous sections, but also the comparative-statics results (Chapter 3) are easier to achieve because the envelope theorem (a consequence of constrained maximization) applies. We shall finally get to the general competitive case below.

If the production possibility frontier in (2.9.3) is derived from technologies and factor market conditions prevailing in the base period, then we have

$$\mathrm{PPF}_G^B = \{\text{maximal } x \mid F^B(x, v) = 0, v = v^{SB}(w) \text{ and } w \cdot v = \hat{C}\},$$

$$(2.9.5)$$

where F^B is the production function facing the economy in the base period,

v^{SB} is the supply schedule it faced in the base period, and $\hat{C}$ denotes base-period money expenditure on factors.

Assume that $\hat{x}$, the actual vector of base-period outputs, maximized revenue at prices $\hat{p}$ subject to the input constraints $v = v^{SB}(w)$ and $w \cdot v = \hat{C}$. Then the three production possibility frontiers, PPF_G^B, (defined in (2.9.4)), PPF_{FC}^B (the PPF for the fully closed economy with actual base-period factor usage), and PPF_{FO}^B (the PPF for the fully open economy with actual base-period factor prices) share a common point, $\hat{x}$. PPF_{FO}^B dominates PPF_G^B, which in turn dominates PPF_{FC}^B.[17] Suppose now that one defines the base-period production possibility frontier for the hybrid case, PPF_H^B, by specifying some factors as fixed at base-period factor prices. Then PPF_H^B also shares the point $\hat{x}$ with PPF_G^B, but in general PPF_G^B cannot be said to be necessarily more or less optimistic than PPF_H^B. In some cases, PPF_G^B dominates PPF_H^B, in other cases, PPF_H^B dominates PPF_G^B, and, in the remaining cases, the two frontiers cross.

Evidently, the analysis of Section 2.5 applies to the production-theoretic output-price and real-output indexes derived from the fully closed, rising-factor-supply-with-monopsony, and fully open cases. We need not repeat the results in detail, they are identical to those given in inequalities (2.8.6)–(2.8.9) for the hybrid case, with the appropriate indexes for the general case of rising factor supplies and monopsony replacing those for the hybrid case.

As usual when dealing with Paasche and Laspeyres indexes, simultaneous lower and upper bounds would apply if the current-period and base-period PPFs were parallel along rays. Unfortunately, the conditions for parallel PPFs seem to be quite restrictive for the case of the monopsonist facing rising supply curves.

2.10. A Digression: Alternative Treatments of Monopoly

This section represents a digression from our analysis of rising supply schedules. We shall return to that theme in Section 2.11.

Our treatment of monopsony just given suggests a somewhat parallel treatment of the case of monopoly. Of course, such a treatment will not be isomorphic to that of monopsony. The problem that is truly isomorphic

---

17. The corresponding ranking in terms of supply schedules is shown in Figure 2.9.1.

to that of the output-price index for the monopsony case treated in the preceding section is that of the input-price index for the monopoly case. The isomorphic problem to that about to be discussed is that of the input-price index for the monopsony case. Nevertheless, the two treatments are similar in that they take full advantage of the monopolist's or monoponist's use of its power over prices.

This was not done in the rather sketchy treatment of market imperfections in Fisher and Shell (1972, pp. 59–61). In that treatment, we handled monopoly (for the fully closed case) by reducing the dosage of factor usage until reaching that level that a perfectly competitive economy would have required to produce value at given prices just equal to the money output actually produced in the presence of monopoly. We then dealt with the PPF for the economy so constructed as though it were the actual one. The misallocation of resources caused by monopoly shows up in this treatment in the fact that the constructed competitive economy will generally require a dosage level less than one, so that a removal of the market imperfection with *actual* factor usage held constant will show up as an expansion of real output – an output vector outside the constructed PPF.

This treatment is not really satisfactory. The whole theory of the output-price index (and of real-output measurement) for a perfectly competitive economy involves the explicit assumption that output prices are taken as given and determined by demand conditions. To put it another way, just as the theory of the cost-of-living index takes prices as representing the trade-offs available to the consumption sector in its purchasing opportunities, so the theory of the output-price and quantity indexes takes prices as representing the trade-offs available to the production sector in its selling opportunities. Under competition, such treatments are correct, at least at the margin, and prices do reflect trade-offs as seen by the participants. Under monopoly, however, this is not the case.

Thus, to deal with the monopoly case by finding a somehow comparable competitive economy is, in a sense, not to deal with it at all. Having found such an economy, we proceed to ask what it would have done had output prices been p'' rather than p'; a monopoly, however, would not have stood still for output prices to be p'' unless those prices happened to be optimal for it. It would have set output prices to suit itself.

This fact points to a direct and relatively satisfactory treatment of the monopoly case, provided that we can assume profit-maximizing behavior. Where prices are under the control of the production sector, it makes no sense to take them as given in constructing that sector's optimum problem. Rather, what must be taken as given are the demand functions facing the production sector. Under competition, as seen by that sector, this reduces to the usual case; under monopoly it correctly reflects the selling opportunities facing the production sector.

Such a treatment may seem a little strange. Prices, as such, are about to disappear from the givens of the output-price-index (or output "deflation") problem. Yet let us keep the purpose of the analysis in mind. The object here is not to deflate any particular price but rather to deflate money output to get a measure of real output in terms of resource usage. The better way to think about this is that, in general, we are constructing an output deflator that in this case is not a (narrowly interpreted) "price index."

Indeed, this very fact reveals itself in the analysis. The incorporation of monopoly in our analysis requires even less change than did that of monopsony. In fact, it requires almost no change at all except in the interpretation of some of the results. Nearly everything we have said in Fisher and Shell (1972, Essay II) or in the present book remains valid with marginal revenues replacing prices throughout.

Incorporating monopoly into our analysis turns out to be so easy that we content ourselves with setting up the output-deflation problem and then commenting on the differences that the change in set up makes. All versions of the theoretical output-price index we have so far treated begin with two output prices, p^A and p^B, and a reference PPF. Explicitly or implicitly, we define

$$y^A = \max_x p^A \cdot x \quad \text{for } x \text{ inside or on the reference PPF}$$

and   (2.10.1)

$$y^B = \max_x p^B \cdot x \quad \text{for } x \text{ inside or on the reference PPF}$$

The production-theoretic output-price index (or output deflator) is then y^A/y^B.

To generalize this to include monopoly, let $R(x)$ be the total revenue function[18] as seen by our monopolist producer, where x is the output vector, with superscripts A and B continuing to denote conditions in the two periods

---

18. The revenue function plays a role in the monopoly producer case similar to that played by profit function in the competitive producer case. Monopoly revenue functions and monopsonistic cost functions are treated in Lau (1974), Epstein (1981), and Diewert (1982).

to be compared. The system (2.10.1) is generalized to

$$y^A = \max_x R^A(x) \quad \text{for } x \text{ inside or on the reference PPF}$$

and (2.10.2)

$$y^B = \max_x R^B(x) \quad \text{for } x \text{ inside or on the reference PPF}$$

Then the theoretical output deflator is y^A/y^B. For the monopolist, the output deflator is based on two revenue functions, R^A and R^B, each defined over the output vector x and on a single PPF, which defines a surface in output space.

Note that, whereas the competitive economy produces on its PPF, the economy with monopoly power need not do so. Hence the possibility that x may be inside rather than on the reference PPF is a real one in (2.10.2) rather than a mere formality as in (2.10.1).

Assume, for example, that the deflator defined in (2.10.2) is derived from conditions that the monopolist faced in situation B, say, the base period. Then the PPF is PPF^B and x^B is equal to $\hat{x}$ actual base-period production, which is such that $y^B = R^B(x^B) = p^B \cdot x^B$, where p^B is the vector of output prices prevailing in the base period and y^B is actual base-period money output. Since the monopolist maximizes revenue, given the PPF, we have $R^B(x^B) = p^B x^B \geq R^B(x)$ for x lying on PPF^B.

The usual Laspeyres index does not in general serve in the monopoly case as a lower bound for the production-theoretic deflator derived from base-period conditions. There is, however, a quasi-Laspeyres index $\tilde{L}$ that serves as a general lower bound, namely,

$$\tilde{L} = \frac{R^A(x^B)}{R^B(x^B)} \leq \frac{R^A(x^A)}{R^B(x^B)}. \tag{2.10.3}$$

The inequality follows because theoretical output x^A maximizes $R^A(x)$ subject to x being on or inside PPF^B. The quasi-Laspeyres index $\tilde{L}$ is not of much use in practice, however, because it cannot be easily related to the usual Laspeyres index. Although we have $R^B(x^B) = p^B \cdot x^B$, it is in general not the case that we have $R^A(x^B) = p^B \cdot x^B$.

Similarly, a quasi-Paasche index $\tilde{P}$ serves as an upper bound for the production-theoretic output deflator derived from production conditions prevailing in the current period. Let that period be period A; then we have

$$\tilde{P} = \frac{R^A(x^A)}{R^B(x^A)} \geq \frac{R^A(x^A)}{R^B(x^B)}. \tag{2.10.4}$$

Since the theoretical index is derived from PPF^A, we have $R^A(x^A) = p^A \cdot x^A$, where p^A is the observed vector of current-period prices and x^A is the observed vector of current-period outputs. Now, the vector x^B is unobserved, and in general it is not true that $R^B(x^A) = p^B \cdot x^A$, where p^B is the vector of observed base-period prices. Hence the quasi-Paasche index cannot be simply related to the usual Paasche index.

When monopoly is replaced by competition, we expect outputs to rise. Will this be captured in our treatment? Unfortunately, the answer is not simple.[19]

To fix ideas, suppose that the base-period situation involved monopoly whereas the current-period situation does not, but that no other changes occurred between the two periods. Construct the production-theoretic output-price deflator as above *as though there had been monopoly in both periods*. Obviously, that deflator will be unity. Evidently, the breaking up of monopoly will be represented by the change in money output in that situation.

This seems attractive, but there is a problem. Although it is true that, for any *given* price vector, the competitive production system will produce a larger value of output than the monopolized one, it does not follow that the breakup of monopoly leads to a higher value of output at *competitive* prices than the monopolized economy would have produced at *monopoly* prices. Hence it is not guaranteed that this method necessarily indicates a positive increase in output from the replacement of monopoly with competition.

An alternative method does come to mind, however, at least in principle. Calculate the prices that the monopolized economy would have charged in the current period. Call that price vector p_m^*. Consider the value of output that the competitive economy would have produced had prices been p_m^*. The ratio of this to the value of output that the monopolized economy would have produced in the current period will certainly be greater than unity, and this can at least in part be attributed to the expansion of output due to the introduction of competition.

This is somewhat more appealing than the first alternative. If we drop the assumption that nothing changed between the two periods other than the removal of monopoly, the same principle can be applied. Now, however, we must note that there are two possible measures of monopoly restriction,

19. This problem should not be confused with that of analyzing the different production-theoretic output-price and output-quantity indexes that the same set of demand conditions would produce under competition and under monopoly. This is a matter of comparing the index constructed in (2.10.1) where competition is present in both periods with that constructed in (2.10.2) with monopoly present in both periods.

one using the base-period and one the current-period PPF. Indeed, for each such PPF there are two measures of monopoly restriction, one based (as just described) on current-period demand conditions and one using base-period demand conditions.

This multiplicity of measures poses no problem. Each measure answers a different question. For example, the measure using the current-period PPF and base-period demand conditions goes to the question of the extent to which monopoly with current-period production resources and technology would restrict output were it to face base-period demand conditions. That is not the same question and does not have the same answer as the extent to which monopoly with current-period production resources and technology would restrict output facing current-period demand conditions.

The problem is not that there are several alternative questions and answers. It is rather that the answers seem somewhat artificial. To return to the original example and notation, under competition the production sector would *not* maximize the value of output at the monopoly prices p^* but at some competitive prices, and the resulting value might be higher or lower.

This problem may be inescapable. It is only apparently avoided in the treatment given in Fisher and Shell (1972, Essay II, pp. 59–61). As described above, this treatment finds a competitive economy that would have been just capable of producing the same value as the monopolized one had it faced the monopoly prices. This treats monopolization as an explicit reduction in resources. Even there, however, the constructed competitive economy maximizes value at monopoly prices, not at the prices that would occur under competition and the same demand conditions.

It may be that we are asking too much in seeking to avoid this problem. The problem appears to come about because of the somewhat arbitrary separation between production and demand required to make sense of producer or consumer index-number construction in the first place.[20] When monopoly is involved, the separation becomes artificial because prices no longer serve to decentralize information between sectors.

2.11. The General Competitive Case

We now return to the case of competitive output markets and, indeed, to competitive input markets as well. In the present section, we develop the

---

20. This also reminds us that the distinction between outputs and inputs can be arbitrary; see Shell (1975).

theory of output-price and real-output indexes applicable to a competitive economic unit (say, an industry) facing rising factor-supply schedules. The fully closed economy, the fully open economy, and the hybrid economy are each special cases of this.

As can be seen from considering the preceding section, the absence of monopoly power in the output markets simplifies the analysis. Unfortunately, the absence of monopsony power in the input markets complicates it considerably. Although our industry is assumed to face a rising supply schedule (as in Section 9), it takes no account of this fact. Because competitive firms do not "see" the full factor-supply schedule, they optimize taking prevailing factor prices as fixed. Firms thus have a more optimistic assessment of global production possibilities than is warranted by the conditions facing the industry. This implies that the construction of the production-theoretic output-price index is no longer merely a problem in constrained optimization; it also involves a fixed-point argument that ensures that the demand and supply of factors are equal. Further, as we shall see in the next chapter, since the index is not derived from a pure constrained optimization problem, comparative-statics analysis is much more difficult. As a result, Paasche and Laspeyres bounds need no longer apply.

In a way, these difficulties stem from an aggregation problem. For the first time, we are encountering a case in which the firm and the industry face meaningfully different supply conditions. An analysis actually conducted at the level of the individual agent is bound to run into problems when this happens.

We use the notation of Section 9, repeated here for convenience. Technological opportunities are summarized by the production relation

$$F(x, v) = 0, \tag{2.11.1}$$

where x is an r-vector of outputs and v is an m-vector of inputs (factors). Let w denote the corresponding m-vector of factor prices. Factors are supplied to our industry according to the schedule

$$v = v^S(w). \tag{2.11.2}$$

If, for some factor, the supply is fixed, then the corresponding component of v^S is a constant (independent of w). If some factor is supplied at a constant price, then the corresponding component of v^S is zero below that price, infinite above it, and any value in $[0, +\infty)$ at that price.

Firms in the competitive industry face a given vector of factor prices w *and act as if they do not affect w.* Thus, the firms perceive themselves as operating in a fully open economy in the sense of Section 7. The *perceived* production possibility frontier for the industry facing factor prices w and limited to money expenditures on factors C is

$$\text{PPF}_{\text{FO}}(w) = \{\text{maximal } x \mid F(x, v) = 0 \text{ and } w \cdot v = C\}. \qquad (2.11.3)$$

For fixed money expenditure C we can derive from (2.11.3) the implied industry demand schedule for factors,

$$v = v^D(w). \qquad (2.11.4)$$

Unfortunately, we cannot base the analysis of our competitive industry solely on the production possibility frontier defined in (2.11.3). First, $\text{PPF}_{\text{FO}}(w)$ is derived for fixed factor prices w; this is a false assumption on the industry level. Second, $\text{PPF}_{\text{FO}}(w)$ does not include the industry-wide constraint that supply and demand for factors be equal (i.e., that $v^S(w) = v^D(w)$. Both these facts mean that $\text{PPF}_{\text{FO}}(w)$ does not actually represent the production possibilities open to the industry.

In particular, the constraint that supply and demand for factors be equal, and the fact that it is not recognized by the competitive industry, makes the analysis complex. This is because the equilibrium factor prices equating factor supplies and demands themselves depend on output prices, since factor demands also depend on output prices. This means, for example, that it is erroneous to suppose that we can proceed by defining the PPF for the competitive general case to be $\{\text{maximal} x \mid x \text{ belongs to } \text{PPF}_{\text{FO}}(w) \text{ for some } w$ with the property that $w \cdot v^S(w) = C\}$. The competitive industry does not solve the problem of maximizing value at fixed output prices subject to such a PPF because *which w* is relevant to $\text{PPF}_{\text{FO}}(w)$ depends on output prices. To put it differently, not all points on $\text{PPF}_{\text{FO}}(w)$ for a given w are in fact achievable because, were output prices different, w would also be different and the competitive economy would "solve" a different maximum problem.

We must therefore proceed differently. We do so by providing a definition of the production-theoretic output-price indexes in which the fixed-point aspect is clearly displayed.

In defining the production-theoretic output-price index for the competitive general industry, I_{CG}, we are given the production relation (2.11.1), money expenditure on factors, C, the factor-supply schedule (2.11.2), and two output-price vectors, p^A and p^B.

First, take the factor price vector w as a parameter and let

$$y^A(w) = \max_{x, v} p^A \cdot x \quad \text{subject to } F(x, v) = 0 \text{ and } wv = C. \qquad (2.11.5)$$

Let the maximizing output vector be $x^A(w)$ and the resulting vector of optimal factor demands be $v^{DA}(w)$. Let w^A be the factor-price vector (assumed to be unique) that equates supply and demand (i.e., that solves the equation $v^{DA}(w) = v^S(w)$). (Note that the competitive industry facing prices p^A in fact ends up solving problem (2.11.5) for $w = w^A$.) In similar fashion, let

$$y^B(w) = \max_{x,v} p^B \cdot x \quad \text{subject to } F(x, v) = 0 \text{ and } wv = C.$$

(2.11.6)

Let the maximizing output vector be $x^B(w)$ and the resulting vector of optimal factor demands be $v^{DB}(w)$. Now, find w (assumed to be unique) that solves $v^{DB}(w) = v^S(w)$; call it w^B. (Note that the competitive industry facing prices p^B in fact ends up solving (2.11.6) for $w = w^B$.) The production-theoretic output-price index appropriate to the competitive general case I_{CG} is then defined by

$$I_{CG} = y^A(w_A)/y^B(w^B).$$

(2.11.7)

This is right in line with our general production-theoretic approach. The numerator and denominator of I_{CG} give the value of output that the competitive industry would have produced when faced with prices p^A and p^B, respectively, given the production technology and factor supply situation posited.

There is an equivalent way of proceeding that uses the fully closed economy rather than the fully open one. First, take factor supplies v as a parameter. Let

$$\tilde{y}^A(v) = \max_x p^A \cdot x \quad \text{subject to } F(x, v) = 0.$$

(2.11.8)

Let the maximizing output vector be $x^A(v)$. Associated with each fixed factor in this maximization problem will be a shadow price – the marginal revenue product of the factor. Call the vector of such shadow prices $w^{*A}(v)$. Let $C^{*A} = w^{*A}(v)v$. Note that the competitive industry that takes $C^{*A}(v)$ and $w^{*A}(v)$ as given will solve (2.11.8) when maximizing value at prices p^A. Further, the value of the solution to that maximum problem will be homogeneous of degree zero in $C^{*A}(v)$ and $w^{*A}(v)$. Accordingly, define

$$w^A = [C/C^{*A}(v)]w^{*A}(v).$$

(2.11.9)

Now find that value of v such that $v = v^S[w^A(v)]$ and denote it v^A. Similarly, solve the same problem with p^B replacing p^A. Call the solution v^B and the corresponding maximized value of output $\tilde{y}^B(v^B)$.

The production-theoretic output-price index for the competitive general case $\tilde{I}_{CG}$ can then be defined by

$$\tilde{I}_{CG} = \tilde{y}^A(v^A)/\tilde{y}^B(v^B). \qquad (2.11.10)$$

It is evident that we have

$$\tilde{I}_{CG} = I_{CG}, \qquad (2.11.11)$$

where I^{CG} is defined in (2.11.7), since the solution to the fully open maximization problems (2.11.5) and (2.11.6) will lead to the factor usages v^A and v^B, respectively, when factor prices are equal to (or proportional to) the appropriate shadow prices.

Thus, the competitive general case can be analyzed using either the fully open or the fully closed case. It can also be analyzed using the hybrid case, but the details are left to the reader.

Now, if the economic unit in question really faced factor-supply schedules that were all flat, all vertical, or a mixture of both, then there would be no further difficulty. This is because given the shadow prices of the perfectly inelastically supplied factors and factor prices of the perfectly elastically supplied ones, the competitive unit would end up solving the same problem as it would if it took full account of supply conditions. Furthermore, those conditions would be the same independent of output prices. In the relevant sense – that of the definition of the PPF – factor supplies will end up the same at both prices p^A and prices p^B. This is because (as we have seen in analyzing them) such cases can be reduced to the fully closed case with the perfectly elastically supplied factors considered together as a single factor represented by the fixed amount of money to be spent on them.

In the competitive general case, however, factor supplies at prices p^A and p^B will differ. No matter whether one expresses the problem solved by the competitive unit as a fully open, fully closed, or hybrid one, the problem solved by the unit in maximizing value at prices p^A differs in more than its maximand from the problem the unit solves in maximizing value at prices p^B. For example, start with the PPF *perceived* by the competitive unit to be the same as some fully open one (as in (2.11.3)). At output prices p^B the production unit ends up believing it faces $PPF_{FO}(w^B)$, whereas at output prices p^A it ends up believing it faces $PPF_{FO}(w^A)$, and these are generally not the same because they involve different points on the factor supply curves.

This difference is perhaps most easily seen if we think of the case of two factors, 1 and 2. At prices p^B with equilibrium factor prices w^B, equilibrium in factor markets produces factor usages v_1^B and v_2^B say. Similarly, at prices p^A with equilibrium factor prices w^A, equilibrium in factor markets produces factor usages v_1^A and v_2^A, say. If the supply of each factor depends only on the price of that factor (the simplest case, but not a necessary assumption), then with $w^A \neq w^B$ and costs C being the same for both maximization problems, (2.11.5) and (2.11.6), it is plain that $v_1^B/v_2^B \neq v_1^A/v_2^A$. Hence, even with constant returns-to-scale, it will generally be the case that the two resulting PPFs, $\text{PPF}_{\text{FC}}(v^A)$ and $\text{PPF}_{\text{FC}}(v^B)$ will intersect. Moreover, so will $\text{PPF}_{\text{FO}}(w^A)$ and $\text{PPF}_{\text{FO}}(w^B)$.

The most important implication of this fact is that the usual Laspeyres and Paasche bounds are not guaranteed to hold for the competitive general case. To see this, let situation B be the base period and consider the problem (2.11.6) faced by the competitive unit in that situation. The maximand, $y^B(w^B)$, which is the denominator of I_{CG} will also be the denominator of the Laspeyres price index. However, the usual method of establishing the bound would be to show that the *numerator* of I_{CG}, $y^A(w^A)$, was the value of the solution to a maximum problem in which x^B (output in the base period) was feasible. This is no longer guaranteed. Figure 2.11.1 shows a situation in which the value of x^B at prices p^A (represented by the slope of the dashed lines) is higher than $y^A(w^A)$. Furthermore, (just for good measure), the value of x^A at prices p^B (represented by the slope of the solid lines) is higher than $y^B(w^B)$. Plainly, Laspeyres and Paasche bounds are inapplicable here.

It is instructive to realize that this negative conclusion cannot be avoided by use of constructions such as that of Figure (2.5.1) involving relatively optimistic and pessimistic assessments of technology. For example, the problem solved by the competitive unit in the base period involves $\text{PPF}_{\text{FO}}(w^B)$. That fully open case, however, is neither more optimistic nor more pessimistic as regards technology assessments in the current-period than is the frontier that the competitive unit *then* believes it is facing, $\text{PPF}_{\text{FO}}(w^A)$. A similar statement applies to the fully closed cases and to the hybrid cases.

It is tempting to suppose, nonetheless, that some bounds can be established using the monopsony case of Section 9. After all, the monopsonist, who takes the rising supply curves into account, can do a better job of maximizing value than the competitive unit, which does not. Unfortunately, this proves to be at little help. Although the monopsonist can do a better job of maximizing value than the competitive unit faced with the same rising supply curves, he can do better in *both* the base and the current-period. To put it differently, the actual position achieved by the competitive

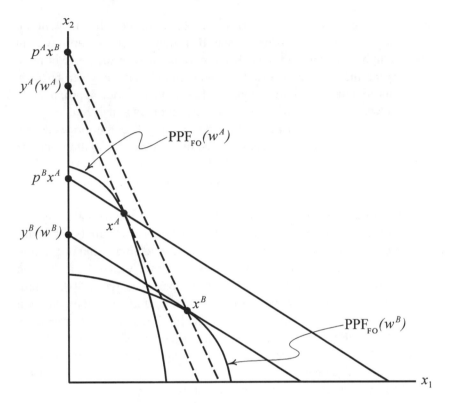

Figure 2.11.1

unit in the base period will generally not be the same as that achieved by a monopsonist with the same supply conditions at the same prices. Indeed, the two PPFs involved will not generally have a point in common, and the construction of Figure 2.5.1 will not be applicable.

We are left with the following position: If we are studying a competitive unit sufficiently small as to be able to purchase factors at constant factor prices, then our analysis of the fully open case applies and Laspeyres and Paasche bounds are applicable. If we are studying a unit large enough to be considered a closed economy, then our analysis of the fully closed case applies and Laspeyres and Paasche bounds are again applicable. If we are studying a unit such as a country, which has some factor supplies fixed but can purchase others at constant world prices, then our analysis of the hybrid case applies and the bounds are again applicable. For the case of units of intermediate size (industries, for example), those bounds will not apply unless either the units understand their monopsony power or we can take the hybrid case as a reasonable approximation over the range of price shifts being indexed. This would mean assuming that any given factor is either approximately fixed in supply or has its factor price approximately independent of the demand of the economic unit being analyzed.

Such an assumption may not be too bad in fact. If output prices do not change very much, then the constant-factor-price approximation may be appropriate.[21] If prices change rapidly, but we are only considering a short time period, then the assumption of approximately constant-factor supplies may be satisfactory.

In the absence of such assumptions, it appears to be the case that one cannot proceed without detailed knowledge of the factor-supply schedules involved. Note that this is the case even though the economic unit in question is made up of smaller units (firms, for example) for which the fully open assumption would be appropriate and is itself a part of a larger unit (the entire economy of the country or the world) to which the fully closed assumption applies. Paasche and Laspeyres bounds hold for the smaller and larger units but not for intermediate ones. In particular, they do not apply to industries or sectors large enough to have rising factor-supply curves but not so large as to have vertical ones.

It is interesting that such aggregation problems arise at an intermediate level but not at a completely macro level. This is because the closed competitive economy, like the small competitive firm, solves a maximization problem using a PPF defined in a way that is directly relevant for purposes of index-number construction.

Aggregation problems are discussed in some detail in Chapter 6.

---

21. It is the extent of changes in the output prices of the unit being analyzed that matters. What is involved here is not actual factor-price changes but the change that would have been induced by the change in the output prices, other things being equal.

3   Comparative Statics: Outputs

3.1. Introduction: The Production Possibility Map

As we stressed in the previous chapter, the production-theoretic output-price and real-output indexes depend on the particular PPF used to construct them. In the present chapter, we investigate the comparative statics of how the indexes vary as the PPF is varied. We assume smoothness and other regularities that allow us to employ basic techniques from differential calculus. This could be of interest for at least three reasons:

1. There is some direct interest in knowing how such dependence operates. If we know how two PPFs differ (for example, the PPFs of two different countries) or how the PPF changes over time, then we may want to use this information to assess how real-output measurement differs or changes.
2. A by product of our analysis will be results on how production of particular goods changes when the PPF changes and how such changes in production are related to the effects of changes in prices on factor usage. These comparative statics are of general interest in areas of microeconomics other than index-number construction.
3. We have seen that the Laspeyres price index often serves as a lower bound for the production-theoretic price index constructed using the base-period PPF. Similarly, the Paasche quantity index often forms a lower bound for the corresponding production-theoretic quantity index. The Paasche price index and Laspeyres quantity index, however, do not provide bounds on the *same* production-theoretic indexes but only (respectively) on the production-theoretic price and quantity

indexes constructed from the current-period PPF. Since it is obviously desirable to bound the production-theoretic indexes from both sides, it is useful to know how the production-theoretic indexes and their associated Paasche and Laspeyres bounds change when moving from the base to the current period (or from one country to another).[1]

To accomplish this end requires the concept of the family of PPFs – a production possibility map (PPM) – introduced in Chapter 2. If the PPM is homothetic (i.e., all the PPFs that comprise it are parallel along rays through the origin), then, as we have seen, production-theoretic output-price and output-quantity indexes constructed using any one member of the family coincide respectively with those constructed using any other member. This fact facilitates much of the following comparative statics.

This discussion will be most easily understood in terms of a concrete example. As before, we begin with the case of the fully closed economy (the case treated extensively in Fisher and Shell (1972, Essay II). Throughout this chapter, hats over variables are used to denote base-period levels. Unhatted variables are either general or represent their current-period levels.

The construction of a particular PPM for the fully closed economy was given in Section 2.6 for the case of constant returns-to-scale and base-period factor proportions. We use the same notation here.

The m-vector of inputs is denoted by v, and the r-vector of outputs by x. The base-period technology is given by

$$F(x, v) = 0. \tag{3.1.1}$$

Suppose, for the time being, that inputs are supplied in the fixed amounts given by the vector v^0. Then the PPF would be

$$\text{PPF} = \{\text{maximal } x \mid F(x, v^0) = 0\}. \tag{3.1.2}$$

Now consider all the PPFs that can be generated by factor supplies in the same proportions as the elements of the vector v^0 but in different absolute amounts. That is, consider, for all positive scalars μ, the set of PPFs given by

$$\text{PPF}(\mu) = \{\text{maximal } x \mid F(x, \mu v^0) = 0\}. \tag{3.1.3}$$

---

1. As briefly discussed in the preceding chapter (and in Fisher and Shell (1972, pp. 56–57)), we take the position that indexes using the base-period PPF are the more interesting ones. Accordingly, the discussion in the present chapter focuses on these indexes. The analysis applies to the indexes based on the current-period PPF, mutatis mutandis.

This set is the production possibility map (PPM) generated in the fully closed economy in which factor proportions are given by v^0.

The scalar μ can be interpreted as the "dosage" of factors (in the proportions given by v^0), and it is determined by x (with v^0 fixed). Thus

$$\mu = \phi(x, v^0). \tag{3.1.4}$$

The function ϕ is the factor-requirements function. It gives the minimum dosage required to produce the output vector x. The production possibility map (given v^0) can then be defined by

$$\text{PPM} = \{(x, \mu) \mid \phi(x, v^0) = \mu \text{ and } \mu \in \mathbb{R}_{++}\}. \tag{3.1.5}$$

We now define the production-theoretic output-price index for the fully closed economy in terms of the PPM given in (3.1.5). (As mentioned, this will be the index using the base-period PPF.) We are given the vector of base-period output prices $\hat{p}$, base-period money output $\hat{y}$, and the vector of current-period prices p. We are also given the vector of factor proportions v^0. We first find the output vector $\hat{x}$ that solves

$$\min_{\hat{x}} \mu \quad \text{subject to } \hat{p} \cdot \hat{x} = \hat{y}. \tag{3.1.6}$$

Let $\hat{\mu}$ denote the minimized value of μ. Next, find the value of x that solves

$$\max_{x} p \cdot x \quad \text{subject to } \phi(x) = \hat{\mu}. \tag{3.1.7}$$

Let y denote the maximized value of $p \cdot x$. Then the production-theoretic output-price deflator I satisfies $I = (y/\hat{y})$.

This apparently cumbersome description is needed for the following reason. When $v^0 = \hat{v}$ (the vector of actual base-period factor supplies), the PPM used is that which actually obtained when $\hat{y}$ was produced at prices $\hat{p}$. In this case, the described procedure obviously amounts to finding the actual base-period PPF (and actual base-period outputs $\hat{x}$) and forming the production-theoretic output-price index as described in previous chapters. In this case, x is *not* the vector of outputs actually produced in the current-period but rather the vector that would have been produced at current-period prices with the base-period PPF.

Suppose, however, that $v^0 = v$ (the vector of actual current-period factor supplies). Then the PPM used is that which actually obtained in the current period. In that case, *provided that the PPM is homothetic,* the described procedure generates the production-theoretic output-price index based on the actual current-period PPF. In this case, $\hat{x}$ is not the vector of outputs actually produced in the base period but rather the vector that would have been produced at base-period prices with the current-period PPM had the dosage of current-period factor supplies been just sufficient to generate $\hat{y}$ as the value of money output at those base-period prices.

The latter situation is pictured in Figure 3.1.1. The actual PPF is the outer one. Actual output at prices p (represented by the slope of the dashed lines) is at x' and money output at y'. Had prices been $\hat{p}$ (represented by the slope of the solid lines), actual production would have been at $\hat{x}'$ and money output at $\hat{y}'$. Clearly, the theoretical output-price index based on this map is $(y'/\hat{y}')$, and this is the same as $(y/\hat{y})$ if the map is homothetic. Actual production in the base-period, however, need not have been at $\hat{x}$, because

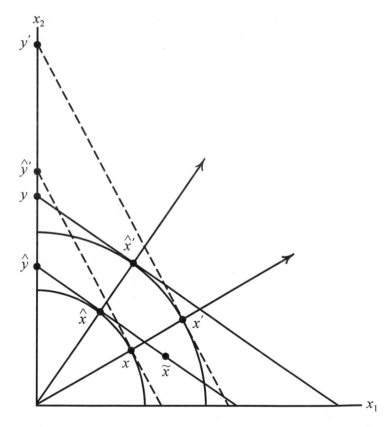

Figure 3.1.1

the PPM was different in the base period. In general, it was at some other point on the same value line, say $\tilde{x}$.

This is the basis of our comparative-statics analysis. We vary the PPF. Among other things, we study the effects on the production plan of variations in the technology. In particular, we seek to explain the difference (if any) between the observed base-period output $\tilde{x}$ and its theoretical counterpart $\hat{x}$. (See Figure 2.1.1.) When the observed output vector $\tilde{x}$ is not proportional to the theoretical output vector $\hat{x}$ then we cannot depend on the Laspeyres and Paasche indexes to serve as bounds for the *same* production-theoretic index. By studying the effects on the production-theoretic index of changing the PPF, we are frequently able to analyze how Paasche and Laspeyres indexes should be corrected in order to restore their (joint) bounding properties.

In this chapter, we focus on homothetic PPMs derived from the technology prevailing in the base period. In these cases, the uncorrected Laspeyres price index typically serves as a lower bound for the production-theoretic output-price index. We then show how the Paasche price index must be corrected to serve as an upper bound for the production-theoretic output-price index.

Our explicit discussion runs in terms of the production-theoretic output-price index and its accompanying Paasche and Laspeyres price indexes. Note, however, that the change in money output equals the product of the production-theoretic output-price and real-output indexes. Recall that the same change is also the product of the Paasche price and Laspeyres quantity indexes as well as the product of the Laspeyres price and Paasche quantity indexes. Consequently, our results for price indexes immediately imply corresponding results for quantity indexes, mutatis mutandis. We do not bother to state such results explicitly, since they can easily be deduced by the reader.

We shall begin this discussion by continuing with the case of the fully closed economy. We shall go on to consider the other cases discussed in the preceding chapter. Such cases will have PPMs generated in different ways from that of the fully closed economy, but provided the PPMs are homothetic, the same general principles of construction will be valid.

One more word is needed before proceeding. Homotheticity obviously plays an important role here, and we shall assume it throughout (and we shall discuss the role of this assumption when appropriate). Not all our results require homotheticity; without homotheticity, our results can be useful in the analysis of *small* changes from base-period conditions. Where homotheticity (or even constant returns-to-scale) is explicitly required in the proofs, we shall say so.[2,3]

3.2. The Fully Closed Economy: Hicks-Neutral Technical Change

In this section, we begin the discussion of comparative-static analysis for the fully closed economy. This was the case covered in Fisher and Shell (1972, Essay II), and the results in the present volume are not new but drawn directly from our earlier work, which gives a more extensive discussion of this case than is given here. We summarize the main points and do not repeat the (occasionally extensive) proofs. The general technique of proof is the same as for the new results given later in the chapter.[4]

It is necessary to deal with the derivation of the PPF from underlying production functions. We assume that the output of the ith good ($i = 1, 2, \ldots, r$) depends only on the amounts of factors devoted to production of that good with no externalities in production. The base-period production possibility map is then determined by

$$x_i = g^i(v_{i1}, \ldots, v_{im})$$

$$\sum_{i=1}^{r} v_{ij} \leq v_j^0, \quad v_{ij} \geq 0 \tag{3.2.1}$$

for $i = 1, \ldots, r$ and $j = 1, \ldots, m$.

Here, v_{ij} is the amount of factor j allocated to production of good i, and g^i is the production function for the ith good. As before, the vector v^0 gives the proportions in which factors are supplied. In the base period, we have $\hat{v} = v^0$.

---

2. We note in passing that homotheticity of both the base-period and current-period PPMs is not required for comparisons such as made in Figure 3.1.1. Homotheticity of either one of them will suffice. We make no use of this below.

3. In general, homotheticity is weaker than constant returns-to-scale.

4. Since, as observed in the preceding chapter, both the fully closed and fully open economies are special cases of the hybrid economy, it would be possible to proceed directly to analysis of the hybrid case and then to specialize the results. Expository considerations, however, have persuaded us not to do so. First, the fully closed and fully open cases have their own special importance and their own interesting features. Second, the homotheticity issues involved are different in each case. Third, the notation for the hybrid case is necessarily cumbersome. It is therefore simpler to work with the special cases first, going to the more elaborate notation only where necessary.

We begin by studying the effects of Hicks-neutral technical change[5] in the production function of the first good. We do so by replacing the first production-function equation in (3.2.1) by

$$x_1 = ag^1(v_{11}, \ldots, v_{1m}), \tag{3.2.2}$$

where a is a parameter equal to unity in the base period. Hicks-neutral technical progress in the production of the first good is represented by a positive change in a. In terms of the notation developed in the preceding section, it is easy to see that the production possibility map for both the current and the base periods is given by

$$\text{PPM} = \{(x, \mu) \mid \phi(x_1/a, x_2, \ldots, x_r, \hat{v}) = \mu \text{ and } \mu \in \mathbb{R}_{++}\}. \tag{3.2.3}$$

The production-theoretic output-price deflator I satisfies $I = (y/\hat{y})$, where $\hat{y}$ is given, and y is defined as the maximized value of $p \cdot x$ in (3.1.7).

Define the supply elasticity η_{ij} by

$$\eta_{ij} = (p_j/x_i)(\partial x_i/\partial p_j)_{\hat{v} \text{ constant}} \tag{3.2.4}$$

for $i, j = 1, \ldots, r$. This is the elasticity of the supply of the ith good with respect to the jth price, holding factor supplies constant.

Further, define α_i, share of the ith good in money output, by

$$\alpha_i = p_i x_i/y \tag{3.2.5}$$

for $i = 1, \ldots, r$. The following result is proved in Fisher and Shell (1972, p. 73).

Theorem 3.2.1: *Assume that the PPM is homothetic. Then*

A. *Suppose we have $p_i = \hat{p}_i$ for $i = 2, \ldots, r$. Then $(\partial y/\partial a)$ and $(p_1 - \hat{p}_1)$ share the same sign.*

B. *Suppose we have $p_i = \hat{p}_i$ for $i \neq j$ and $j \neq 1$. If we have $(\eta_{j1} - \alpha_1) > 0$, then $(\partial y/\partial a)$ and $(p_j - \hat{p}_j)$ share the same sign. If we have $(\eta_{j1} - \alpha_1) < 0$, then $(\partial y/\partial a)$ and $(p_j - \hat{p}_j)$ are of opposite sign. If we have $(\eta_{j1} - \alpha_1) = 0$, then $(\partial y/\partial a) = 0$.*

C. *The results of B also hold with $(\eta_{1j} - \alpha_j)$ replacing $(\eta_{j1} - \alpha_1)$.*

Since an increase in a single price leads to an increase in the price index, these results have a simple interpretation. First, Hicks-neutral technical

5. This notion of neutrality was introduced in Hicks (1932). See Burmeister and Dobell (1970, pp. 69–75) for a discussion.

change amplifies the effect of changes in the price of the first good on the production-theoretic output-price index. Second, this technical change increases or decreases the "weight" of the price of the jth good ($j \neq 1$) according to whether the (factor-supply-constant) elasticity of supply of the jth good with respect to the first price is greater than or less than the share of the first good in money output. Finally, this criterion can be replaced with that of whether the (factor-supply-constant) elasticity of supply of the first good with respect to the jth price is greater or less than the share of the jth good in money output.

It is further shown (Fisher and Shell (1972, pp. 70–72)), that the effect of the technical change on the production of good i, $(\partial \hat{x}_i / \partial a)$, is positive if and only if the conditions just given imply an increase in the importance of the price of good i in the production-theoretic output-price index ($i = 1, \ldots, r$). This is as one should expect, since $\hat{x}_i$ is proportional to the weight given to the ith price in a Laspeyres price index. Hence Theorem 3.2.1 shows the direction in which a Laspeyres price index must be changed to retain its property as a lower bound on the production-theoretic output-price index formed using the current-period PPF. Similar results apply to the Paasche price index and the production-theoretic output-price index using the base-period PPF.

3.3. The Fully Closed Economy: Changing Factor Supplies and Factor-Augumenting Technical Change

Having finished with our review of Hicks-neutral technical change in the fully closed economy, we now return to (3.2.1) as the specification of the PPF. In this section, we review some related cases of changes in the PPF. These involve changes in factor supplies and changes in factor efficiencies. We begin with the case of a change in the supply of the mth factor (say, labor).

The problem involves evaluating the derivative $(\partial y / \partial v_m^0)$. The following results are derived in Fisher and Shell (1972, pp. 81–88). Let $\hat{w}_m$ and w_m denote the wage of the mth factor in the base period and the current period, respectively. Define $\hat{\beta}_m$ and β_m by

$$\hat{\beta}_m = (\hat{w}_m \hat{v}_m / \hat{y}) \quad \text{and} \quad \beta_m = (w_m v_m / y). \tag{3.3.1}$$

These are the shares of the mth factor in money output in the base period and the current period, respectively.

Theorem 3.3.1: *Under constant returns-to-scale, we have*

$$\partial y / \partial v_m^0 = (y/v_m^0)(\beta_m - \hat{\beta}_m).$$ (3.3.2)

That is, the effect of an increase in the supply of the mth factor increases or decreases the production-theoretic output-price index according to whether the share of that factor is greater or less at current-period prices than at base-period prices.

This leads immediately to our next result.

Theorem 3.3.2: *Assume constant returns-to-scale. If a rise in the price of the kth output ($k = 1, \ldots, r$) (other prices constant) would increase (decrease) the share of the mth factor, then an increase in the supply of the mth factor leads to an increase (decrease) in the relative importance of the kth price in the production-theoretic output-price index.*

As we should expect from this result, it is also true that those goods for which a rise in their prices would increase the share of the mth factor are precisely those goods whose outputs are increased when the supply of the mth factor rises – the goods for which their weights in a Laspeyres price index increases. Other general results for nonconstant returns-to-scale and special results for the two-sector model can also be derived.

Now, so far as the issues we are discussing are concerned, it makes no difference whether labor supply actually increases or whether all labor simultaneously becomes more productive by the same percentage (one new worker doing the work of b old ones, $b > 1$). A stronger result can be derived if we consider efficiency gains in the production of a single output: the case of factor-augmenting change.

For this purpose, replace the production function of the first output by

$$x_1 = g^1(v_{11}, \ldots, v_{1m-1}, bv_{1m}).$$ (3.3.3)

We are interested in $(\partial y / \partial b)$, where $b > 0$ is a shift parameter denoting an mth factor-augmenting technical change in the production of the first good.

Define the fractions $\hat{\beta}_{1m}$ and β_{1m} by

$$\hat{\beta}_{1m} = (\hat{w}_m \hat{v}_{1m}/\hat{y}) \quad \text{and} \quad \beta_{1m} = (w_m v_{1m}/y).$$ (3.3.4)

These are, respectively, the base-period share and current-period share in money output of the mth factor employed in the production of the first good (for example, the share in national output of steelworkers). Theorem 3.3.1 generalizes to the following theorem:

Theorem 3.3.3: *Assume constant returns-to-scale. Then we have*

$$\partial y/\partial b = (y/b)(\beta_{1m} - \hat{\beta}_{1m}). \tag{3.3.5}$$

Similarly, Theorem 3.3.2 generalizes to the following:

Theorem 3.3.4: *Assume constant returns-to-scale. If a rise in the price of the kth good ($k = 1, \ldots, r$) (with other prices being constant) would increase (decrease) the share in money output of the mth factor employed in the production of the first good, then an mth-factor-augmenting technical change in the production of the first good leads to an increase (decrease) in the relative importance of the kth price in the production-theoretic output-price index.*

As before, the prices that become more important in the production-theoretic output-price index as a result of the change correspond to just those goods whose production is increased by the change.

Further results for nonconstant returns-to-scale and for a two-sector model are also available but will not be reviewed here.

3.4. The Fully Closed Economy: General Technology Change

Before ending our review of the fully closed case, there is one general result worth discussing. We have already considered the effects of a Hicks-neutral and a factor-augmenting technical change in the production function of the first good. Consider now a general technical change in the first production function. Replace the production function for the first good by

$$x_1 = g^1(v_{11}, \ldots, v_{1m}, b), \tag{3.4.1}$$

where b is a technological parameter. We denote the partial derivative of g^1 with respect to b by g_b^1, using a hat to denote the value of the derivative evaluated at the base-period levels. The following results are proved in Fisher and Shell (1972, pp. 97–99).

Theorem 3.4.1: *Under constant returns-to-scale, we have*

$$\frac{\partial y}{\partial b} = p_1 g_b^1 \left(\frac{p_1 g_b^1}{\hat{p}_1 \hat{g}_b^1} - \frac{y}{\hat{y}} \right).$$ (3.4.2)

The magnitude $p_1 g_b^1$ is the first-order effect of the technical change on the value of output – the marginal revenue product of the technical change.

Hence, this result can be interpreted as folows:

Theorem 3.4.2: *If a rise in the price of the kth good ($k = 1, \ldots, r$) (with other prices held constant) would increase (decrease) the ratio of the marginal revenue product of the technical change to money output, then the technical change leads to an increase (decrease) in the importance of the kth price in the production-theoretic output-price index.*

As we should expect, it is just those goods for which an increase in their prices results in an increase in the ratio mentioned in the theorem that have the property that their production is increased by the technical change, raising the weights of their prices in a Laspeyres index.

This completes our review of the results obtained in our earlier work for the fully closed economy. We now turn to new material.

3.5. The Fully Open Economy: The PPM and Homotheticity

As discussed in Chapter 2, the opposite polar case to the fully closed economy is the case of the fully open economy (also the case of the small firm or industry) to which factors are supplied perfectly elastically at exogenously given prices. For such an economy, how should the production possibility map be defined?

In the fully open case, efficient production plans are described by

$$F(x, v) = 0,$$ (3.5.1)

where, as before, x is the r-vector of outputs and v is the m-vector of inputs.

We are given base-period output prices $\hat{p}$, base-period money output $\hat{y}$, and current-period output prices p. We are also given factor prices w (the same for each period), which are used for describing output opportunities.

We find the vector $(\hat{x}, \hat{v})$ that solves

$$\text{Minimize } w \cdot \hat{v} \quad \text{subject to } F(\hat{x}, \hat{v}) = 0 \text{ and } \hat{p} \cdot \hat{x} = \hat{y}. \tag{3.5.2}$$

Let $\hat{C}$ denote the resulting minimized value of $w \cdot \hat{v}$. We next find the vector (x, v) that solves

$$\text{Maximize } p \cdot x \quad \text{subject to } F(x, v) = 0 \text{ and } w \cdot v = \hat{C}. \tag{3.5.3}$$

Let y denote the resulting maximized value of $p \cdot x$. The production-theoretic output-price index is then $I = (y/\hat{y})$.

For later reference, it will be convenient to write out the Lagrangians corresponding to the two optimization problems, (3.5.2) and (3.5.3). The Lagrangian function for Problem (3.5.2) is

$$\hat{\Lambda} = w \cdot \hat{v} + \hat{\delta} F(\hat{x}, \hat{v}) - (1/\hat{\lambda})(\hat{p} \cdot \hat{x} - \hat{y}), \tag{3.5.4}$$

where $\hat{\delta}$ and $(1/\hat{\lambda})$ are Lagrange multipliers. (The latter multiplier is written as a reciprocal for reasons of symmetry.) The Lagrangian function for Problem (3.5.3) is

$$\Lambda = p \cdot x + \delta F(x, v) - \lambda(w \cdot v - \hat{C}), \tag{3.5.5}$$

where δ and λ are Lagrange multipliers.

We can describe what is involved here in the following fashion. Given factor prices, base-period output prices, and the base-period money output, we first find the level of costs required to produce that value of output efficiently. That level of costs then determines what we shall continue to call a PPF – the locus of outputs that could have been produced with the same expenditure on factors. Given this PPF, we find the value of output, y that would have been produced had prices been p instead of $\hat{p}$. The change in the value of output from $\hat{y}$ to y then represents a pure price phenomenon, since it is a change along a PPF. Any additional change is to be considered to be a change in real output.

Put somewhat more succinctly, the question posed is: What is the capacity of the economy, which produced value $\hat{y}$ when prices were $\hat{p}$, to produce value when prices are p? This is the same question we posed in the fully closed case (and will pose again in later cases). The difference is that in the fully open case, constant capacity means constant total factor costs rather than constant-factor supplies.

If we think of the production-theoretic output-price index I as constructed with actual base-period technology and factor prices, then the construction above results in finding the PPF through the actual production point $\hat{x}$.

Where technology or factor prices differ from the base-period, then $\hat{x}$ in the solution above will not be the actual base-period production point but will be the vector of outputs that the new economy would have produced at prices $\hat{p}$ in order to produce money output $\hat{y}$. Constructing the problem this way enables us to have tangency of the PPF to the value lines at both $\hat{x}$ and x and thus to retain symmetry between the base period and current period. As was the case in Section 3.1, if the PPM (in at least one of the periods) exhibits appropriate homotheticity properties, then the comparison by means of the differential calculus of the production-theoretic output-price indexes based on differing technologies is facilitated and leads to results on the use of Laspeyres and Paasche indexes.

The exact nature of the required homotheticity needs some explanation. What is needed in the present fully open case is homotheticity of the production possibility map generated by considering the different PPFs corresponding to different levels of cost. After discussing what this means, we shall assume it directly; where it is specifically needed for particular results (as opposed to being generally needed for interpretative purposes as in Figure 3.1.1) we shall so indicate.

What does such "cost homotheticity" of the PPM amount to in terms of the production relation (3.5.1)? To answer this, it is natural to deal with the general version of homotheticity[6] which is based on the following definition:

Definition 3.5.1: The efficient production frontier defined in (3.5.1) is said to exhibit *output homotheticity* if and only if for each positive scalar α and each vector of inputs v, there exists a positive scalar $\beta = \beta(\alpha, v)$ such that $F(x, v) = 0$ implies $F(\beta x, \alpha v) = 0$.

The interesting question is the extent to which β can be allowed to depend on v. Before considering this directly, observe that Definition 3.5.1 only makes sense if β is restricted so that the equation

$$\beta(\alpha_1, v)\beta(\alpha_2, \alpha_1 v) = \beta(\alpha_1\alpha_2, v) \tag{3.5.6}$$

holds for positive scalars α_1 and α_2 and input vector v. Note that Equation (3.5.6) entails $\beta(1, v) = 1$ for all v (from setting $\alpha_1 = \alpha_2 = 1$).

If the PPM were to be generated by changing inputs along a ray in input space, as was done for the closed-economy case, there would be no need to restrict β any further. It is clear, however, that further restrictions will be necessary to guarantee homotheticity of the PPM generated by changing cost levels in the present, fully open case.

---

6. For general analyses of output homotheticity, input homotheticity, and related concepts, See Färe and Mitchell (1993) and Färe and Primot (1995a, b).

One obvious possibility is to go to the extreme and assume β to be independent of v. In this case, one can easily show that $\beta(\alpha, v) = \alpha^\gamma$ for some fixed positive constant γ.[7] We shall refer to this occasionally below as the "homogeneous case," it includes constant returns-to-scale.

This is clearly more restrictive than necessary. It would obviously suffice that β be the same for all v corresponding to a given value of cost. Even this would be overly restrictive, since what we care about is not the PPF corresponding to each equal-cost v but the outer envelope of those PPFs.

To see that this distinction can matter, consider the *very* special case in which $F(x, v) = \phi(x) - \psi(v)$ and ϕ is homothetic in the usual sense of being a monotonic transformation of a function homogeneous of degree one. Then, given cost minimization, the value of ψ will depend only on C, and it is obvious that the PPM generated by varying C will be homothetic without any further restrictions.

In the next section, we assume that the PPM for the fully open case is homothetic.

3.6. The Fully Open Economy: Changing Factor Prices

Because, with factor prices fixed, the fully open economy can be considered as a special case of the fully closed economy with a single factor, called "cost," we should expect that a number of the results obtained for the fully open case will resemble those described above for the fully closed one. This turns out to be true, but it is instructive (and most interesting) to begin by analyzing the effects of a shift that has no direct parallel in the fully closed case: a change in the price of some factor. Our first result follows.

Theorem 3.6.1: $\partial y/\partial w_i = \lambda(\hat{v}_i - v_i)$ *for* $i = 1, \ldots, m$. *Hence, if a rise in the price of the kth good* $(k = 1, \ldots, r)$ *would increase (reduce) usage of the ith factor, then a rise in the wage of the ith factor will reduce (increase)*

---

7. Assume that β is independent of v and let $f(\alpha) = \log \beta(\alpha, v)$. Write (3.5.6) in terms of logarithms and differentiate with respect to α_1, obtaining

$$f'(\alpha_1) = \alpha_2 f'(\alpha_1 \alpha_2). \tag{3.5.7}$$

Set $\alpha_1 = 1$, integrate the resulting differential equation, and use the fact that $\beta(1, v) = 1$ to obtain the desired result.

the importance of the price of the kth good in the production-theoretic output-price index.

Proof: We evaluate $\partial y / \partial w_i$ by application of the Envelope Theorem first to Problem (3.5.5) and then to Problem (3.5.2) to yield

$$\partial y / \partial w_i = \partial \Lambda / \partial w_i = -\lambda(v_i - \partial \hat{C} / \partial w_i) = \lambda(\partial \hat{C} / \partial w_i - v_i)$$

$$= \lambda(\hat{v}_i - v_i) \tag{3.6.1}$$

Note that λ is positive, since, by (3.5.5), it is the shadow price of the cost constraint in (3.5.3).

Now, suppose that $p_j = \hat{p}_j$ for $j \neq k$, but that $p_k > \hat{p}_k$. (An exactly symmetric argument follows if $p_k < \hat{p}_k$.) Then the effect of the change in the kth price is to raise the production-theoretic output-price index above unity. If that increase in the kth price also increases the usage of the ith factor, then $v_i > \hat{v}_i$, and it follows from (3.6.1) that the production-theoretic output-price index calculated after an increase in w_i will be less than the one calculated before that increase (although still greater than unity). Because, in this situation, the entire increase above unity in the production-theoretic output-price index comes from the increase in the kth output price, this means that the increase in w_i reduces the importance of the kth output price in the production-theoretic price index.   ∎

Two remarks are in order before proceeding. First, arguments such as that given in the last paragraph of the proof will recur throughout this chapter. In view of their similarity, we shall not spell them out in full each time.

Second, comparison of Theorem 3.6.1 with Theorem 3.3.2, which is its closest analogue in the closed-economy case, shows an apparent difference. Theorem 3.3.2 states that (under constant returns-to-scale) a decrease in the supply of the ith factor, which is as close as we can come in the closed-economy model to an increase in its price, would reduce (increase) the importance of the kth output price in the production-theoretic output-price index if and only if an increase in the kth output price would increase (reduce) the share of the ith factor in total money output. In contrast, Theorem 3.6.1, although while generally corresponding to this, makes no mention of factor shares. We postpone discussion of this apparent difference until we reach the more exactly comparable case of factor-augmenting technical change, where we shall see that the difference is in fact illusory.

We should naturally suspect that Theorem 3.6.1 has a companion theorem stating that an increase in the kth output price will increase usage of the

ith factor if and only if an increase in the ith factor price will reduce production of the kth good relative to national output. This expectation arises because (x_k/y) is the weight given to p_k in a Paasche index and because of the many similar results obtained for the fully closed economy described above.

In what follows (and in parallel later theorems), the reader should bear in mind that differentiation of y here involves differentiation *with costs constant*, since we are interested in how output decisions change, given the PPF. This is different from the case involved in Theorem 3.6.1 where we were also interested in the effect of a change in w_i on the PPF itself.

Before presenting the theorem, we will state and prove three simple lemmas.

Lemma 3.6.1: *Since the PPM is homothetic, we have*

$$\partial \Lambda/\partial p_k = \lambda(x_k/y).$$

Proof: Differentiating (3.5.5) yields

$$\partial \Lambda/\partial p_k = x_k \quad \text{and} \quad \partial \Lambda/\partial \hat{C} = \lambda. \tag{3.6.2}$$

Hence we have

$$\partial \lambda/\partial p_k = \partial^2 \Lambda/\partial \hat{C}\partial p_k = \partial x_k/\partial \hat{C}. \tag{3.6.3}$$

We evaluate $(\partial x_k/\partial \hat{C})$ in two steps. First, note that for the fully open case, different PPFs from the same PPM correspond to different levels of $\hat{C}$. Consider the effects on x_k of an outward shift in the value-of-production plane, allowing $\hat{C}$ to vary. That is, consider $(\partial x_k/\partial y)$ where prices are held constant and we look at the expansion path defined by the points of tangency between the iso-value lines and the PPFs as $\hat{C}$ is varied. Since the PPM is homothetic, we have

$$\partial x_k/\partial y = (x_k/y). \tag{3.6.4}$$

To evaluate $(\partial x_k/\partial \hat{C})$, it will thus suffice to evaluate $(\partial y/\partial \hat{C})$ that is, to evaluate the rate at which total value shifts outward along points of tangency as $\hat{C}$ increases. From the Envelope Theorem applied to (3.5.5), we have $(\partial y/\partial \hat{C}) = \lambda$. Hence we have

$$\partial x_k/\partial \hat{C} = (\partial x_k/\partial y)(\partial y/\partial \hat{C}) = \lambda(x_k/y). \tag{3.6.5}$$

∎

Lemma 3.6.2: *Since the PPM is homothetic, we have*

$$\frac{\partial x_k}{\partial w_i} = -\lambda \left(\frac{\partial v_i}{\partial p_k} + \frac{v_i x_k}{y} \right).$$

Proof: Differentiate (3.5.5) (bearing in mind that $\hat{C}$ is to be taken as constant) to obtain

$$\partial \Lambda / \partial p_k = x_k \quad \text{and} \quad \partial \Lambda / \partial w_i = -\lambda v_i. \tag{3.6.6}$$

Hence, we have

$$\frac{\partial x_k}{\partial w_i} = \frac{\partial^2 \Lambda}{\partial w_i \partial p_k} = \frac{\partial (-\lambda v_i)}{\partial p_k} = -\lambda \left(\frac{\partial v_i}{\partial p_k} + \frac{v_i x_k}{y} \right), \tag{3.6.7}$$

where the last step follows from Lemma 3.6.1.   ■

Theorem 3.6.2: *Since the PPM is homothetic, we have*

$$\frac{\partial (x_k / y)}{\partial w_i} = \frac{-\lambda (\partial v_i / \partial p_k)}{y}.$$

Proof: Differentiating (x_k / y) with respect to w_i yields

$$\frac{\partial (x_k / y)}{\partial w_i} = \frac{y(\partial x_k / \partial w_i) - x_k (\partial y / \partial w_i)}{y^2}$$

$$= \frac{-\lambda (\partial v_i / \partial p_k) - (\lambda v_i x_k / y)}{y} + \frac{\lambda x_k v_i}{y^2}$$

$$= \frac{-\lambda (\partial v_i / \partial p_k)}{y}, \tag{3.6.8}$$

using Lemma 3.6.2 and applying the Envelope Theorem to (3.5.5).   ■

   The interpretation of this theorem has already been given. Taken in combination with Theorem 3.6.1, it shows that the kth output price will be increased in importance in the production-theoretic output-price index by an increase in w_i if and only if the "weight" (x_k / y) that should be given to that price in the total value of output and in a Paasche price index is also increased. This will happen if and only if an increase in the kth price would reduce usage of the ith factor. We believe that this and similar results below hold without the explicit use of homotheticity, but we have been unable to find a proof.

3.7. Fully Open Economy: Factor-Augumenting Technical Change

We now consider the case of a factor-augmenting technical change.[8] We begin by supposing that such a change is economy wide. In this circumstance, such a change in the mth factor's efficiency can be represented as a change in the positive scalar b in representation of the set of technologically feasible points given by the production relation

$$F(x_1, \ldots, x_r, v_1, \ldots, bv_m) = 0. \tag{3.7.1}$$

The following corollary follows directly from the setup in Section 5.

Corollary 3.7.1: $(\partial y/\partial b) = (\lambda w_m/b)(v_m - \hat{v}_m)$.   *It follows that if a rise in the price of the kth good $(k = 1, \ldots, r)$ would increase (reduce) usage of the mth factor, then economy-wide, mth-factor-augmenting technical progress will increase (reduce) the importance of the kth price in the production-theoretic output-price index.*

Proof: The result may be obtained in (at least) three ways. First, one can differentiate (3.5.5) and then (3.5.4) and apply the first-order conditions. Second (and perhaps more instructive), observe that an increase in b is equivalent to a decrease in the wage of the mth factor *when that factor is measured in efficiency units*. Working in efficiency units, the wage per efficiency unit becomes (w_m/b), whereas the amount of the mth factor is $b\hat{v}_m$ or bv_m. The desired result now follows from applying Theorem 3.6.1 to the remeasured factor and its remeasured wage. Third, since a uniform economy-wide factor-augmenting technical change is equivalent to such a change in each firm or industry taken separately, the same result follows as a corollary to Theorem 3.6.1 above, taking into account the different notation.   ∎

A result parallel to that of Theorem 3.6.2 also holds but will not be stated separately.

As indicated above, Theorem 3.6.2 appears to contrast with Theorem 3.3.2 for the closed-economy model. The latter result runs in terms of the effect of the kth price on the *share* of the mth factor in the value of total

---

8. See Burmeister and Dobell (1970, pp. 67–69) for a general discussion of factor-augmenting technical change and its relationship to Harrod-neutral and Solow-neutral technical change.

output, whereas the former results runs in terms of the effects of the kth price on the *usage* of the mth factor. This difference is apparent, rather than real, however.

To see this, observe that the general result that leads to Theorem 3.3.2 runs in terms of the share of the mth factor in total factor payments valued at shadow prices.[9] Under constant returns-to-scale, such total factor payments just exhaust the value of output, leading to the result cited in Theorem 3.3.2. In the present, fully open economy, the same thing is true. Payments to the mth factor *at the correct shadow price* are not simply $w_m v_m$ (or $w_m \hat{v}_m$), because the factor prices are determined exogenously and total factor costs are fixed in the second optimization problem (3.5.3). Hence, there is a shadow price associated with the cost constraint in that problem; its value is λ. Similarly, there is a shadow price associated with the cost constraint in the first optimization problem; its value is $\hat{\lambda}$. Valued at shadow prices, therefore, the share of the mth factor in total factor payments is $(\hat{\lambda} w_m \hat{v}_m / \hat{\lambda} \hat{C})$ and $(\lambda w_m v_m / \lambda \hat{C})$, in the base-period and the current-period, respectively. Since w_m and $\hat{C}$ are the same in both expressions[10] and the Lagrange multipliers cancel out, that share changes in the same direction as the usage of the mth factor itself.

Thus, the two results are basically the same. This will be seen again when we consider the more general case of the hybrid economy. In that case it will again be possible to assume constant returns-to-scale and express the results in terms of output (although payments to factors purchased at exogenous prices will still have to be valued at shadow prices). We have avoided doing this here because of the complications caused by indeterminacy of scale in the constant returns-to-scale fully open economy.

We now turn to the somewhat more interesting case of a factor-augmenting technical change that affects only the production of a particular good.[11] To do this requires that we again go behind the aggregate representation of technology given by (3.5.1) or (3.7.1) and deal with the production functions for individual outputs. We define the production functions

9. See Fisher and Shell (1972, pp. 83–85).
10. This is so even in the case considered in Section 3.6, where the change in wages applies equally to both periods.
11. It is easy to generalize to consider a change that affects only the production of some subset of goods. Similarly, we have assumed in the text that each of the production functions is characterized by a single output rather than involving multiple outputs. This is not essential and does not affect the results. (A similar remark applies to the analysis in Fisher and Shell (1972, Essay II).)

$g^1, \ldots, g^i, \ldots, g^r$ by

$$x_1 = g^1(v_{11}, \ldots, v_{1m-1}, bv_{1m})$$

and   (3.7.2)

$$x_i = g^i(v_{i1}, \ldots, v_{im}) \quad \text{for } i = 2, \ldots, r,$$

where v_{ij} is the amount of the jth factor used in the production of the ith output and b is a positive scalar, the increase in which corresponds to mth-factor-augmenting technical progress in the production of the first output. Materials balance requires that we have

$$v_{ij} \geq 0 \quad \text{and} \quad \sum_{i=1}^{r} v_{ij} \quad \text{for } i = 1, \ldots, r \text{ and } j = 1, \ldots, m.$$

(3.7.3)

Production is described by (3.7.2) and (3.7.3). The efficient frontier for the economy (3.5.1) is obtained by fixing all the v_j and all the x_i save one and maximizing the remaining output. As usual, hats will denote base-period values. We can now rewrite the Lagrangians (3.5.4) and (3.5.5) in the following way:

$$\hat{\Lambda} = w \cdot \hat{v} + \hat{\delta}_1 [\hat{x}_1 - g^1(\hat{v}_{11}, \ldots, b\hat{v}_{1m})]$$

$$+ \sum_{i=2}^{r} \hat{\delta}_i [\hat{x}_i - g^i(\hat{v}_{i1}, \ldots, \hat{v}_{im})] - (1/\hat{\lambda})(\hat{p} \cdot \hat{x} - \hat{y}) \qquad (3.7.4)$$

and

$$\Lambda = p \cdot x + \delta_1 [x_1 - g^1(v_{11}, \ldots, bv_{1m})]$$

$$+ \sum_{i=2}^{r} \delta_i [x_i - g^i(v_{i1}, \ldots, v_{im})] - \lambda(w \cdot v - \hat{C}), \qquad (3.7.5)$$

where λ, $(1/\hat{\lambda})$, the δ_i, and the $\hat{\delta}_i$ are the relevant Lagrange multipliers.

Next, we state, prove, and discuss two comparative-statics results for the fully open economy.

Theorem 3.7.1: $(\partial y / \partial b) = (\lambda w_m / b)(v_{1m} - \hat{v}_{1m})$. *Hence, if a rise in the price of the kth good ($k = 1, \ldots, r$) would lead to an increase (reduction) in the employment of the mth factor in the first industry, then mth-factor-augmenting technical progress in the first industry will increase (decrease) the importance of the kth output price in the production-theoretic output-price index.*

Proof: Using the Envelope Theorem, we have

$$\partial y/\partial b = \partial \Lambda/\partial b = -\delta_1 v_{1m} g_m^1 + \lambda(\partial \hat{C}/\partial b), \qquad (3.7.6)$$

where g_m^1 denotes the partial derivative of g^1 with respect to its mth argument (rather than with respect to v_{1m}). Similarly, we have

$$\partial \hat{C}/\partial b = \partial \hat{\Lambda}/\partial b = -\hat{\delta}_1 \hat{v}_{1m} \hat{g}_m^1, \qquad (3.7.7)$$

where the hat in $\hat{g}_m^1$ denotes the derivative evaluated at the "hatted" values of the arguments of g^1 (and similarly from now on). From the first-order conditions for the two optimization problems, we obtain

$$\hat{\delta}_1 b \hat{g}_m^1 = w_m \quad \text{and} \quad \delta_1 b g_m^1 = -\lambda w_m. \qquad (3.7.8)$$

Substituting (3.7.7) into (3.7.6) and using (3.7.8) yields the desired result. ■

As before, there is no real difference of substance between this result and that obtained for the closed-economy case (Theorem 3.3.4), which is in terms of the share (in national output) of the mth factor employed in the first industry.

We now prove a companion theorem to Theorem 3.7.1 showing that the kth price will gain importance in the theoretical output-price index as a result of the technical change being considered if and only if that change would increase the weight that one would naturally associate with that price, namely, x_k/y. This will happen if and only if an increase in the kth price would increase usage of the mth factor in the first industry.

To do this, observe that Lemma 3.6.1 remains valid in the present notation. We replace Lemma 3.6.2 by

Lemma 3.7.1: *Since the PPM is homothetic, we have*

$$\frac{\partial x_k}{\partial b} = \left(\frac{\lambda w_m}{b}\right)\left(\frac{\partial v_{1m}}{\partial p_k}\right) + \frac{\lambda w_m v_{1m} x_k}{by}.$$

Proof: Differentiate (3.7.5), holding $\hat{C}$ constant, to obtain

$$\frac{\partial \Lambda}{\partial p_k} = x_k \quad \text{and} \quad \frac{\partial \Lambda}{\partial b} = -\delta_1 v_{1m} g_m^1 = \frac{\lambda w_m v_{1m}}{b} \qquad (3.7.9)$$

from (3.7.8). Hence, using Lemma 3.6.1, we have

$$\frac{\partial x_k}{\partial b} = \left(\frac{\partial^2 \Lambda}{\partial p_k \partial b}\right) = \frac{\partial(\lambda w_m v_{1m}/b)}{\partial p_k}$$

$$= \left(\frac{\lambda w_m}{b}\right)\left(\frac{\partial v_{1m}}{\partial p_k}\right) + \frac{\lambda w_m v_{1m} x_k}{by} \tag{3.7.10}$$

■

We use this lemma to prove the following theorem.

Theorem 3.7.2: *Since the PPM is homothetic, we have*

$$\frac{\partial(x_k/y)}{\partial b} = \left(\frac{\lambda w_m}{by}\right)\left(\frac{\partial v_{1m}}{\partial p_k}\right).$$

Proof:

$$\frac{\partial(x_k/y)}{\partial b} = \left(\frac{1}{y^2}\right)\left[y\left(\frac{\partial x_k}{\partial b}\right) - x_k\left(\frac{\partial y}{\partial b}\right)\right]$$

$$= \left(\frac{1}{y^2}\right)\left[\left(\frac{\lambda y w_m}{b}\right)\left(\frac{\partial v_{1m}}{\partial p_k}\right) + \frac{\lambda x_k w_m v_{1m}}{b} - \frac{\lambda x_k w_m v_{1m}}{b}\right]$$

$$= \left(\frac{\lambda w_m}{by}\right)\left(\frac{\partial v_{1m}}{\partial p_k}\right), \tag{3.7.11}$$

making use of Lemma 3.7.1, (3.7.9), and the Envelope Theorem applied to (3.7.5). ■

Not surprisingly, this result has a strong family resemblance to that of Theorem 3.6.2, particularly if we think of factors and factor prices expressed in efficiency units.

As the last topic in this section, we return to the representation of technology given in (3.5.1) and consider the case of an equal factor-augmenting change in the efficiency of *every* factor. (This can be thought of as one form of a Hicks-neutral technical change for the whole open economy – an interpretation of some interest if the open economy being studied is thought of as a single firm or sector in a larger economy.) Thus, we alter (3.5.1) to get

$$F(x, bv) = 0. \tag{3.7.12}$$

Our next corollary follows immediately.

Corollary 3.7.2: *A uniform, economy-wide, factor-augmenting technical change in all factors does not change the production-theoretic output-price index.*

Proof: Applying the results of Corollary 3.7.1 in the obvious way for the present situation yields

$$\partial y / \partial b = (\lambda / b)(w \cdot v - \hat{w} \cdot \hat{v}) = (\lambda / b)(\hat{C} - \hat{C}) = 0. \qquad (3.7.13)$$

∎

This is not a surprising result. If we consider the PPM for this economy, the map showing the different PPFs corresponding to different cost levels, we see that an increase in b, like a uniform proportional change in all factor prices, merely changes the cost associated with each PPF without changing the PPM in any other way. Thus the same PPF will be used to construct the theoretical output-price index both before and after the change.

Another way of looking at this situation is as follows. At fixed factor prices, the PPF depends only on $\hat{C}$. We might indeed think of $\hat{C}$ as a single factor of production, with the usage of the actual factors determined, given their prices, by the requirements of efficiency. A uniform, economy-wide, factor-augmenting change in all factors can then be thought of as a factor-augmenting change in the single factor $\hat{C}$ when the production surface is reexpressed in this way. This is the fully closed economy, however, with a single factor of production. Now, as already discussed, the effect of a factor-augmenting technical change in the closed-economy case depends on the effect of prices on the share of the augmented factor in total factor payments (at shadow prices if constant returns-to-scale is not assumed). Obviously, that effect must be zero here. (Note that in this derivation the result does not depend on assuming homotheticity of the PPM.)

If we interpret this change as a Hicks-neutral change in the technology of a particular industry (the open economy under consideration), then this result shows that such a change produces no change in the production-theoretic output-price index constructed for this industry alone. Such a change would, however, alter the weight given to this industry in the production-theoretic output-price index constructed for any larger sector of economy of which this industry is a part. We have already seen this in Section 3.2 for the case in which the larger economy is fully closed. We shall see it again in the next section for the case in which the larger economy is itself fully open.

3.8. The Fully Open Economy: Hicks-Neutral Technical Change

We now turn to the case in which Hicks-neutral change occurs in the production of a particular output. We modeled this case for the fully closed economy in Section 3.2 above. Fortunately, it is not necessary to model it again and to analyze by brute force the effects of such a change on the production-theoretic output-price index in the fully open economy.

As we observed at the end of the preceding section, with factor prices fixed, one can think of the set of efficient outputs (i.e., the PPF) as being entirely determined by the amount of a single composite factor: total cost. Since a Hicks-neutral change in the production function for the first output (a change in the parameter a in (3.2.2) and (3.2.3)) does not affect the exogenously given factor prices and does not affect the way in which individual factors enter the technology, this is an appropriate tack to take here. If we do so, however, we have reduced the problem to that of the closed-economy case and the results must be identical to those in Section 3.2.[12] We thus restrict our remarks here to the matters of interpretation.

The results summarized in Section 3.2 run in terms of elasticities of supply taken with factor supplies held constant. It is also possible to state results (indeed, results that do not explicitly require homotheticity) in terms of elasticities of supply taken holding the value of total output y constant (Fisher and Shell, 1972, pp. 67–73). In the general-equilibrium context of the fully closed economy, supply elasticities with factor supplies constant seem natural ones to work with (although they are not the ones typically estimated in econometric studies).

In the fully open economy, however, this is not true. Supply elasticities evaluated holding total cost and factor supply constant do not seem any more natural than supply elasticities holding constant money output. Clearly, the most natural supply elasticities to work with would be those taken holding only factor prices constant and letting total cost vary. The relation between these and either the gross or the net elasticities just described is not easily determined, however.

One other remark on Hicks-neutral technical change seems worth making. At the end of the preceding section, we saw that an economy-wide, uniform, factor-augmenting change in all factors has no effect on the

---

12. A similar remark holds for the extension of the results of Section 3.4 (on general technical change) to the fully open case. In that case, the results are so general that there does not seem to be much point in discussing issues of interpretation.

theoretical output-price index. It might be thought that this is also true of an economy-wide, uniform, Hicks-neutral technical change in all outputs. After all, from the point of view of the PPF, a Hicks-neutral technical change is effectively an "output-augmenting" technical change – a change represented by changing a parameter multiplying the affected output(s) in the description of the technology (see (3.2.3)). Hence one might think the two types of economy-wide, uniform changes as just two ways of describing the same thing: a Hicks-neutral change in the overall technology of the entire economy being studied.

This is clearly true in the homogeneous case briefly discussed in Section 3.5. This is the case in which there exists a positive scalar γ such that, for all nonnegative x and v, and any positive scalar α, $F(x, v) = 0$ implies $F(\alpha^{\gamma} x, \alpha v) = 0$. In this case (which includes constant returns) an economy-wide, uniform, output-augmenting change is equivalent to an economy-wide, uniform, factor-augmenting change.

More generally, as long as the PPM is homothetic, it will be true that an economy-wide, uniform, Hicks-neutral technical change will not affect the production-theoretic output-price index. Unlike the similar result for economy-wide, uniform, factor-augmenting changes, however, this result does require homotheticity. This is because, after the change, production of the base-period's value of output will result in a different cost and a different PPF from before. This PPF will be used to define the production-theoretic output-price index. Unless the PPM is homothetic, however, this change in the PPF will make a difference. Such was not true of the case of a uniform factor-augmenting change because such a change altered only the cost associated with the base-period's value of output but not the PPF corresponding to that value.

This completes our discussion for the fully open economy.

3.9. The Hybrid Economy: General Considerations

In the more general case of the hybrid economy, the productive unit being analyzed can buy some, but not all, factors at exogenously given prices. The remaining factors are fixed in amount. We shall refer to these as "variable" factors and "fixed" factors, respectively. As described in Chapter 2, the PPF to be used in constructing the theoretical output-price index is the locus of outputs that can be feasibly produced at given levels of the fixed factors and with given cost of the variable factors. This seems straightforward enough.

A subtle issue arises, however, when we consider how to obtain this PPF through an optimization process such as that described in (3.1.6) or (3.5.2). The first obvious thought is to do so by minimizing the cost of the variable factors, given base-period prices, the value of base-period output, and the amounts of the fixed factors. Such an approach certainly locates the base-period PPF, but (as we shall see) it runs into difficulty when used in comparative static exercises such as those given in preceding sections. Also, although generalizing the fully open economy case, it fails to have a clear relation to the fully closed economy case, in which there is no variable cost to minimize.

The difficulty in undertaking the comparative-statics analysis has to do with homotheticity of the PPM, which, as we have seen, is an important and often crucial property. Not only do some of our results depend explicitly on that homotheticity, but also the whole enterprise of using the calculus (or more generally duality theory) in this manner to make comparisons between theoretical output-price indexes based on different PPMs implicitly rests on the assumption that at least one of them is homothetic. Without homotheticity of the PPM, the procedure that starts by finding the PPF tangent to the base-period value-of-output hyperplane and then altering conditions to match current-period ones will not end up with the same production-theoretic output-price index that begins with the current-period value-of-output hyperplane and its tangent PPF.

If the optimization problem that finds the tangent PPF is that of minimization of the cost of the variable factors, however, then the different PPFs of the PPM correspond to different levels of variable cost but the same levels of the fixed factors. Homotheticity ensures that for every primal optimization problem there is an interesting dual problem and that the optimum of the primal objective is equal to the optimum of the dual objective.[13] Unfortunately, homotheticity of the map we are interested in here fails to be a plausible assumption unless *all* factors are variable.

Obviously, the plausible homotheticity assumption is some suitable restriction of Definition 3.5.1 above. Suppose, as in the discussion of output-augmenting technical change above, we think of the total cost of the variable factors as itself a factor of production. That is, given the exogenously set factor prices, the feasible set of outputs will be entirely determined by the levels of the fixed factors and the level of cost of the variable factors. We can

13. See Diewert (1982) and Newman (1987) for discussions on the use of duality in economic theory.

think of rewriting the technology to obtain a "partially indirect" PPF, where variable cost is just another input and the levels of the variable factors do not appear explicitly; the PPF simply reflects the way in which this "input" is used.

Now construct a composite factor by fixing the proportions of the fixed factors *and* of variable cost. That is, choose a ray in the space of the fixed factors and variable cost. Consider the PPM generated by taking the PPFs corresponding to different points on this ray. It is this PPM that we shall assume to be homothetic; this is a natural generalization of the homotheticity assumptions of both the closed and the fully open economy cases.

Accordingly, we shall set up our optimization problem for finding the appropriate PPF by choosing such a composite factor and minimizing its dosage, given base-period prices and money output. This procedure locates the actual base-period PPF if base-period proportions are chosen (as will the cost minimization procedure above) and will make sense for comparative-statics comparisons. In essence, we measure changes in real output by how much more dosage of the composite factor would be required to produce the new output; this is more sensible than measuring such changes by how much more variable cost would be required with fixed factors given.

Note that this procedure (like the corresponding homotheticity assumption) provides a natural generalization of both the procedure used in the open-economy case and that used in the case of the closed economy. In the fully open case, it reduces to cost minimization; in the fully closed case, it reduces to minimizing the dosage of fixed factors.

We make two more points before proceeding to the formal analysis. First, if the reader still wonders where the cost-minimization analysis would lead, we have already provided much of the answer. With the levels of the fixed factors given, the technology can be expressed in terms of outputs and variable factors only. The fully open case then becomes directly applicable (although homotheticity no longer is plausible). The obvious comparative-statics exercises that cannot be read out of the analysis of the fully open case involve changes in the PPM produced by changes in the amounts of the fixed factors or by fixed-factor-augmenting technical change. (It is difficult to see how to parametrize these conveniently while working in the space of outputs and variable factors.)

Second, the "dosage" approach that we shall pursue is isomorphic to that used in the treatment of the closed economy. In analyzing many, although not all, changes in the PPM, the fact that one of the fixed "factors" is total variable cost is important. Accordingly, there is no need to repeat the analysis of the closed economy case to obtain the identical results for changes in the amount of a fixed factor or for fixed-factor-augmenting technical change, whether economy-wide or industry specific. Further, there is no need to separately analyze output-augmenting technical change, except to observe that the crucial supply elasticities must now be interpreted holding constant fixed-factor levels, variable factor-prices, and the level of variable costs.

This is not to say that every change in the PPF of the hybrid economy can be studied in terms of the fully closed case. It remains to analyze the effects of a change in the price of a variable factor and the effects of variable-factor-augmenting technical change in the domestic economy and in a specific industry, since these changes cannot be expressed as simple (e.g., efficiency-unit) changes in the technology. We will analyze these cases below, generalizing our analysis of the fully open economy.

We proceed to the formal model. We must now distinguish between variable and fixed factors. Continue to denote the variable factors by v, and denote an additional vector of s fixed factors by u. The efficient technological frontier is described by the production function F with

$$F(x, v, u) = 0. \tag{3.9.1}$$

We denote by u^0 the vector of reference amounts of fixed factors and by C^0 the reference level of costs of variable factors. The PPM is generated by varying the positive scalar μ, with

$$u = \mu u^0 \quad \text{and} \quad w \cdot v = C = \mu C^0, \tag{3.9.2}$$

where μ is the dosage level of the composite factor. For many purposes, u^0 and C^0 can be thought of as simply the *actual* base-period values of u and C, respectively.

We set up our initial optimization problem (using hats, as before, to denote (theoretical) base-period values) by minimizing the ratio of $\hat{u}_1$ to u_1^0 constraining the ratio of every other $\hat{u}_j$ to u_j^0 as well as that of $\hat{C}$ to C^0 by

$$\left(\hat{u}_j/u_j^0\right) = \left(\hat{u}_1/u_1^0\right) = \left(\hat{C}/C^0\right) \quad \text{for } j = 2, \ldots, s. \tag{3.9.3}$$

This procedure is obviously equivalent to minimizing μ. Because we wish to study the effects of changes in factor prices, it is notationally simpler to set up the problem in the apparently asymmetric form of minimizing $(\hat{u}_1/u_1^0)$ rather than in the form of minimizing $(\hat{C}/C^0)$. The latter provides the readiest parallel with (3.5.2) above. The two forms are equivalent, given (3.9.3), so that this choice (unlike our earlier choice as to how to generate the PPM) does not matter.

We can now state the optimization problems that replace (3.5.2) and (3.5.3), respectively, as follows: We are given initial prices $\hat{p}$, initial money output $\hat{y}$, and a second set of prices p. We are also given factor prices w. We begin by finding the vector of outputs $\hat{x}$ and the vectors of inputs $\hat{v}$ and $\hat{u}$ that solve the problem

$$\text{Minimize } \mu = \hat{u}_1/u_1^0$$

$$\text{subject to (3.9.3), } F(\hat{x}, \hat{v}, \hat{u}) = 0, \text{ and } \hat{p} \cdot \hat{x} = \hat{y}. \quad (3.9.4)$$

Let $\hat{u}$ denote the resulting value of μ. Now find the output vector x and the input vectors v and u that solve the problem

$$\text{Maximize } y = p \cdot x$$

$$\text{subject to } F(x, v, u) = 0, u = \hat{\mu}u^0, \text{ and } C^0.^{14} \quad (3.9.5)$$

The Lagrangian for (3.9.4) is

$$
\hat{\Lambda} = \left(\hat{u}_1/u_1^0\right) + \sum_{j=2}^{s} \hat{\eta}_j \left[\left(\hat{u}_j/u_j^0\right) - \left(\hat{u}_1/u_1^0\right)\right]
$$

$$
+ \hat{\rho}\left[(w \cdot \hat{v}/C^0) - \hat{u}_1/u_1^0\right]
$$

$$
+ (\hat{\rho}/\hat{\lambda}C^0)(\hat{p} \cdot \hat{x} - \hat{y}) + \hat{\delta}F(\hat{x}, \hat{v}, \hat{u}), \quad (3.9.6)
$$

where $\hat{\rho}$, $(\hat{\rho}/\hat{\lambda}C^0)$, $\hat{\delta}$, and the $\hat{\eta}_j$ are Lagrange multipliers.

The multiplier for the constraint $\hat{p} \cdot \hat{x} = \hat{y}$ has been written as $(\hat{\rho}/\hat{\lambda}C^0)$ to facilitate the interpretation of $\hat{\lambda}$, as follows. The constraint for the "cost" factor is written as $(w \cdot \hat{v}/C^0 - \hat{u}_1/u_1^0) = 0$. Define $\bar{C}$ by $\bar{C} = C^0(\hat{u}_1/u_1^0)$ and rewrite the constraint as $(w \cdot \hat{v}/C^0 - \bar{C}/C^0) = 0$. By the Envelope Theorem, we have

$$\partial\hat{\mu}/\partial\bar{C} = -\hat{\rho}/C^0 \quad \text{and} \quad \partial\hat{\mu}/\partial\hat{y} = -\hat{\rho}/\hat{\lambda}C^0. \quad (3.9.7)$$

Hence, holding $\hat{\mu}$ constant, we have $\partial\hat{y}/\partial\bar{C} = \hat{\lambda}$, and hence, as in earlier sections, $\hat{\lambda}$ is thus the marginal product of the "cost" factor.

The Lagrangian for (3.9.5) is much simpler. It can be written as

$$
\Lambda = p \cdot x - \sum_{j=1}^{s} \eta_j \left(u_j - \hat{\mu}u_j^0\right) - \lambda(w \cdot v - \hat{\mu}C^0) + \delta F(x, v, u), \quad (3.9.8)
$$

---

14. This of course amounts to imposing $u = \hat{u}$ and $C = \hat{C}$. We proceed in this apparently cumbersome way because it is relatively easy to use the Envelope Theorem to examine the effects of various changes on $\hat{\mu}$ and relatively tedious directly to evaluate the effects of such changes on $\hat{v}$, $\hat{u}$, and $\hat{C}$.

where the Greek letters other than $\hat{\mu}$ are Lagrange multipliers. Notice that, like $\hat{\lambda}$, λ can be interpreted as the marginal product of "cost" in the relevant situation.

3.10. The Hybrid Economy: Changing Factor Prices

We now generalize the results of Section 3.6. Let $\hat{Q}$ and Q denote total factor payments at shadow prices in the base period and current period, respectively. Then we have the following lemma:

Lemma 3.10.1:

$$\partial y/\partial \hat{\mu} = Q/\hat{\mu} \quad and \quad \partial \hat{\mu}/\partial \hat{y} = \hat{\mu}/\hat{Q}.$$

Proof: This lemma can be proved by applying the Envelope Theorem to (3.9.6) and (3.9.8) and using the first-order conditions to interpret the Lagrange multipliers. (This is the procedure followed in Fisher and Shell (1972, pp. 83–84) to obtain a similar result.) Alternatively, that interpretation can be derived by careful manipulation of the Envelope Theorem along the lines used in (3.9.7) above. It is simpler to avoid the necessity for such interpretations, however, by reasoning as follows.

An increase in $\hat{\mu}$ means a multiplicative increase in the amount of every factor (counting cost as a factor). Since $\hat{\mu}$ multiplies the reference amount of each factor in (3.9.8), $(\partial y/\partial \hat{\mu})$ must consist of a sum of terms, each of which is the shadow price of some factor times the reference amount of that factor (indeed, this is obvious from differentiating (3.9.8)). The first equation in Lemma 3.10.1 follows after observing that the actual amount of each factor employed is $\hat{\mu}$ times the reference amount.

The second equation follows from symmetry or by (tedious) direct computation from (3.9.6).   ∎

From this we can establish the following theorem:

Theorem 3.10.1:

$$\partial y/\partial w_i = (Q/w_i)(\hat{\lambda} w_i \hat{v}_i/\hat{Q} - \lambda w_i v_i/Q).$$

Hence, if a rise in the price of the kth good (k = 1, ... , r) would lead to an increase (decrease) in the share of the ith factor in total factor payments

*at shadow prices, then an increase in the wage of the ith factor will reduce
(increase) the importance of the kth output price in the production-theoretic
output-price index.*

Proof: Applying the Envelope Theorem to (3.9.8) yields

$$\partial y / \partial w_i = -\lambda v_i + (\partial y / \partial \hat{\mu})(\partial \hat{\mu} / \partial w_i)$$

$$= -\lambda v_i + (Q / \hat{\mu})(\partial \hat{\mu} / \partial w_i), \tag{3.10.1}$$

using the first part of Lemma 3.10.1. From the Implicit Function Theorem,
we have

$$\frac{\partial \hat{y}}{\partial w_i} = -\frac{\partial \hat{\mu} / \partial w_i}{\partial \hat{\mu} / \partial \hat{y}} \tag{3.10.2}$$

along a surface on which $\hat{\mu}$ is constant. Applying the Envelope Theorem to
(3.9.6) and substituting into (3.10.2) yields

$$\partial \hat{y} / \partial w_i = -\hat{\lambda} \hat{v}_i. \tag{3.10.3}$$

Thus, combining (3.10.2) and (3.10.3) and using the second half of Lemma
3.10.1, we have

$$\frac{\partial \hat{\mu}}{\partial w_i} = \frac{\hat{\lambda} \hat{v}_i \hat{\mu}}{\hat{Q}}. \tag{3.10.4}$$

This yields the desired result when substituted into (3.10.1) and appropriately manipulated.   ∎

Corollary 3.10.1: *If the technology is homogeneous (of any degree), we
have*

$$\frac{\partial y}{\partial w_i} = \frac{y}{w_i} \left(\frac{\hat{\lambda} w_i \hat{v}_i}{\hat{y}} - \frac{\lambda w_i v_i}{y} \right)$$

*so that the results of Theorem 3.10.1 can be interpreted in terms of the ith
factor's payments at shadow prices expressed as a share of money output.*

Proof: If the technology is homogeneous of degree γ (that is, if in the
definition of homotheticity (Definition 3.5.1) adapted to the present case,
$\beta = \alpha^\gamma$), then we can think of y as being produced as a single output
from a production function homogeneous of degree γ. Then, by Euler's

Theorem, we have $Q = \gamma y$ and $\hat{Q} = \gamma \hat{y}$. Substitution into the statement of Theorem 3.10.1 establishes the result.[15]   ∎

Theorem 3.10.1 is the general form of Theorem 3.6.1 above. (We have already discussed the reasons for the apparent differences.) We now proceed similarly to generalize Theorem 3.6.2. (Recall in what follows that we are now interested in the effects of changes in w_i with $\hat{\mu}$ constant.) We need two lemmas before we state the theorem.

Lemma 3.10.2:

$$\partial(\lambda v_i)/\partial p_k = -\partial x_k/\partial w_i.$$

Proof: From (3.9.8), we have

$$\partial \Lambda/\partial p_k = x_k \quad \text{and} \quad \partial \Lambda/\partial w_i = -\lambda v_i. \tag{3.10.5}$$

The lemma follows from the symmetry of cross–second partial derivatives.   ∎

Lemma 3.10.3: *Since the PPM is homothetic, we have*

$$\partial Q/\partial p_k = x_k Q/y.$$

Proof: From (3.9.8), we have

$$\partial \Lambda/\partial p_k = x_k \quad \text{and} \quad \partial \Lambda/\partial \hat{\mu} = \partial y/\partial \hat{\mu} = Q/\hat{\mu} \tag{3.10.6}$$

using the Envelope Theorem and Lemma 3.10.1. By homotheticity, as in the proof of Lemma 3.6.1, we have

$$\partial x_k/\partial \hat{\mu} = (\partial x_k/\partial y)(\partial y/\partial \hat{\mu}) = (x_k/y)(\partial y/\partial \hat{\mu}) = x_k Q/y\hat{\mu}, \tag{3.10.7}$$

again making use of Lemma 3.10.1. The desired result now follows from the symmetry of cross–partial derivatives and the fact that $\hat{\mu}$ is independent of p_k.   ∎

Theorem 3.10.2: *Since the PPM is homothetic, we have*

$$\frac{\partial(x_k/y)}{\partial w_i} = -\left(\frac{Q}{w_i y}\right)\left(\frac{\partial(\lambda w_i v_i/Q)}{\partial p_k}\right).$$

---

15. Similarly, the results of Fisher and Shell (1972, Essay II), which appear to depend on constant returns-to-scale for statement in terms of y rather than Q, in fact require only homogeneity of arbitrary degree.

Proof: Direct differentiation yields

$$\frac{\partial(x_k/y)}{\partial w_i} = \frac{y(\partial x_k/\partial w_i) - x_k(\partial y/\partial w_i)}{y^2}$$

$$= (1/y)(\partial x_k/\partial w_i) + \lambda x_k v_i/y^2, \tag{3.10.8}$$

using the Envelope Theorem. However, we also have

$$\frac{\partial(\lambda w_i v_i/Q)}{p_k} = w_i \frac{Q[\partial(\lambda v_i/\partial p_k)] - \lambda v_i(\partial Q/\partial p_k)}{Q^2}$$

$$= -\left(\frac{w_i}{Q}\right)\left(\frac{\partial x_k}{\partial w_i} + \frac{\lambda x_k v_i}{y}\right), \tag{3.10.9}$$

using Lemmas 3.10.2 and 3.10.3. Comparison of (3.10.8) and (3.10.9) yields
the desired result.   ■

As expected, an increase in w_i increases the importance of p_k in the
theoretical output-price index if and only if the same increase would increase the weight to be given to p_k in a Paasche index (x_k/y). This happens if and only if an increase in p_k would reduce the share of the ith
factor in total factor payments at shadow prices. Note that, because w_i
is taken as constant in this evaluation, at issue is whether an increase in p_k
decreases the weight that would naturally be given to w_i in an index of input
prices $(\lambda v_i/Q)$. Indeed, under constant returns-to-scale, the result of
Theorem 3.10.2 allows us to state this duality in its purest form; we do
this in the following corollary.

Corollary 3.10.2: *Under constant returns-to-scale, we have*

$$\frac{\partial(x_k/y)}{\partial w_i} = -\frac{\partial(\lambda v_i/Q)}{\partial p_k}.$$

Proof: The proof follows from Theorem 3.10.2 and the fact that, under
constant returns-to-scale, we have $Q = y$.   ■

3.11. The Hybrid Economy: Factor-Augmenting
Technical Change

Having generalized the results of Section 3.6, we now briefly generalize those of Section 3.7 and consider factor-augmenting technical change.
There is no need to consider technical changes that augment the fixed factors, since the analysis of the fully closed economy case given in Section 3.3

carries over without change. We therefore restrict attention to technical changes that augment one of the variable factors, say the *m*th. As in Section 3.7, we represent such augmentation by multiplying v_m by a parameter b and we first consider economy-wide augmentation, so that the multiplication is done in the overall representation of the technology (3.9.1). As in Section 3.7, this is merely a change in the wage of the *m*th factor per efficiency unit, so that Theorem 3.10.1 implies the following corollary.

Corollary 3.11.1:

$$\frac{\partial y}{\partial b} = \frac{Q}{b} \left(\frac{\lambda w_i v_i}{Q} - \frac{\hat{\lambda} \hat{w}_i \hat{v}_i}{\hat{Q}} \right).$$

Hence, if a rise in the price of the kth good would increase (reduce) usage of the mth factor, then economy-wide, mth-factor-augmenting technical progress will increase (reduce) the importance of that price in the production-theoretic output-price index.

This result also follows from Theorem 3.11.1 below, allowing for the change in notation. The task of stating and proving results parallel to Corollary 3.10.1, Theorem 3.10.2, and Corollary 3.10.2 is left to the reader.

Corollary 3.11.1 shows most clearly that although some factors are purchased at exogenously given prices this makes no difference to the analysis of factor-augmenting technical change, since the same result holds for fixed factors and for the closed-economy case. (See Section 3.3 above and Fisher and Shell (1972, p. 90).) In each case, what matters is the effect of output prices on the share at shadow prices of the factor being augmented.

We now consider the case of *m*th-factor-augmenting technical progress in a particular industry, say the first. To do this, as in (3.7.4) and (3.7.5), we must go to explicit representation of the technologies of the individual industries and replace in (3.9.8) the term $F(x, v, u)$ with

$$\delta_1[x_1 - g^1(v_{11}, \ldots, bv_{1m}, u_{11}, \ldots, u_{1s})]$$

$$+ \sum_{i=2}^{r} \delta_i[x_i - g^i(v_{i1}, \ldots, v_{im}, u_{i1}, \ldots, u_{is})],$$

where the notation should be clear from the parallel with Section 3.7. A similar substitution with hatted values is made in (3.9.6). We can now generalize Corollary 3.11.1 to give us the following theorem.

Theorem 3.11.1:

$$\frac{\partial y}{\partial b} = \frac{Q}{b}\left(\frac{\lambda w_m v_{1m}}{Q} - \frac{\hat{\lambda} w_m \hat{v}_{1m}}{\hat{Q}}\right).$$

Hence, if a rise in the price of the kth good would lead to an increase (re-duction) in the share of the mth factor employed in the first industry in total factor payments at shadow prices, then mth-factor-augmenting technical progress in the first industry will increase (decrease) the importance of the kth output price in the production-theoretic output-price index.

Proof: By the Envelope Theorem applied to the altered version of (3.9.8), we have

$$\partial y/\partial b = -\delta_1 g_m^1 v_{1m} + (\partial y/\partial\hat{\mu})(\partial\hat{\mu}/\partial b). \tag{3.11.1}$$

From the first-order conditions, we have

$$-\delta_1 g_m^1 b = \lambda w_m. \tag{3.11.2}$$

Now, applying the Envelope Theorem to the altered version of (3.9.6) yields

$$\partial\hat{\mu}/\partial b = -\hat{\delta}_1 \hat{g}_m^1 \hat{v}_m^1, \tag{3.11.3}$$

and from the first-order conditions and (3.9.7), we have

$$\hat{\delta}_1 \hat{g}_m^1 b = w_m \hat{\rho}/C^0 = \hat{\lambda}(\partial\hat{\mu}/\partial\hat{y}). \tag{3.11.4}$$

Using (3.11.2)–(3.11.4) in (3.11.1) and applying Lemma 3.10.1 establishes the result.   ■

Corollary 3.11.2: *If the technology is homogeneous of any degree, then y and $\hat{y}$ can replace Q and $\hat{Q}$, respectively, in Theorem 3.11.1.*

We can similarly generalize the duality result, Theorem 3.7.2. To do this, it will be convenient first to establish the following lemma.

Lemma 3.11.1:

$$\frac{\partial x_k}{\partial b} = \left(\frac{1}{b}\right)\frac{\partial(\lambda w_m v_{1m})}{p_k}.$$

Proof: Differentiating (3.9.8) (and holding $\hat{\mu}$ constant), we have

$$\partial \Lambda / \partial p_k = x_k \quad \text{and} \quad \partial \Lambda / \partial b = -\delta_1 g_m^1 v_{1m} = (\lambda w_m v_{1m}/b),$$

(3.11.5)

using (3.11.2). The lemma now follows from the symmetry of cross–second partial derivatives.   ∎

We generalize Theorem 3.7.2 in the next theorem.

Theorem 3.11.2: *Since the PPM is homothetic, we have*

$$\frac{\partial (x_k/y)}{\partial b} = \frac{Q}{by} \frac{\partial (\lambda w_m v_{1m}/Q)}{\partial p_k}.$$

Proof: Differentiating and applying the Envelope Theorem yields

$$\frac{\partial (x_k/y)}{\partial b} = \frac{y(\partial x_k/\partial b) - x_k(\partial y/\partial b)}{y^2}$$

$$= \left(\frac{1}{y}\right)\left(\frac{\partial x_k}{\partial b}\right) - \frac{x_k w_m v_{1m}}{by^2}.$$

(3.11.6)

Using Lemmas 3.11.1 and 3.10.3, we also have

$$\frac{\partial (\lambda w_m v_{1m}/Q)}{\partial p_k} = \frac{Q \partial (\lambda w_m v_{1m})/\partial p_k - \lambda w_m v_{1m}(\partial Q/\partial p_k)}{Q^2}$$

$$= \left(\frac{b}{Q}\right)\left(\frac{\partial x_k}{\partial b} - \frac{\lambda x_k w_m v_{1m}}{by}\right).$$

(3.11.7)

Comparison of (3.11.6) and (3.11.7) completes the proof.   ∎

As before, this result is simpler under constant returns-to-scale, as can be seen in the next corollary.

Corollary 3.11.3: *Under constant returns-to-scale, we have*

$$\frac{\partial (x_k/y)}{\partial b} = \left(\frac{1}{b}\right)\left(\frac{\partial (\lambda w_m v_{1m}/Q)}{\partial p_k}\right).$$

Proof: In this case, we can again use the "adding up" result, $Q = y$.   ∎

3.12. The General Competitive Case

We now turn to the analysis, begun in Section 2.11, of the competitive industry facing rising factor-supply schedules. Because the definition of the production-theoretic output-price index is quite involved for this case – involving not only simple optimization problems but also fixed-point arguments – comparative-statics results are not easy to achieve. (Of course, the fully closed, fully open, and hybrid cases analyzed above in detail are special cases of the general compctitive case.)

The efficient technological frontier is given by

$$F(x, v) = 0, \tag{3.12.1}$$

where x is an r-vector of outputs and v an m-vector of factors. We denote the corresponding m-vector of factor prices by w.

Factors are supplied to the industry according to

$$v^S = v^S(w). \tag{3.12.2}$$

We are given base-period prices $\hat{p}$, current-period prices p, base-period money output $\hat{y}$, and a level of reference costs C^0. Note that factor prices in the base period are not given (although for some versions of what follows they reemerge rather quickly).

Two steps are required for the construction of the production-theoretic output-price index.

Step 3.12.1: Choose a factor price vector $\hat{w}$. Define $\hat{C}$ and μ by

$$\hat{C} = \hat{w} \cdot \hat{v} \quad \text{and} \quad \mu = \hat{C}/C^0. \tag{3.12.3}$$

Then choose $\hat{v}$ and $\hat{x}$ to minimize μ subject to (3.12.1) and

$$\hat{p} \cdot \hat{x} = \hat{y}. \tag{3.12.4}$$

Call the resulting factor demands $\hat{v}(\hat{w})$, the resulting minimized costs $\hat{C}(\hat{w})$, and the resulting minimized value of μ, $\mu(\hat{w})$. Now find that value of $\hat{w}$, say $\hat{w}^*$, that satisfies

$$\hat{v}(\hat{w}^*) = \mu(\hat{w}^*)v^S(\hat{w}^*). \tag{3.12.5}$$

Step 3.12.2: Choose a factor price vector w. Define y and C by

$$y = p \cdot x \quad \text{and} \quad C = w \cdot v. \tag{3.12.6}$$

Choose v and x to maximize y subject to (3.12.1) and

$$C = \mu(\hat{w}^*)C^0 = \hat{C}(\hat{w}^*) = \hat{w}^* \cdot \hat{v}(\hat{w}^*). \tag{3.12.7}$$

Call the resulting factor demands $v(w)$ and the resulting maximized value of y, $y(w)$. Now find that value of w, say w^*, that satisfies:

$$v(w^*) = \mu(\hat{w}^*)v^S(w^*). \tag{3.12.8}$$

(Notice that $\mu(\hat{w}^*)$, not $\mu(w^*)$, is involved here.) The production-theoretic output-price index is now determined as $(y(w^*)/\hat{y})$. For convenience, we assume that $\hat{w}^*$ and w^* are unique.

Obviously, if $\mu(\hat{w}^*) = 1$, then (3.12.5) and (3.12.8) are merely equating supply and demand in all factor markets. If we are working with the actual base-period technology, actual base-period factor-supply curves, and actual base-period costs as a reference, then $\hat{w}^*$ will turn out to be base-period wages and $\mu(\hat{w}^*) = 1$. In this case, we are merely asking what value of output would have been produced at prices p by the base-period economy facing the same supply conditions that it actually did face. For comparative-static exercises, however, the technology or the factor-supply curves can differ between the base period and the current period. To better understand such cases, we first examine how this setup generalizes the special cases already discussed.

Consider first the fully closed case. Here, at the $\hat{w}^*$ that solves the problem of Step 3.12.1, (3.12.5) implies that factor usage must be proportional to fixed factor supplies. Moreover, the factor of proportionality, $\mu(\hat{w}^*)$, must be minimized subject to (3.12.1) and (3.12.4). In view of (3.12.8), the solution to the problem of Step 3.12.2 just maximizes y given (3.12.1) and the same factor usages that result for Step 3.12.1. This is obviously equivalent to the version in Section 3.1 above.

Now consider the fully open economy. Factors are supplied at exogenously given factor prices. This means that v^S is a correspondence, whose ith component is zero if w_i is below the exogenously given wage, infinity if w_i is above that wage, and any point in $[0, +\infty)$ if w_i equals that wage. It is plain, however, that the solution of the problem in Step 3.12.1 must be at those same exogenous factor prices. To see this, observe that if $\hat{w}_i^*$ were lower than the corresponding exogenous wage, then (3.12.5) would imply that the corresponding factor demand was zero. Then that demand would continue to be zero (and would not affect anything) at higher wages up to the exogenously given one. In contrast, if $\hat{w}_i^*$ were higher than the corresponding exogenously given wage, the corresponding factor supply would be infinite. Since, given (3.12.1), (3.12.3), and (3.12.4), the optimal value of μ cannot be zero, the finite factor demands that result from minimizing μ could not satisfy (3.12.5). Hence Step 3.12.1 reduces to minimizing costs at the exogenously given factor prices. Similarly, Step 3.12.2 reduces to maximizing the value of output given costs at those same factor prices.

The hybrid, partly open case is a combination of these two cases. Here, it is easy to see that (3.12.5) implies that at $\hat{w}^*$ the demand for fixed factors must be proportional to reference amounts, with the factor of proportionality the same as the ratio of total costs to reference costs. Evidently, that same ratio (which is to be minimized) must be the ratio of the costs of the variable factors to their reference costs (defined as total reference costs C^0 less the value of the reference amounts of the fixed factors at the solution wages). Step 3.12.2 then involves the maximization of money output given the demands for fixed factors and the costs that solved Step 3.12.1.

In general, we have the following situation: We know that if we start with actual base-period conditions, Step 3.12.1 amounts to asking what would money output have been had the base-period economy been faced with prices p instead of prices $\hat{p}$. Where we start with conditions other than those of the base period, we first ask by what factor $\mu(\hat{w}^*)$ the supply functions and costs of the base period would have to be multiplied so that a competitive production system with the resulting conditions would have produced value $\hat{y}$ when prices were $\hat{p}$. We then ask what value of output the same competitive production system would have produced under the same conditions and with the same costs had prices been p.

This way of examining the problem is perhaps most naturally akin to the fully closed case where fixed factor supplies are multiplied by a dosage level to get a reference economy just capable of producing $\hat{y}$. Essentially the same thing is going on here. Aside from the fact that the present version generalizes the fully closed case, this can perhaps be seen most readily by observing that the procedure given is equivalent to the following two-step procedure.

Step 3.12.1′: Choose a factor price vector $\hat{w}$. Consider $v^S(\hat{w})$ and treat it as fixed. Solve the standard first problem for the fully closed case, that is, minimize the common ratio of factor usages to corresponding "fixed" factor supplies subject to (3.12.1) and (3.12.4). Call the resulting value of this ratio $\hat{\mu}(\hat{w})$. Now, efficiency requires that the marginal revenue product of each factor be the same in every use. Construct new factor prices $\tilde{w} = (\tilde{w}_1, \ldots, \tilde{w}_i, \ldots, \tilde{w}_m)$ such that

$$\tilde{w}_i = \tilde{\lambda}\mathrm{MRP}_i, \tag{3.12.9}$$

where MRP_i is the marginal revenue product of factor i, for $i = 1, \ldots, m$, and $\widetilde{\lambda}$ is given by

$$\widetilde{\lambda} = \frac{\widetilde{\mu}(\hat{w})C^0}{\displaystyle\sum_j \text{MRP}_j v_j^S(\hat{w})}. \qquad (3.12.10)$$

Find that value of $\hat{w}$ for which $\widetilde{w} = \hat{w}$. Call it $\hat{w}^{**}$.

Step 3.12.2′:   Choose a factor price vector w. Treat $v^S(w)$ as fixed and solve the standard second problem for the fully closed case, that is, maximize y subject to (3.12.1) and factor usages equal to $\widetilde{\mu}(\hat{w}^{**})v^S(w)$. Again calculate marginal revenue products and set wages as in (3.12.9) and (3.12.10), with w replacing $\hat{w}$. Find that value of w, say w^{**}, such that $\widetilde{w} = w^{**}$. The index is given by the corresponding value of $y/\hat{y}$.

It is not hard to see that this way (given by Steps 3.12.1′ and 3.12.2′) of defining the production-theoretic output-price index is equivalent to the first way (given by Steps 3.12.1 and 3.12.2). Consider the solution to the problem in Step 3.12.1′, $\hat{w}^{**}$. At $\hat{w}^{**}$, factor usages are proportional to factor supplies, so that (3.12.5) is satisfied. The constraints (3.12.1) and (3.12.4) are certainly satisfied. Marginal revenue products are the same in every use and are proportional to the elements of $\hat{w}^{**}$, so that production is efficient. Finally, the factor of proportionality in (3.12.9) is such as to make the ratio of costs to reference costs the same as the common ratio of factor usages to factor supplies. But these are precisely the conditions that determine $\hat{w}^*$ as the outcome of Step 3.12.1, and all the other magnitudes involved in the problems must similarly coincide, respectively. A similar statement holds for the relations between Steps 3.12.2′ and 3.12.2.

In essence, Steps 3.12.1′ and 3.12.2′ turn the analysis into a series of fully closed problems, whereas Steps 3.12.1 and 3.12.2 turn it (perhaps more naturally in the case of a competitive economy) into a series of fully open ones. It is also possible to perform the analysis as a series of hybrid problems treating some factors as in Steps 3.12.1 and 3.12.2 and the remainder as in Steps 3.12.1′ and 3.12.2′, but such treatment, although most general, is least natural and is not particularly convenient. It is left as an exercise to the reader.

Returning to the discussion of Steps 3.12.1 and 3.12.2, consideration of the fully closed, fixed-factor case makes it evident why we cannot proceed by simply minimizing costs subject to (3.12.4) and actual supply conditions and then maximizing the value of output at the new prices subject to (3.12.7) and those same supply conditions. The difficulty has to do with the appearance of $\mu(\hat{w}^*)$ in (3.12.5) and (3.12.8). When using actual base-period conditions, $\mu(\hat{w}^*)$ will be unity. When departing from those conditions, however, the presence of factors not in perfectly elastic supply would create feasibility problems in Step 3.12.1 if supply conditions as well as costs were not multiplied by $\mu(\hat{w}^*)$.

More important than this, however, is the simple fact that to proceed without such multiplication would be to ignore the fact that with rising factor-supply curves, even under constant returns-to-scale, a doubling of costs does not represent a doubling of resource use, as it does in the fully open case. Similarly, simply to maximize the value of output at output prices $\hat{p}$ and p, respectively, under actual supply conditions and treat the difference as purely a price level effect would be to ignore the fact that, unlike in the fully closed case, an increase in cost does mean an increase in resource use. The simplest example of this is that of an outward shifting factor-demand curve with a given rising (but not perfectly inelastic) factor-supply curve.

In general, it is easy to see that a constant returns-to-scale technology implies constant returns to $\mu(\hat{w}^*)$ in this problem (i.e., to a proportional change in all factor supplies and in cost). If we wish to increase or decrease the base-period economy proportionally, such proportional changes that must be made (and it is these that will enable us to take advantage of any homotheticity properties of the PPM). This is what Step 3.12.1 accomplishes.

Each of the two ways of looking at the problem (Steps 3.12.1 and 3.12.2 or Steps 3.12.1′ and 3.12.2′) has its own advantages. Steps 3.12.1 and 3.12.2 have the natural feature of cost minimization, whereas Steps 3.12.1′ and 3.12.2′ clearly show the proportional increase in supply conditions.

Unfortunately, as mentioned before, doing comparative statics in the competitive general case is likely to be difficult, as can be seen by the following argument: Consider Steps 3.12.1 and 3.12.2. At the equilibrium factor prices, $\hat{w}^*$ and w^*, we can think of the economy as optimizing subject to the (fixed) given factor prices. If, therefore, we knew how a particular change affected *equilibrium* factor prices, we could use the Envelope Theorem to analyze the effects of such changes on the optimization problems, essentially as we analyzed the effects of exogenously given factor price changes in the fully open case. The trouble is that most parameter changes affect equilibrium factor prices in a complex way, since the derivation of factor demands is part of the solution to Steps 3.12.1 and 3.12.2. Even where some factor is in perfectly elastic supply and the others are not, we run into a problem in analyzing the effects of a change in the price of the elastically supplied factor because such a change will also alter other equilibrium factor prices.

Similarly, consider dealing with the matter by way of Steps 3.12.1′ and 3.12.2′. If we knew how a particular change affected equilibrium factor supplies, we could use the Envelope Theorem to analyze the effects of such changes on the optimization problems, essentially as we analyzed the effects of changing exogenously given factor supplies in the fully closed case. But most parameter changes affect equilibrium factor supplies in a complicated way, unless the economy truly is a fully closed one.

In general, the best we seem able to do in this regard is to analyze the hybrid case given above, where for each factor either its price or its supply is exogenously given. Therefore, we will not elaborate further the details of the procedures described in the preceding two paragraphs.

3.13. The Monopsony Case

Of course, the distinguishing feature of the competitive case with general supply curves (and the feature that makes comparative-statics difficult) is that the production system takes factor prices as given and takes no account of the effect of its own factor demands on these prices. In the present section, we deal with the case of monopsony in which the fact that supply schedules are rising is taken into account. This turns out to be quite easy to do and it makes comparative-statics exercises easier, rather than harder, to perform, because more is determined in the context of the optimization problems involved.

It is very easy to adapt Steps 3.12.1 and 3.12.2 to handle the cases of monopsony. Suppose that the first t factors are monopsonized ($t \leq m$), so that the effects on factor demands of the corresponding factor prices are taken into account by the production system.[16] Then, in Step 3.12.1, only the last $(m - t)$ elements of $\hat{w}$ and, in Step 3.12.2, only the last $(m - t)$ elements of w are to be set outside the optimization problems. The first t elements of the two factor price vectors are to be treated as choice variables

16. For convenience, we shall proceed in the comparative-statics analysis below as though the taken-into-account effects of a particular factor demand on factor prices were restricted only to the effects on that factor's own price, but this is not necessary.

in minimizing costs and maximizing value, respectively. In doing this in Step 3.12.1, the factor prices must satisfy

$$\hat{v}_j(\hat{w}) = \mu(\hat{w})v_j^S(\hat{w}) \quad \text{for } j = 1, \dots, t. \tag{3.13.1}$$

Similarly, in Step 3.12.2, the factor prices must satisfy

$$v_j(w) = \mu(\hat{w}^*)v_j^S(w) \quad \text{for } j = 1, \dots, t. \tag{3.13.2}$$

The special feature of monopsony is that (3.13.1) and (3.13.2) are taken into account in the respective optimization problems rather than being imposed afterwards with factor prices varied parametrically to clear markets, as is done with the remaining factor prices in (3.12.5) and (3.12.8). There is no other difference from the competitive case. Notice the appearance of μ in (3.13.1) and (3.13.2). Supply conditions are still being varied up or down proportionally, and it is the resulting supply curves that the monopsonist takes into account. As always, we work with a reference economy differing by scale from the actual economy.

Because the monopsonist takes its effects on factor prices into account in its optimization problem, comparative-statics analysis is easier to perform than in the fully competitive case. This is so because we can employ the Envelope Theorem and not have to worry *separately* about effects on equilibrium factor prices. As this suggests, however, the assumption of monopsony is most helpful if we have either $t = m$, so that monopsony is complete, or else every nonmonopsonized factor has its supply curve either flat or vertical so that we can deal with the problem as in the hybrid case considered earlier.

We shall do this in a moment. It is disappointing that this is the most general case that can be considered conveniently. In particular, it keeps us from being able to analyze the effects of a change in industrial structure from monopsony to competition, other things equal. (Such a change will generally increase output but will do so in both the base period and the current period, so that the net effect on the index is unclear.) The closest we can come to such an analysis is to ask what the effect would be of an increase in the slope of the supply curve of a monopsonized factor, and this is not the same thing.

The comparative-statics exercises that do seem feasible under monopsony are very easy adaptations of our analysis of the hybrid model in Sections 3.9 and 3.10, above. We use the notation of those sections, but suppose that the first t of the m variable factors are monopsonized. This leads to the following changes in the Lagrangians, (3.9.6) and (3.9.8).

Consider first (3.9.6). Since factor prices will not be the same in both periods, denote base-period variable-factor prices by w. Add to the right-hand side of (3.9.6) the term

$$\sum_{j=1}^{t} \hat{\alpha}_j \left[\frac{\hat{v}_j}{v_j^S(\hat{w})} - \frac{\hat{u}_1}{u_1^0} \right],$$

(3.13.3)

where the $\hat{\alpha}_j$ are Lagrange multipliers. This imposes the constraint (3.13.1). Note the similarity to the treatment of fixed factors.

Similarly, add to the right-hand side of (3.9.8) the term

$$-\sum_{j=1}^{t} \alpha_j \left[v_j - \hat{\mu} v_j^S(w) \right],$$

(3.13.4)

where the α_j are Lagrange multipliers. This imposes the constraint (3.13.2).

Note that in this setup any result based on the Envelope Theorem *and* not involving changes in the terms in (3.13.3) and (3.13.4) must still apply. This is true for all the results on factor-augmenting technical change considered in Section 3.11, which depend only on the Envelope Theorem and on Lemma 3.9.1. The latter Lemma, however, extends to the present case, although the shadow price of the monopsonized factor now involves its shadow marginal cost, as it were, rather than merely its shadow price.[17]

Thus, all the results of Section 3.11 on factor-augmenting change in the competitive hybrid case must still apply. The only question is their interpretation in the present case.

In cases where the factor being augmented is not one of the monopsonized factors, there is no problem at all. The results of Section 3.11 stand. Further, since uniform factor augmentation is equivalent to a supply increase, the same is true for changes in the supply of a fixed factor.

In cases where the factor being augmented is one of the monopsonized factors, however, a little care is required. The verbal statements of the various results remain correct in this case, but the appearance in the mathematical statements of terms such as $\lambda w_m v_{1m}$ is not. (The reason for this was given above.)

Consider the proof of Theorem 3.11.1, for example. The term in question appears from the use of the first-order conditions in (3.11.2). But, in the monopsonized case, the marginal revenue product of a monopsonized factor

---

17. Using the revised version of (3.9.8), for example, the shadow price of factor j is now $(\alpha_j + \lambda w_j)$ rather than merely λw_j, as before.

will not equal its shadow factor *price* but rather its full shadow *marginal cost*, including the Lagrange multiplier α_j. What matters in the theorem, therefore, is still the share of the factor in question in total payments to factors at shadow prices, but those shadow prices must be taken to include the monopsonistic effects.

One must be very careful, however, when extending this result on factor augmentation to one involving a change in the supply curve of a monopsonized factor. Although one might think that (as in the case of fixed factors) uniform factor augmentation of a monopsonized factor is equivalent to a multiplicative increase in supply (that is, to the multiplication of the relevant $v_j^S(w)$ by some parameter), this is not the case. Although, as far as production is concerned, a uniform factor-augmenting change is just like having more of the factor at any given factor price, such a change does not affect the marginal cost at which more of the factor can be hired in the same way as does a shift in supply. This means that supply shifts must be separately analyzed. We do this next.

This analysis will also assist us in considering the effect of a change in one of the factor prices. Unlike the results of Section 3.11 on factor-augmenting change in the competitive hybrid case, the results of Section 3.10 on the effects in that case of a change in factor prices are not necessarily immediately applicable here. Obviously, it makes no sense to examine changes in the factor prices of monopsonized factors, as these are not given exogenously. Even a change in a factor price that is exogenously given may present problems, however, because of the possibility that such a change affects the supply of one of the monopsonized factors and thus enters in (3.13.3) and (3.13.4). Where this is not the case, the results of Section 3.10 immediately apply. Further, even where it is the case, we can think of the effects of a change in such a factor price as consisting of two parts, the first being the one examined in Section 3.10 with monopsony absent and the second being the one that occurs through a shift in the supply curve of a monopsonized factor.

This brings us to an analysis of the effect of supply shifts. In our analysis, the effect of monopsony emerges very plainly. We first consider a general parametric change in the supply function for the first factor (which we assume to be monopsonized). We write that supply function as

$$v_1^S = v_1^S(w, \sigma), \tag{3.13.5}$$

where σ is a shift parameter, and we will make the appropriate changes in notation wherever needed. We denote with hats the value of any function or derivative evaluated in the base period, saving unhatted values for the current period.

Next, observe that the marginal revenue product of any factor will be the same in every use. We denote by $\hat{\gamma}_1$ and γ_1 the marginal revenue products of the first factor in the base period and current period, respectively. (The exact expressions for $\hat{\gamma}_1$ and γ_1 are not important. They can be obtained from the fact that the first-order conditions must imply that marginal revenue product is equal to marginal factor cost.) We then have the following theorem:

Theorem 3.13.1:

$$\frac{\partial y}{\partial \sigma} = \hat{\mu} Q \left[\frac{(\gamma_1 - \lambda w_1)(\partial v_1^S / \partial \sigma)}{Q} - \frac{(\hat{\gamma}_1 - \hat{\lambda} \hat{w}_1)(\partial \hat{v}_1^S / \partial \sigma)}{\hat{Q}} \right].$$

Proof: Applying the Envelope Theorem to (3.9.8) expanded to include (3.13.4) yields

$$\partial y / \partial \sigma = \hat{\mu} \alpha_1 \left(\partial v_1^S / \partial \sigma \right) + (\partial y / \partial \hat{\mu})(\partial \hat{\mu} / \partial \sigma). \tag{3.13.6}$$

Similarly, applying the Envelope Theorem to (3.9.6) expanded to include (3.13.3) yields

$$\frac{\partial \hat{\mu}}{\partial \sigma} = -\alpha_1 \left(\hat{v}_1 / \left(\hat{v}_1^S \right)^2 \right) \left(\partial \hat{v}_1^S / \partial \sigma \right) = -\hat{\mu} \left(\hat{\alpha}_1 / \hat{v}_1^S \right) \left(\partial \hat{v}_1^S / \partial \sigma \right),$$

$$\tag{3.13.7}$$

using (3.13.1). From the first-order conditions, however, we have

$$\alpha_1 = \gamma_1 - \lambda w_1 \tag{3.13.8}$$

and

$$\hat{\alpha}_1 / \hat{v}_1^S = (\rho / \hat{\lambda} C^0)(\hat{\gamma}_1 - \hat{\lambda} \hat{w}_1). \tag{3.13.9}$$

The desired result now follows from the substitution of (3.13.7) and (3.13.8) into (3.13.6) and the use of (3.13.7), Lemma 3.10.1, and (3.9.7).   ∎

The appearance of terms such as $(\gamma_1 - \lambda w_1)$ in this result shows very clearly the presence of monopsony. This term is the difference between the marginal revenue product and the "competitive" factor price of the first factor [recalling that the "competitive" factor price (or imputed factor price) includes the shadow price of the cost constraint]. Hence it represents "monopsony profits" per unit of the first factor.

This result should be compared with Theorem 3.3.1 and Corollary 3.11.1. In those cases, monopsony effects are absent, factor price effects are not taken into account in the optimization problem, and hence only marginal revenue products appear in the results.

Theorem 3.13.1 is our direct result for general shifts in supply. Define N_1 by

$$N_1 = (\gamma_1 - \lambda w_1)(\partial v_1^S / \partial \sigma). \tag{3.13.10}$$

Then Theorem 3.13.1 states that if an increase in the kth price would increase (N_1/Q), then an increase in the parameter σ will make the kth price more important in the production-theoretic output-price index.

If the PPM could be taken to be homothetic, this result would also correspond to an extension of our various duality results to the present case, that is, we would obtain the result that a shift in supply increases N_1/Q if and only if it also increases x_k/y, the weight given to p_k in a Paasche index.

Unfortunately, as observed in Section 2.9, homotheticity is not a particularly natural assumption for the case of a monopsonist facing rising supply curves. We do not know whether or not the result on Paasche indexes extends to the nonhomotheticity case. We suspect that the ratio nature of x_k/y does indeed make this result dependent on the homotheticity assumption. Of course, as is well known, failure of homotheticity greatly reduces interest in Paasche and Laspeyres price indices – precisely because of the ratio nature of the weights involved.[18]

Theorem 3.13.1 sets forth the analysis for the case of a general shift in supply. Plainly, how interesting that analysis is in any particular case depends on what N_1 turns out to be. We consider two leading cases of shifts in the supply schedule v_1^S: (i) a multiplicative shift and (ii) an additive shift. For these cases, we provide the following explicit statements of corollaries of Theorem 3.13.1.

Corollary 3.13.1: *The effect on the production-theoretic output-price index of a multiplicative increase in v_1^S has the sign of*

$$\frac{(\gamma_1 - \lambda w_1)v_1}{Q} - \frac{(\hat{\gamma}_1 - \hat{\lambda}\hat{w}_1)\hat{v}_1}{\hat{Q}}.$$

In other words, the kth price will become more important as a result of the

---

18. As we have observed, this fact also reduces interest in comparative-statics analyses. The analysis in this section should therefore be taken as directly interesting only if applied to small changes. It retains some indirect interest, however, because of the contrast it provides to our earlier results.

shift if and only if an increase in the kth price would increase the ratio of *total* first factor monopsony profits to total shadow valuation of factors.

Corollary 3.13.2: *The effect on the production-theoretic output-price index of an additive increase in v_1^S has the sign of*

$$\frac{\gamma_1 - \lambda w_1}{Q} - \frac{\hat{\gamma}_1 - \hat{\lambda}\hat{w}_1}{\hat{Q}}.$$

In other words, the kth price will become more important as the result of the shift if and only if an increase in the kth price would increase the ratio of first factor monopsony profits *per unit of factor* to total shadow valuation of factors.

3.14. Monopoly

We now turn to the analysis of monopoly along the lines discussed in Section 2.10.[19] We take as given two revenue functions instead of two output-price vectors.

Let $R(x, S)$ be the total revenue function as seen by the (monopolized) production sector, where x, as always, is the vector of outputs and S is a vector of shift parameters. The role of S is to capture shifts in demand conditions between the two periods, and, accordingly, we shall denote its base-period value by $\hat{S}$, reserving the unhatted notation for the current period. If some output prices are taken as given, then those prices are elements of S. Where monopoly is present, shifts in S parametrize shifts in the demand curve facing the monopolist. It will be convenient to assume $R(x, S)$ to be increasing in the elements of S.

We now generalize our analysis to include monopoly by beginning with the constraint

$$\hat{y} = R(\hat{x}, \hat{S}), \tag{3.14.1}$$

where $\hat{y}$ is given, and then by maximizing

$$y = R(x, S). \tag{3.14.2}$$

In other words, we now seek the value of output that the economy that produced value $\hat{y}$ when demand conditions were characterized by $\hat{S}$ would have

---

19. We remind the reader that this approach is quite different from that taken in Fisher and Shell (1972, pp. 59–61).

produced had demand conditions been characterized by S. That economy includes all relevant monopoly elements.

How does the substitution of (3.14.1) and (3.14.2) for $\hat{y} = \hat{p} \cdot \hat{x}$ and $y = p \cdot x$, respectively, affect our analysis? Examination of the comparative-statics results of earlier subsections reveals remarkably little change. Naturally, R_i, the marginal revenue product of the ith good, replaces p_i in the various results; similarly, $\hat{R}_i$ replaces $\hat{p}_i$. Very little else is altered, save the interpretation.

One change that does occur is as follows. In various places, use has been made of the first-order conditions for the optimum problems involving statements that marginal revenue product equals factor price. This remains true, even though marginal revenue products are now not simply the values of marginal physical products. However, even under constant returns-to-scale, total factor payments at shadow prices W will no longer equal the value of output y, so that (as the inequality is general in the nonconstant returns-to-scale environment) it is total factor payments at shadow prices rather than total output values that appear in the theorems. Substitutions such as that made in Corollary 3.10.1 above are no longer valid (except where revenue $R(x, S)$ is homogeneous of some degree in x, which is not a particularly interesting case).

The interpretation of the various comparative-statics results changes but in an obvious way. Whereas previously those results ran in terms of various changes making particular prices more or less important in the production-theoretic output-price index, now prices are not among the givens of the problem unless they are elements of the shift parameter S. It is the latter elements that are the givens, as it were. Accordingly, our basic comparative-statics theorems now describe the circumstances under which a given parametric change makes shifts in particular elements of S more or less important in the production-theoretic output-price index. To take an example, in the extension of Theorem 3.6.1 to the present case, a rise in the price of the ith factor will reduce the importance of changes in S_k in the production-theoretic output-price index if and only if an increase in S_k would increase the usage of the ith factor.[20] Of course, for the nonmonopolized part of the economy, prices are taken as given and are among the elements of S. For those prices, there is no change in the interpretation of the results.

Our various duality results also change and become less directly interesting. In general, these now run as follows: The effect of some parametric

20. Recall that $R(x, S)$ is increasing in the elements of S.

change on the production-theoretic output-price index always turns out to depend on the derivative of the Lagrangian for the current-period optimum problem with respect to that parameter. The duality results obtained in earlier sections all involved differentiating that derivative with respect to one of the prices, say p_k, and then observing, since cross–second partials are equal, that this is also the derivative of x_k with respect to the parameter in question. This fact is then used to relate the effect of the parameter on (x_k/y), the natural weight given to p_k in a Paasche index, to the effects of the parameter on the importance of p_k in the production-theoretic output-price index as described in the corresponding primal theorem.

In the monopoly case, however, the primary changes are those in the elements of S, not those in prices. It remains true, of course, that the cross–second partial derivative of the Lagrangian with respect to some parameter and S_k (say) is independent of the order of differentiation, but although the effects of S_k on the derivative of the Lagrangian with respect to that parameter is of interest because of the primal theorem involved, the effects of the parameter on the derivative of the Lagrangian with respect to S_k is not. Where S_k is not itself a price, the latter derivative is not x_k and plainly bears no relation to the weight one would give to S_k in a Paasche index, since the nonprice S_k do not enter such an index.

Moreover, even where S_k is a price, say p_k, the duality results lose much of their importance. Although it remains true that one is now relating the results of the primal theorems to the effects of the relevant parameters on x_k, it is no longer true that these are directly related to effects on (x_k/y), the natural weight of p_k in a Paasche index, because revenue will no longer be homothetic in inputs even if outputs are.

This is as it should be. Even if effects on (x_k/y) were related to the effects in the primal theorems, that would not matter because (x_k/y) is no longer of much interest. A Paasche index in the present monopoly case clearly does not have the same meaning as in the competitive case. As suggested in Section 2.10,[21] the bounding relations between Paasche and Laspeyres indexes and our production-theoretic output-price index do not hold for the monopoly case.

To see this, consider the case of a Laspeyres index. Here, the denominator, the value of base-period outputs at base-period prices, will continue to be $\hat{y}$, the denominator for our production-theoretic index. The bounding property of the Laspeyres index comes from the fact that the economy that maximized

---

21. See also our earlier treatment of monopoly, Fisher and Shell (1972, pp. 59–61).

y, defined at fixed prices p, could have chosen to continue to produce $\hat{x}$ and earned $p \cdot \hat{x}$ by so doing.

In the present case, however, this is not true. It is certainly true that the economy could have chosen to continue producing $\hat{x}$. Had it done so, however, it would have earned $R(\hat{x}, S) \leq R(x, S)$. But $R(\hat{x}, S)$ is not in general equal to $p \cdot \hat{x}$, because prices would have been different if output had been $\hat{x}$ rather than x.

There is a quasi-Laspeyres index that will continue to bound the production-theoretic output-price index, namely $R(\hat{x}, S)/R(\hat{x}, \hat{S})$; a similar quasi-Paasche index can be defined as $R(x, S)/R(x, \hat{S})$, as shown in Section 2.10. Where monopoly is present in one or more output markets, Paasche and Laspeyres output-price indexes are suspect even where factor-supply curves are either all vertical or flat.

This completes our detailed analysis of monopoly and monopsony. There is one question we have left untouched, however. What if factor supplies themselves are monopolized? This problem will also arise if the productive unit being considered buys from an upstream monopolist of an intermediate good.

There are two cases to consider. On the one hand, if the production sector also has monopsony power in the monopolized factor market, then we have a case of bilateral monopoly and cannot expect to make any progress. On the other hand, if the production sector is a price taker in the monopolized market, then its optimization problems are unaffected by the presence of the factor monopoly. One might therefore expect that our analysis of the competitive general case given in Section 3.12 would apply.

Things are not so simple, however. The difficulty arises in the side conditions (3.12.5) and (3.12.8), since the monopolized factor will not have a supply curve. It is not clear how to deal with this absence. One suggestion is as follows. For the monopolized factor, consider the supply curve it would have if its owner behaved competitively (if the factor is supplied by a firm, this is that firm's marginal cost curve). Then use this function multiplied by μ to give a proportional change in supply conditions. Equilibrium requires that factor prices be such that, after such multiplication, the monopolized factor is at its equilibrium factor price and usage point (including the effects of monopoly). The details (which do not appear very revealing) are left to the reader.

4   Principles of Price and Quantity
Measurement: Inputs

4.1. Introduction

We now turn to the detailed analysis of production-theoretic input-price and input-quantity (or real-input) indexes. Input-price indexes can be used, for example, to deflate costs of production in order to measure real resource use (i.e., to construct the corresponding quantity index). Input-price indexes can also be used in an attempt to see how much of a price increase in a given sector or industry is directly attributable to increases in the prices of the inputs it uses. One example of this (with the productive sector being the entire U.S. economy) is the analysis of the extent to which increases in the price of crude petroleum accounted for inflation in the 1970s. As this suggests, input-price indexes for an economy can be interpreted as import-price indexes.

Naturally, the theory of input-price indexes is largely isomorphic to that of output-price indexes, which we have already developed.[1] In particular, the central role of the PPF in the theory of output-price indexes is replaced in the theory of input-price indexes by a reference isoquant (given different interpretations in different parts of the theory). Revenue maximization with given inputs or cost is replaced by cost minimization for given outputs or revenue. We shall exploit this isomorphism in our treatment of the subject. Doing so will allow us to shorten the analysis considerably: We shall often be able to obtain results simply by reinterpreting the corresponding results about output-price indexes.

---

1. This was first noted and exploited by Muellbauer (1972), but he only dealt with the case isomorphic to that of the fully closed economy. As explained in the next paragraph, this is of limited interest.

124

Pure reliance on the isomorphism, however, although formally correct, does not always lead to asking the most interesting questions. Let us take the leading example: The fully closed economy is an interesting case for output-price index-number theory. It involves the PPF constructed in the usual manner with factor supplies fixed. The isomorphic case for input-price index-number theory, in contrast, is of very little interest. It would involve the isoquant that is the locus of points in input space that can efficiently produce a fixed bundle of outputs. Even when the economy is closed, however, it makes no sense to suppose that demand for all goods is perfectly inelastic as this case would require. As a result, we shall not bother exploring the results obtainable through isomorphism in such a case. The natural case to study first is the one isomorphic to the fully open economy. Other examples where particular isomorphic statements fail to be of much interest occur elsewhere in the theory, and new, nonisomorphic results arise.

We now proceed to a formal general description of the theory of input-price deflation along the lines given for output-price deflation in Chapter 2. The central role of the PPF – the maximal set of outputs that can be produced with inputs satisfying certain conditions – will now be taken by an isoquant – the *minimal* set of inputs that are required to produce outputs satisfying certain conditions. For the present we need not be specific as to what these conditions are; for brevity, we shall refer to the production of "given output," even though, as we have already seen, this will not turn out to be the interesting case (unless "output" is interpreted as "money output").

Figure 4.1.1 shows such an isoquant drawn with the usual shape. v_1 and v_2 denote the amounts of the two factors of production whose prices will enter the index. Points such as $v^C = (v_1^C, v_2^C)$, which lie above and to the right of the isoquant, correspond to input combinations that can produce the given output but that are inefficient in that they involve more inputs than are needed. Points such as $v^D = (v_1^D, v_2^D)$, which lie below and to the left of the isoquant, correspond to input combinations that are insufficient to produce the given output.

We take the position that, *based on the given isoquant*, v^C represents the greatest "overall" input and v^D the least "overall" input of the points explicitly labeled in the diagram. Points v^A and v^B represent equivalent "overall" inputs. This is because they lie on the same isoquant and thus the economy could choose either one efficiently to produce the same output – so far as technology is concerned. The choice between v^A and v^B depends only on factor prices. Hence, the difference in costs between the two points when each of the two points is chosen at the prices that make it efficient

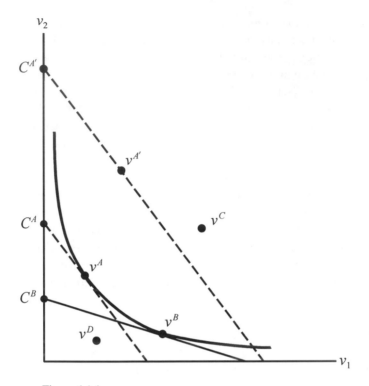

Figure 4.1.1

to do so should be considered solely a price effect and not a change in real-input use.

Thus, suppose that, as usual, money costs are represented on the vertical axis (i.e., the second factor is chosen as the numéraire). The slope of the solid line corresponds to the factor-price ratio at which v^B would be chosen to produce the given output; the slope of the dashed lines corresponds to the price ratio at which v^A would be chosen. Denoting the two sets of factor prices by w^B and w^A, respectively, $C^B = w^B \cdot v^B = w_1^B v_1^B + w_2^B v_2^B$ and $C^A = w^A \cdot v^A = w_1^A v_1^A + w_2^A v_2^A$ are the total costs in the two respective situations.

Now suppose that factor prices in the base-period were w^B and inputs correspondingly v^B, with total cost C^B. Suppose that factor prices then changed to w^A. In this circumstance, the same economy or sector that produced the given output with inputs v^B would have – had it continued to produce the same output – shifted to v^A and had total cost C^A. Since v^B and v^A are on the same isoquant, we consider this change as representing only a factor-price change and not a change in real-input use. Hence, the production-theoretic input-price deflator in this situation is (C^A/C^B). Thus, if the shift in factor prices from w^B to w^A is accompanied in fact by a shift in factor usage to some point other than v^A, say $v^{A'}$, with associated total cost $C^{A'} = w^{A'} \cdot v^{A'}$, the change in costs from C^B to $C^{A'}$ is to be thought of as composed of two parts. We have the identity

$$C^{A'}/C^B = (C^A/C^B)(C^{A'}/C^A), \tag{4.1.1}$$

and (i) C^A/C^B is the index of the change in factor prices, whereas (ii) $C^{A'}/C^A$ represents the increase in real-input usage.

Obviously, this comparison depends on the isoquant used. If we were to start with the isoquant through $v^{A'}$ (not drawn) and consider the change to v^B when prices change from w^A to w^B, we would be asking a different question. If the two isoquants were not parallel along rays (as in a homothetic isoquant map), we would get a different answer. One interpretation of our comparative-statics analysis in the next chapter is as the analysis of how such answers differ when the isoquants differ in particular ways.

It is easy to see how the production-theoretic input-price index relates to Laspeyres and Paasche factor-price indexes. In Figure 4.1.2, v^A, v^B, C^A, and C^B are depicted once more. So is C^{A^*}, the cost of the base-period input bundle v^B at second-period prices w^A. It is evident that we have $C^{A^*} > C^A$. Indeed, it will always be true (even for more than two goods) that $C^{A^*} \geq C^A$, since C^A is the minimum input cost of a particular input bundle on this isoquant. To put it differently, C^{A^*} takes no account of the cost-saving possibilities that can be achieved through substitution among inputs. The Laspeyres input-price index L is given by

$$L = (w^A \cdot v^B/w^B \cdot v^B) = C^{A^*}/C^B \geq C^A/C^B, \tag{4.1.2}$$

so that the Laspeyres price index bounds the production-theoretic input-price index from above. (This is the same sense of the inequality as in the cost-of-living index but in the opposite one from the case of the production-theoretic output-price index.) It is obvious that the inequality in (4.1.2) will be strict if the two sets of prices are not proportional for all nonzero inputs and the isoquant is strictly convex to the origin.

Note that the inequality just established places a Laspeyres upper bound on the production-theoretic input-price index constructed using the actual base-period isoquant. By a similar argument, it is evident that a Paasche input-price index places a lower bound on the production-theoretic input-price index constructed using the actual current-period isoquant. Unless those isoquants are parallel to each other along rays, however, it will

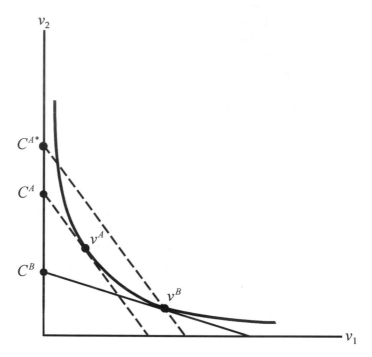

Figure 4.1.2

generally not be the case that the two production-theoretic indexes are the same, so the two bounds need not be simultaneously applicable.

This completes our general introductory discussion of production-theoretic input-price indexes. Before proceeding further in the analysis of these matters, we briefly discuss some issues that apply at this general level. These are the issues involved in corner solutions and, especially, in quality improvement in factors and goods.

4.2. Corner Solutions

The issues involved in corner solutions here are easily resolved. The iso-morphic case to that of new or disappearing goods in the analysis of the cost-of-living index or of the production-theoretic output-price index is that of a new or disappearing factor of production. This does not seem to be a particularly interesting case unless we are considering not primary factors but inputs of goods or materials that one sector or country buys from another. If we do consider such cases, then it is not difficult to imagine a technical discovery that, in effect, produces a good that serves as a previously unknown factor of production from the point of view of the sector or economy that purchases it.

Despite such cases, there is no need to give a lengthy analysis – in part because of the isomorphisms between the theory of input-price indexes and that of output-price indexes. It is plain from consideration of Section 2.3 above[2] that the problem of what factor price to use for a new factor is only a problem for a Paasche index and not for the production-theoretic input-price index. The bounding property of a Paasche index will be preserved if the factor price chosen is any price at or above its base-period demand reservation price. (This is the price at which the productive sector being considered would be just indifferent between employing the factor and not doing so; it is the intercept on the base-period factor demand curve.) Of all prices in this range, the demand reservation price produces the most efficient Paasche lower bound. Further, that price can also be interpreted as the shadow price of the constraint involved in not being able to employ the factor in question in the base period.

It is important to realize, however, that corner solutions arising because of the appearance of new goods or the disappearance of old ones do not raise similar problems. This is because the isoquant relative to which the production-theoretic, input-price deflator is calculated is defined for a given set of output conditions. Just how those conditions are properly defined is a matter we consider below, but however they are defined they will be the same for both periods. New goods do therefore raise a question; the appearance of a new good, like any other technical change, will generally alter the isoquant that determines the production-theoretic input-price index. To evaluate the effect on that index then involves comparative-statics analysis, which involves quite a different class of issues from those solely based on corner solutions in *factor* space.[3]

To take the simplest (and least interesting) example, suppose that the relevant isoquant describes the efficient factor combinations for producing a given set of goods in specified quantities. This set of goods either includes the new one or it does not. The specific goods comprising the set certainly affect the shape of the isoquant and the value of the resulting input-price

2. Or from Fisher and Shell (1972, pp. 99–105).
3. We consider comparative statics in Chapter 5. The particular problem mentioned in the text is not explicitly studied, however, because it is not clear how to parametrize conveniently the change in the isoquant caused by the appearance of the new factor.

deflator, but the fact that a different set of goods would produce a different isoquant and a different deflator raises no problem for the construction of the deflator using the given isoquant corresponding to a given set of goods.

4.3. Quality Change: The Repackaging Theorem

The other general issue that we discuss at this point is that of the analysis of quality change. It presents somewhat deeper problems than does the analysis of corner solutions.

In the theory of the cost-of-living index, a fairly natural issue is the treatment of quality change in one or more of the goods consumed. Although such changes can be handled in principle as the disappearance of one good (with the old quality) and the appearance of a new good (with the new quality), this is not done in practice and, indeed, is rather awkward. In the theory of the cost-of-living index, quality improvement in a consumed good is equivalent to an improvement in the opportunity set facing consumers and therefore equivalent to a fall in the cost of living if prices remain constant. In Fisher and Shell (1972, pp. 26–37), we analyzed these effects and considered whether one can treat a quality improvement as equivalent to a virtual price decrease in the good whose quality had changed. We showed (as our principal result) that, although this could generally be done, it could only be done with the virtual price change involved independent of all other prices and amounts consumed (e.g., dependent only on the physical nature of the quality change) under very special circumstances. The necessary and sufficient conditions for such treatment are that the consumer view the new quality of the good as exactly equivalent to a fixed number of units of the old quality, that is, that the quality change enter the utility function as a shift in a good-augmenting parameter (as b in $U(bx_1, x_2, \ldots, x_n)$, where x_i is the quantity consumed of good i and U is the utility function). We called this case "repackaging" since the consumer regards the new quality good as a "repackaged" version of the old one, so to speak.

The case of output-price deflation has an isomorphic problem (which we considered in Fisher and Shell (1972, pp. 105–107)). There it turns out that one would still wish to treat a quality change as equivalent to a price decrease. This is because the resources used to produce the new quality of the good could have been used to produce different amounts of the original quality had consumers desired it. In effect, quality change is interpreted as simply a shift in demand. The isomorphic statement to the repackaging theorem is that quality improvement can be treated as a virtual decrease in the price of the good whose quality has changed independent of prices and quantities of all goods produced only under special circumstances. The necessary and sufficient conditions for this treatment to be appropriate are that the PPF with the new quality good differ from the PPF with the old one by a shift in a good-augmenting parameter. This is equivalent to requiring that the production functions for the new and old quality good differ by a Hicks-neutral technical change so that, in terms of resource use (rather than utility), one unit of the new quality of good is equivalent to a fixed number of units of the old.

Leaving the repackaging theorem aside for the moment, it is important to recognize the difference between the treatment of quality change and that of technological change in the theory of output deflation. The production-theoretic output-price deflator is constructed from the point of view of a specific production possibility frontier. A technical change will shift that PPF and (usually) change the deflator. However, the PPF used to construct the deflator will be constant when comparing base-period prices with current-period prices – even if the technical change occurred between the two periods. This is because the question to be answered concerns the responses that an economy with a given PPF would have made when faced with two sets of prices. A shift in the PPF may increase real output – if it leads to larger money output than would have been achieved with the base-period PPF and the current-period prices – but this is *not* because the change is equivalent to a price decrease. With base-period and current-period prices the same, the deflator will be unity *whichever* PPF is used to construct it.

Quality change, in contrast, is treated as unambiguous. It is treated as though the choice between new and old quality of goods reflected not a change in supply but a change in *demand* conditions. Hence, a quality change requiring more resources to produce the new quality than to produce the old leads to an unambiguous increase in real output if the number of units of the new quality of good produced in the current period is the same as the number of units of the old quality of good produced in the base period, with the production of all other goods held constant. The quality change is thus equivalent to a price decrease. Indeed, prices will be treated as declining solely because of the quality change, even if money prices remain the same in the two periods.

Obviously, it is important to decide whether a given change should be treated as technological and due to supply or as a quality change and due to demand. (Similarly, in the theory of the cost-of-living index, it is important to decide whether a given change is a taste change, due to demand, or a quality change due to supply.[4]) The basic question to be asked is always whether, if prices do not change, one wishes to consider the value of the deflator as necessarily altered by the change under consideration. If so, then it is a quality change.

The question of how a given change should be treated arises again when we consider input deflation. Here the question to ask is whether, with money input prices the same, we wish to say that input prices have gone down as a result of the change. If so, then the change will be treated as a quality change; if not, then it will be treated as a technical change.

It is important to realize here that a change that occurs inside the unit whose input prices are to be deflated will be treated as a technical change (just as such a change in the case of households is treated as a shift in taste). In general, the discovery of a more efficient process within the production unit itself will not be considered as a decrease in input prices. An input-price index measures the cost of inputs, not the usefulness of inputs once they are used. A quality change, however, means a decrease in input costs for *any* technology used by the production sector. Thus, the kind of quality change with which we are concerned here is change in *input* quality. Changes in output quality will simply be treated as technical changes for purposes of input deflation. It is not reasonable to treat an output quality improvement as a virtual decline in input prices.[5]

To fix ideas, suppose that the change in question concerns the quality of labor, so that labor (with other factors being constant) becomes more productive. If that increase in productivity is due to a discovery on the part of firms as to how to use labor more efficiently, then this will be treated as a technical change and not as a decrease in the effective cost of inputs. If, however, the increase is due to better education of labor, then one may very well wish to treat it as a virtual decrease in input costs and a reduction in the input-price deflator.

---

4. This is not always as simple as it looks. See Fisher and Shell (1972, pp. 7–8).
5. Note the reversal of roles from the case of output-price deflation. There a quality change in an *input* was treated as a technical change – a change in the PPF. Here it is treated as a quality change. In contrast, a quality change in an *output* (there treated as such) is here treated as a technical change (i.e., a change in the isoquant).

The issue is not a simple one. Better educated workers may represent an effective decrease in input prices to the firm that hires them; this is not so (or at least not obviously so) if the education comes through on-the-job training. Now suppose that the production sector whose input costs are being considered is that of the entire economy. Do better educated workers represent lower virtual input prices? Or do they simply reflect a more efficient way of using a given set of inputs – "raw" labor? Either answer is possible.

For those cases in which a given change is treated as a quality change in an input, a result isomorphic to that of the repackaging theorem applies and is very natural. A quality improvement in an input can always be treated as equivalent to a decrease in the price of that input with input quality constant. That price decrease will be independent of input prices and purchases only under special conditions, however. Necessary and sufficient conditions for such independence are that the quality change can be represented within the productive technology as a shift in a parameter augmenting the factor whose quality has changed. In other words, the quality change must be such that one unit of the new quality of factor is exactly equivalent in production to a fixed number of units of the old quality of factor.

It may be thought that this version of the repackaging condition seems more likely to be satisfied in the present case of quality changes in factors than in either the case of good-augmenting changes in the utility function or Hicks-neutral changes in production functions – the conditions that apply to the cost-of-living index and to the production-theoretic output-price deflator, respectively. Once one has decided that a given change is to be considered as a quality change in a factor rather than as a change in technology affecting how that factor is used, it may not seem too stringent to suppose that the change is factor augmenting. But is this really so? Aside from the fact that the decision to treat the change as a quality change already supposes a fairly restrictive set of circumstances (perhaps more restrictive than in the case of output-price deflation or the cost-of-living index), it is not obvious that factor augmentation is then a totally natural assumption. Can an educated worker, for example, really do *everything* better than an uneducated one and better in the same proportion no matter what the task? If not, then the quality change involved in education is not merely factor augmenting in the way required by the repackaging theorem. No simple adjustment in wages will suffice to account for the effect of the change on the production-theoretic input-price deflator or on the corresponding production-theoretic index of real-input use.

4.4. The Fully Open Case

As already indicated, the sensible central case for the analysis of input-price deflation is that corresponding to the fully open economy considered in Section 2.7. In the present circumstances this amounts to assuming that the productive sector can sell all the outputs it wants to at fixed output prices. The isoquant relative to which the input-price deflator is defined then becomes the locus of all efficient input combinations that will produce output bundles of equal value. This is plainly more interesting than basing the analysis on the requirement that a fixed market basket of output be produced (the fully closed case) or on some combination (the hybrid case). Whereas it is sometimes interesting to take total factor supplies as fixed for purposes of output deflation, it is not interesting to take output demands as perfectly inelastic – the isomorphic case for input-price deflation.

We study the fully open case in this section. Later sections use this analysis to study the general competitive case where declining demand curves are faced but not taken into account. The monopoly case where declining demand curves are taken into account is studied separately.

The economic unit's technologically efficient production plans can be summarized in terms of the production relation

$$F(x, v) = 0, \tag{4.4.1}$$

where x is the output vector and v is the input vector. We are also given the vector of output prices $p = (p_1, \ldots, p_r)$ and the money value of output y.

The isoquant to be used in constructing the production-theoretic input-price deflator is defined in the following manner: Choose an output vector x with money output y at prices p. Next, consider the set of v corresponding to this x and the production function $F(x, v) = 0$. This is an isoquant for the production of the given vector x. Consider the family of isoquants generated in this way by varying x over all vectors satisfying $p \cdot x = y$. The isoquant that will be used for input-price deflation is the (lower) envelope of this family. Each v on this envelope also lies on some isoquant defined for some fixed x with money output at the given output prices equal to y. Formally, define the isoquant Ω_{FO} by

$$\Omega_{\mathrm{FO}} \equiv \{v \mid v \text{ is minimal subject to } F(x, v) = 0 \text{ and } p \cdot x = y\}.$$

$$\tag{4.4.2}$$

Given the isoquant Ω_{FO}, the construction of the corresponding production-theoretic input-price index is a straightforward application of the general approach discussed above. We are given two input-price vectors, w^A and w^B.

First we define

$$C^A = \min_{v} w^A \cdot v \quad \text{subject to } v \text{ in } \Omega_{FO}. \tag{4.4.3}$$

Let v^A be the minimizing value of v in Problem (4.4.3). Hence, we have $C^A = w^A \cdot v^A$. Similarly we define C^B by

$$C^B = \min_{v} w^B \cdot v \quad \text{subject to } v \text{ in } \Omega_{FO}. \tag{4.4.4}$$

Let v^B be the minimizing value of v in Problem (4.4.4). Hence, we have $C^B = w^B \cdot v^B$. The production-theoretic input-price index for comparing money costs at input prices w_A to money costs at input prices w^B when outputs can be freely sold at fixed prices p and output value is held constant at y is then (C^A / C^B).

This index is, of course, defined relative to a given isoquant, Ω_{FO}, which is determined by technology (4.4.1), output prices p, and money output y. If these are the actual technology, output prices, and money output of the base period (the period indexed as B), then a Laspeyres input-price index will bound the corresponding production-theoretic index from above. If they are the technology, output prices, and money output of the current period (indexed as A), then a Paasche input-price index will bound the corresponding production-theoretic index from below. If the two isoquants are parallel along rays, then the two production-theoretic indexes will be equal and both bounds will apply.

When will such isoquants be parallel in this way? Sufficient conditions are: (i) The production technology F is common to both periods; (ii) F exhibits constant returns-to-scale; and (iii) the output prices p are proportional in both periods. These conditions, particularly that of constant returns-to-scale, are far stronger than is necessary.

When isoquants are not parallel, the two production-theoretic input-price indexes will differ and the Paasche and Laspeyres bounds need not both apply to the same problem. What form such differences take – and, in effect, how to alter the Paasche or Laspeyres index to restore the bounding property – is a subject of the comparative-statics analysis taken up in Chapter 5.

4.5. General Demand Conditions: The Monopolistic Case

The fully open case, in which output demands are perfectly elastic, is the appropriate one for input deflation when the productive sector involved is small (e.g., a firm, a small group of firms in competition, or a small country in international trade). Larger units or aggregates, however, cannot be treated this simply. We must therefore analyze the case of declining demand curves.

As in the isomorphic case of rising supply curves and output-price deflation, it matters whether or not the producers realize that they face declining demand curves and take this fact into account in their decision making. If they do, we are in the monopoly case, and the analysis is somewhat simpler than if they do not (in the competitive case in which each firm behaves as if it were in the fully open situation). In the present section, we take up the monopoly case. The more difficult (and more interesting) competitive case is treated later.

As before, efficient production plans are given by the relation

$$F(x, v) = 0, \tag{4.5.1}$$

where x is an r-vector of outputs and v is an m-vector of inputs. Let p be the corresponding r-vector of output prices. Outputs are sold by the economic unit in question according to the demand schedule

$$x = x^D(p). \tag{4.5.2}$$

If demand for some good is perfectly elastic at a constant price, then the corresponding component of x^D is infinite below that price, zero above it, and any value in $[0, +\infty)$ at the exogenously given price.

Suppose that we observe an economic unit (the "economy") producing an output vector x^* at prices p^* so that its total revenue is $y^* = p^* \cdot x^*$. Fixing total revenue y^*, what are the output combinations that the economy could have sold? The answer depends on what is assumed about the output demand conditions which the economy faces. In Figure 4.5.1, the point x^* is indicated. For the fully open economy, the dashed line shows the output combinations consistent with total revenue y^*; this line is the set $\{x \mid p^* \cdot x = y^*\}$. Points to the northeast of the dashed line produce more revenue for the fully-open economy than it receives at x^*. The solid curve represents the output combinations consistent with y^* for the economy facing declining demand schedules, that is, this curve is the set

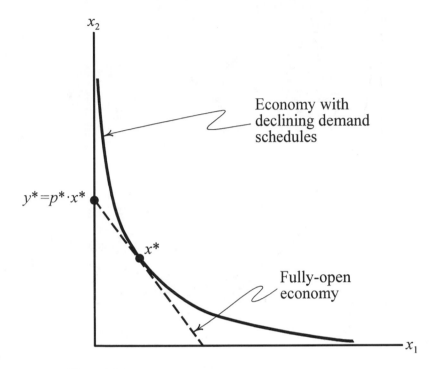

Figure 4.5.1

$\{x \mid x = x^D(p) \text{ and } p \cdot x = y^*\}$, where $x^* = x^D(p^*)$. Except at x^*, the solid curve lies to the northeast of the dashed line, reflecting the fact that increased outputs can only be sold at lower prices.

The input isoquant Ω_M for the general case of a monopoly economic unit facing declining demand curves is defined by

$$\Omega_M = \{v \mid v \text{ is minimal subject to } F(x, v) = 0,$$

$$x = x^D(p), \text{ and } p \cdot x = y\}. \tag{4.5.3}$$

It is important to realize that this isoquant is based on the assumption that the economic unit "sees" and acts upon its entire demand schedule. It does not take output prices as given but rather minimizes its cost subject to the constraint $p \cdot x^D(p) = y$. In other words, in deriving Ω_M, we have assumed that the economic unit has monopoly power in its product markets. The case of competition with declining demand is studied later.

Assume that Ω_M is derived from technological and output market conditions actually prevailing in the base period. Denote these conditions by the

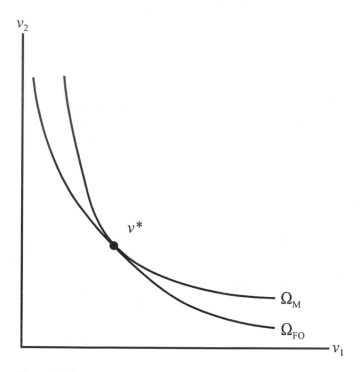

Figure 4.5.2

superscript B, so that the isoquant becomes

$$\Omega_M^B = \{v \mid v \text{ is minimal subject to } F^B(x, v) = 0,$$

$$x = x^{DB}(p), \text{ and } p \cdot x = y\}. \tag{4.5.4}$$

Assume that v^B, the actual vector of base-period inputs, minimizes cost at factor prices w^B subject to the technological constraint $F^B(x, v) = 0$, the demand constraint $x = x^{DB}(p)$, and the revenue constraint $p \cdot x = y^B$. Then the two isoquants, Ω_M^B (defined in (4.5.4)) and Ω_{FO}^B, the corresponding fully open isoquant (see (4.4.2)), share a common point, but Ω_M^B lies above and to the right of Ω_{FO}^B (see Figure 4.5.2).[6] Thus we see that the fully open model of technology provides a more "optimistic" input isoquant than does the declining-demand-schedule model. This is reflected in the fact that the isoquant showing the efficient factor combinations required to generate the

---

6. Ω_M^B would lie below and to the left of a "fully closed" isoquant defined with perfectly inelastic demands – a fixed market basket of outputs – but the latter is of very little interest.

given revenue y^* shows greater required inputs with declining demand than in the fully open case.

Let I_M^B denote the production-theoretic input-price deflator defined relative to the isoquant Ω_M^B and let I_{FO}^B denote the production-theoretic input-price deflator defined relative to the isoquant Ω_{FO}^B. Then we have

$$L \geq I_M^B \geq I_{FO}^B, \tag{4.5.5}$$

where L denotes the Laspeyres input-price index. Similarly, for the indexes derived from current-period conditions (superscripted A), we have

$$P \leq I_M^A \leq I_{FO}^A, \tag{4.5.6}$$

where P denotes the Paasche input-price index.

This completes our treatment of the monopoly case, except for the comparative-statics analysis to which we return in Chapter 5. We add a remark about the treatment of *monopsony* and input-price deflation. The analysis of this problem is isomorphic to that of our treatment of monopoly and output-price deflation in Section 2.10. We shall not comment on it in detail save to say that input prices as such disappear from the input-deflation problem since they are under the control of the economic unit and not part of the environment it faces. The role of a particular factor price in the analysis is taken by the marginal cost of acquiring an additional unit of the factor – a construct that takes into account the rising factor-supply curve that is present under monopsony. As in the output-deflation/monopoly case, ordinary Paasche and Laspeyres bounds no longer apply, and although quasi-Paasche and quasi-Laspeyres bounds can be constructed they do not seem of much practical use. The quasi-Laspeyres index required, for example, would involve the cost in the current period of purchasing the base-period collection of factors, and, given monopsony, this cannot easily be inferred from economic data.

4.6.   The General Competitive Case

We turn now to the important case of a competitive economic unit (an industry, say) facing falling output demand schedules. There is no monopoly (or monopsony) power. The economic unit faces the same general demand conditions as in the preceding section, but it "does not know it." The firms that make up the unit optimize taking output prices as given, as in the fully open case of Section 4.4 above. In fact, however, taken all together, they are not in a fully open environment, since output prices do depend on the sum of their decisions.

As in the parallel case of output-price deflation treated in Section 2.11, this dependence implies that the construction of the production-theoretic input-price deflator is not merely a problem in constrained optimization; this construction also involves a fixed-point argument to ensure equality of supply and demand in all output markets, making comparative statics far more difficult than in the other cases so far considered. Because of the "fixed-point" argument, Paasche and Laspeyres bounds need no longer apply.

As in the preceding section, technology is summarized by

$$F(x, v) = 0^7 \qquad (4.6.1)$$

and output demand by

$$x = x^D(p). \qquad (4.6.2)$$

Firms in our competitive industry face a given output-price vector p *and act as if they do not affect it.* Thus, the firms perceive themselves as operating in a fully open economy as in Section 4.4. If that perception were correct, the isoquant $\Omega_{FO}(p)$ for the industry facing output prices p and earning total revenue y would be given by

$$\Omega_{FO}(p) = \{v \mid v \text{ is minimal subject to } F(x, v) = 0 \text{ and } p \cdot x = y\}. \qquad (4.6.3)$$

By fixing total revenue y and varying output prices p, we can derive from (4.6.3) the implied industry supply schedule for outputs (parametric on y, of course):

$$x = x^S(p). \qquad (4.6.4)$$

We cannot base the analysis of the competitive industry on the isoquant $\Omega_{FO}(p)$ defined in (4.6.3). First, $\Omega_{FO}(p)$ is derived for fixed output prices, and output prices are not fixed at the industry level. Second, $\Omega_{FO}(p)$ does not take into account the industry-wide constraint that supply and demand for outputs must be equal (i.e., that we have $x^D(p) = x^S(p)$).

It is the fact that this constraint is not "recognized" by the competitive industry that makes the analysis complex. This is because the equilibrium

---

7. Note that (4.6.1) gives the production technology for the industry. In the absence of constant returns-to-scale, this will not generally be the technology for the individual firm, although this is not important here.

output prices equating output supplies with output demands themselves depend on factor prices w since output supplies depend on w. Thus, although the competitive industry, given y, minimizes costs while remaining on $\Omega_{\text{FO}}(p)$ for *some* p, which p this is depends on factor prices w. Were w different, p would also be different, and the competitive economy would "solve" a different problem.

We must therefore take this into account and (in principle) use the p that corresponds to equilibrium in output markets given the factor prices involved.

In defining the production-theoretic input-price index I_{CG} for the competitive general case, we are given the production relation (4.6.1), total revenue y, the output demand schedules in (4.6.2), and two input-price vectors w^A and w^B.

First, take the output-price vector p as a parameter and let $C^A(p)$ be defined by

$$C^A(p) = \min_{x,v} w^A v \quad \text{subject to } F(x, v) = 0 \text{ and } p \cdot x = y, \quad (4.6.5)$$

that is, $C^A(p)$ is money cost at factor prices w^A given that inputs are in $\Omega_{\text{FO}}(p)$. Let the minimizing input vector be $v^A(p)$ and the resulting vector of optimal output supplies be $x^{SA}(p)$. Now find the p (for convenience assumed to be unique) that solves the equation $x^{SA}(p) = x^D(p)$; call it p^A.

Similarly, let $C^B(p)$ be defined by

$$C^B(p) = \min_{x,v} w^B \cdot v \quad \text{subject to } F(x, v) = 0 \text{ and } p \cdot x = y. \quad (4.6.6)$$

Let the minimizing input vector be $v^B(p)$ and the resulting vector of optimal output supplies be $x^{SB}(p)$. Now find the p (assumed to be unique) that solves the equation $x^{SB}(p) = x^D(p)$. Call it p^B.

The production-theoretic input-price index I_{CG} appropriate to the competitive general case is then defined by

$$I_{\text{CG}} = C^A(p^A)/C^B(p^B). \quad (4.6.7)$$

The fact that the firms making up the competitive economic unit behave as though they face flat demand curves, whereas the unit as a whole does not, creates practical difficulties for further analysis. First, comparative-statics analysis becomes difficult. The effect of a shift in a given parameter now not only involves changes in the solution to the unit's optimizing problem given that shift (which are readily handled by the Envelope Theorem) but also involves shifts in the other parameters of the unit's optimization problem through changes in the position of equilibrium in all output markets. Without more information as to demand schedules, such shifts cannot be studied.

Second, and more important for the practice of price-index construction, Laspeyres and Paasche bounds are no longer guaranteed to hold. To see this, let B denote actual base-period and A actual current-period conditions, respectively. Then $C^B(p^B)$ (the denominator of I_{CG}), and the denominator of the Laspeyres input-price index will be the same. However, the usual method of establishing the bound would be to show that the numerator of $I_{CG}(C^A(p^A))$ is the value of the solution to a minimum problem in which v^B (the actual input combination used in the base period) was feasible. This is no longer guaranteed. Figure 4.6.1 shows a situation in which the value of v^B at factor prices w^A (represented by the slope of the dashed lines) is lower than $C^A(p^A)$. Also (just for good measure), the value of v^A at prices w^B (represented by the slopes of the solid lines) is lower than $C^B(p^B)$. Plainly, Laspeyres and Paasche bounds are inapplicable here.

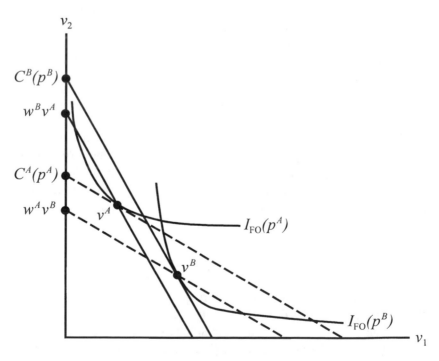

Figure 4.6.1

The moral is clear. Except where demand curves can *in fact* be taken to be approximately flat because the unit is very small, Paasche and Laspeyres input-price indexes will not bound the production-theoretic input-price indexes. The case is even worse than for output-price deflation (see Section 2.11, above). There, if the unit is *large* enough, it is appropriate to treat factor supplies as fixed, generating another case in which Paasche and Laspeyres bounds hold. Here, no matter how big the unit, it is inappropriate to assume that the demand curves it faces are perfectly inelastic.[8]

Paasche and Laspeyres input-price indexes will thus give a misleading picture except for very small economic units. For other cases, detailed knowledge of demand schedules (and, in general, of technology as well) will be required. One cannot assume that changes in input prices leave output prices unaffected, and this creates a serious problem.

Of course, this difficulty with Paasche and Laspeyres indexes is a form of aggregation problem. It comes about because the situation facing an entire industry is not the same as what is perceived by the firms that make it the industry. We discuss aggregation problems further in Chapter 6.

---

8. Similarly, the hybrid case is of no interest here.

5 Comparative Statics: Inputs

5.1. Introduction

We now study the comparative-statics properties of the production-theoretic input-price index, examining what happens when the isoquant on which the index is based changes. Such changes can be due to demand shifts as reflected in output prices or they may be the result of technical change or accumulation of overhead capital.

As in the isomorphic case of output deflation, comparative-statics results for the general competitive case considered in Section 4.6 are difficult to achieve. This is because of the fixed-point nature of the requirement that all output markets clear. More fundamentally, it is because the productive unit fails to realize that it faces declining demand curves but instead behaves as if it were in the fully open case.

Results for the fully open case itself are available through the use of the isomorphism to the problem of output deflation. We will concentrate on this case, but we also analyze monopoly. The fully open economy is of interest in itself and forms part of any comparative-statics analysis for the general competitive case.

In the fully open economy, the case in which appropriate Laspeyres and Paasche bounds do apply, comparative-statics analysis has a role to play relative to those bounds. Where isoquants change, the Laspeyres index bounds from above the production-theoretic input-price index based on the base-period isoquant, whereas the Paasche index bounds from below the production-theoretic input-price index based on the current-period isoquant. In the theory of the cost-of-living index with taste change (Fisher and Shell,

1972, pp. 5–6) and the theory of the production-theoretic output deflator with technical change (Fisher and Shell, 1972, pp. 55–58), we argued that it was consumer satisfaction according to *current* tastes that matter. This enabled us to pick the more interesting of the two theoretic indexes and thus to choose either Paasche (in the cost-of-living case) or Laspeyres (in the output-deflation case) as the bound on the interesting index. We then could motivate comparative-statics results in part as showing the direction in which the other approximating index should be adjusted to restore its bounding property.

In the present case of input deflation, however, a similar argument is not always available. It is true that where isoquants differ because of differences in base-period output prices and current-period output prices, considerations as to tastes as reflected in output prices lead to the production-theoretic input-price deflator based on the current-period isoquant as the interesting one. In turn, this leads to the Paasche approximation as the appropriate bound and the Laspeyres approximation as the bound to be adjusted. However, where isoquants differ for technological reasons, it is at least possible that output prices will be the same in both periods; in the fully open case under study this is even likely. In these circumstances, the two production-theoretic indexes and their bounding approximation stand on an equal footing.

What about comparative statics in such circumstances? The fact that there are two production-theoretic indexes of interest does not make comparative-statics analysis less useful. Since each production-theoretic index has only one approximating bound, consideration of how those indexes differ is required so that the bound on one production-theoretic index can be adjusted to bound the other. This is important since computation of the Paasche and Laspeyres bounds requires far less information than does computation of the production-theoretic input-price indexes themselves.

Unfortunately, as already remarked, comparative-statics results are not readily available for the general competitive case. It is little consolation that, if they were available, they would be less immediately applicable than in the fully open case because Laspeyres and Paasche bounds do not apply in the general case either.

5.2. The Fully Open Case: Formal Model

For simplicity we study the production-theoretic input-price index based on the base-period isoquant, but this is only a matter of notation. Wherever possible we exploit the isomorphism to the theory of the production-theoretic output-price index (Chapter 3) to avoid reproving essentially the same theorems. Instead we concentrate on matters of interpretation.[1]

The productive unit's efficient production plans are described by

$$F(x, v) = 0, \tag{5.2.1}$$

where x is an r-vector of outputs and v an m-vector of inputs. We are given base-period factor prices $\hat{w}$, money cost of base-period production $\hat{C}$, and current-period factor prices w. We are also given output prices p (the same for each period). We find the vector $(\hat{x}, \hat{v})$ that solves

$$\text{Maximize } y = p \cdot \hat{x} \quad \text{subject to } F(\hat{x}, \hat{v}) = 0 \text{ and } \hat{w} \cdot \hat{v} = \hat{C}. \tag{5.2.2}$$

Call the resulting value of y, $\hat{y}$. Then find the vector (x, v) that solves

$$\text{Minimize } \hat{C} = \hat{w} \cdot \hat{v} \quad \text{subject to } F(x, v) = 0 \text{ and } p \cdot x = \hat{y}. \tag{5.2.3}$$

The production-theoretic input-price index is then equal to $(C/\hat{C})$.

The Lagrangian for (5.2.2) is written as

$$\hat{\Lambda} = p \cdot \hat{x} + \hat{\gamma} F(\hat{x}, \hat{v}) - (1/\hat{\mu})(\hat{w}\hat{v} - \hat{C}), \tag{5.2.4}$$

where $\hat{\gamma}$ and $(1/\hat{\mu})$ are Lagrange multipliers (the latter being written as a reciprocal for reasons of symmetry in what follows).

The Lagrangian for (5.2.3) is written as

$$\Lambda = w \cdot v + \gamma F(x, v) - \mu(px - y), \tag{5.2.5}$$

where γ and μ are Lagrange multipliers.

We explain the model as follows. Given base-period factor prices, base-period money cost of production, and base-period output prices, we first find the greatest value of output that could have been produced with that level of costs. This value of output determines an isoquant giving the locus of inputs that could efficiently have produced the output value. Given this isoquant, we find the cost of the inputs that would have been purchased had base-period factor prices been w instead of $\hat{w}$. The corresponding change in input costs from $\hat{C}$ to C then represents a pure factor-price

1. In this regard, note (as in the closely related case of comparative statics for the analysis of the production-theoretic output-price deflator in Chapter 3) that when output prices are fixed, we can take the fully open case to be a fully closed one with a single output, "revenue." Hence many of the results can also be derived from an analysis of the fully closed case, despite the fact that the latter case does not appear to be interesting in its own right. Some of the results in this section are due to Muellbauer (1972).

phenomenon, being a factor-price induced change along the isoquant. Any additional change is to be considered a change in real input. More succinctly, the question posed is: What would the unit that spent $\hat{C}$ when factor prices were $\hat{w}$ have spent to produce the same value of output had factor prices been w?

If, as above, we think of the production-theoretic input-price index $(C/\hat{C})$ as being constructed with actual base-period technology and base-period output prices, then the construction above results in finding the isoquant through the actual vector $\hat{v}$. Where technology or output prices are not the same as in the base period, then $\hat{v}$ in the solution to (5.2.2) will not be the actual base-period input vector but will be instead the vector of inputs that the productive unit would have employed at factor prices $\hat{w}$ with total costs $\hat{C}$. This type of construction enables us to have tangency of the isoquant to the isocost hyperplane at both $\hat{v}$ and v and thus to retain symmetry between actual base and comparison periods. If the technology exhibits appropriate homotheticity properties, then we can use the differential calculus (or duality theory) to study changes in the production-theoretic input-price index despite the fact that the actual isoquant for the comparison period may be quite far from the one tangent to the isocost hyperplane with costs equal to $\hat{C}$.

The required homotheticity is that of the isoquant map. Since an isoquant is here defined as the locus of inputs that will efficiently produce a given value of outputs when output prices are fixed, what is required is that multiplication of all inputs by a scalar multiply the value of the efficiently produced output by some other scalar. This will happen, of course, under constant returns-to-scale. Indeed, it will happen for more general technologies. Our formal definition of input homotheticity (parallel to Definition 3.5.1) follows.

Definition 5.2.1: The production function F is said to exhibit *input homotheticity* if and only if for every scalar $\beta > 0$ and every vector of outputs x, there exists a positive scalar $\alpha = \alpha(\beta, x)$ such that $F(x, v) = 0$ implies $F(\beta x, \alpha v) = 0$.

This definition only makes sense if the function α is restricted by

$$\alpha(\beta_1, x)\alpha(\beta_2, \beta_1 x) = \alpha(\beta_1\beta_2, x) \tag{5.2.6}$$

for any two positive scalars β_1 and β_2 and any output vector x. Note that this implies that $\alpha(1, x) = 1$ for all x. (Set $\beta_2 = 1$.)

Input homotheticity is not sufficient for our purposes: The technology must be further restricted in the extent to which α can depend on x. Consider the extreme case in which α is independent of x. In this case it is easy to show that $\alpha(\beta, x) = \beta^\theta$ for some fixed θ – the "homogeneous case," which includes constant returns-to-scale.[2]   However, this restriction is stronger than necessary (see the closely related discussion in Section 3.5).

5.3. The Fully Open Case: Changing Output Prices

We begin by analyzing the effect of a change in the price of some output on the production-theoretic input-price index.

Theorem 5.3.1: $\partial C / \partial p_k = \mu(\hat{x}_k - x_k)$ *for* $k = 1, \ldots, r$.

Hence, if a rise in the price of the ith factor $(i = 1, \ldots, m)$ *would increase (reduce) output of the kth good, then a rise in the price of the kth good will reduce the importance of the ith factor price in the production-theoretic input-price index.*

Proof: The proof is similar to that given for Theorem 3.6.1.   ■

This theorem has a companion that shows how the weights in a Paasche index change with a change in the kth factor price. It follows.

Theorem 5.3.2: *Under homotheticity, we have*

$$\frac{\partial(v_i/C)}{\partial p_k} = -\frac{\mu(\partial x_k/\partial w_i)}{C}.$$

Proof: The proof is similar to that given for Theorem 3.6.2.   ■

Combining this result with that of Theorem 5.3.1, we see that the ith factor price will be increased in importance in the production-theoretic input-price index by an increase in p_k if and only if the "weight" that should be given to that factor price in total costs (v_i/C) is also increased. This will happen if and only if an increase in the ith factor price would reduce the output of the kth good.

---

2. See the proof of the closely related property in Footnote 5 in Section 3.5.

5.4. The Fully Open Case: Hicks-Neutral Technical Change

We now consider the effects of technical change on the production-theoretic input-price index. We begin with Hicks-neutral technical change in the production function for some output, say the rth. This change can be represented by a shift in the scalar a in a revised representation of the efficient technology given by

$$F(x_1, \ldots, x_r/a, v_1, \ldots, v_m) = 0. \tag{5.4.1}$$

Note that an increase in the parameter a represents Hicks-neutral technical *progress*.

Comparing (5.4.1) with (3.7.1), we see that Hicks-neutral change in the theory of the production-theoretic input-price index is isomorphic to economy-wide, factor-augmenting change in the theory of the production-theoretic output-price index. This isomorphism immediately yields the following corollary.

Corollary 5.4.1:

$$\frac{\partial C}{\partial(1/a)} = \mu a p_r (x_r - \hat{x}_r).$$

Hence, if a rise in the price of the ith factor ($i = 1, \ldots, m$) would increase (reduce) the output of the rth good, then Hicks-neutral technical progress in the production of the rth good will reduce (increase) the importance of the ith factor price in the production-theoretic input-price index.

Proof: The proof is similar to that of Corollary 3.7.1.　　　　■

A similar result to that of Theorem 5.3.2 also holds for this index-number problem.

There appears to be no interesting case here that is isomorphic to that in the theory of the production-theoretic output-price index of factor-augmenting technical change in a particular industry (Theorems 3.7.1 and 3.7.2.) This is because demand for a particular factor cannot generally be thought of as depending on parts of the output vector requiring that factor but rather depends on total outputs. We can state, however, the following corollary.

Corollary 5.4.2: *A uniform Hicks-neutral technical change in the production of* all *outputs does not change the production-theoretic input-price index.*

Proof: The proof is similar to that of Corollary 3.7.2.   ∎

This result is not surprising. Such a uniform change merely changes the money output associated with a given isoquant rather than deforming the isoquant itself. Notice that under constant returns-to-scale we can interpret such a change as uniform factor augmentation in all factors employed by the productive unit. We now turn to a more general analysis of the effects of factor-augmenting technical change.

5.5. The Fully Open Case: Uniform Factor-Augmenting Technical Change

Hicks-neutral technical change is an output-augmenting technical change. Hence it is not surprising that, just as Hicks-neutral technical change in the analysis of the production-theoretic *input*-price index is isomorphic to factor-augmenting technical change in the analysis of the production-theoretic *output*-price index, so factor-augmenting technical change in the analysis of the production-theoretic *input*-price index is isomorphic to Hicks-neutral technical change in the analysis of the production-theoretic *output*-price index.

Revise the representation of the set of technologically efficient combinations so it is given by

$$F(x_1, \ldots, x_r, v_1, \ldots, bv_m) = 0, \tag{5.5.1}$$

where b is the parameter representing augmentation of the mth factor. Note that such augmentation is uniform across the productive unit; we shall later consider augmentation within particular production functions.

Now, since the isoquant on which the production-theoretic input-price index is based is the locus of factor combinations required to produce efficiently a given money output and since output prices are fixed, we can think of production as involving only a single composite output – total revenue, the amount of which is fixed. This makes our problem isomorphic to that of Hicks-neutral change in the fully closed economy in the analysis of the production-theoretic output-price index considered in Fisher and Shell

(1972, pp. 63–75) and summarized in Section 3.2. (Indeed, it is also iso-morphic to the analysis of good-augmenting taste change in the theory of the cost-of-living index. See Fisher and Shell (1972, pp. 7–22).)

Next we define the net elasticity η_{ij} by

$$\eta_{ij} = \frac{w_j}{v_i} \left(\frac{\partial v_i}{\partial w_j} \right)_{y\,const.} . \tag{5.5.2}$$

Hence, η_{ij} is the (derived) demand elasticity for the ith factor with respect to the jth factor price *when the value of output is held constant* (i.e., along a given isoquant). We refer to this as a "net" demand elasticity by analogy to the consumer case (where utility is held constant). We also define β_i, the share of the ith factor in money cost, by

$$\beta_i = w_i v_i / C. \tag{5.5.3}$$

We are ready for the theorem that describes the effects of changes in b on the production-theoretic input-price index.

Theorem 5.5.1: *Assume that the isoquant map is homothetic.*

   (A) *Suppose $w_i = \hat{w}_i$ for $i = 1, \ldots, m - 1$. If $-\eta_{mm} > (1 - \beta_m)$ holds, then it follows that $(\partial C / \partial b)$ and $(w_m - \hat{w}_m)$ share the same sign. If $-\eta_{mm} < (1 - \beta_m)$ holds, then it follows that $(\partial C / \partial b)$ and $(w_m - \hat{w}_m)$ are of opposite sign. If $-\eta_{mm} = (1 - \beta_m)$ holds, then we have $(\partial C / \partial b) = 0$.*

   (B) *Suppose $w_i = \hat{w}_i$ for $i = 1, \ldots, m-1, i \neq j$, and $j \neq m$. If $\eta_{mj} > \beta_j$ holds, then it follows that $(\partial C / \partial b)$ and $(w_j - \hat{w}_j)$ are of opposite sign. If $\eta_{mj} < \beta_j$ holds, then it follows that $(\partial C / \partial b)$ and $(w_j - \hat{w}_j)$ share the same sign. If $\eta_{mj} = \beta_j$ holds, then we have $(\partial C / \partial b) = 0$.*

   (C) *Suppose $w_i = \hat{w}_i$ for $i = 1, \ldots, m - 1, i \neq j$, and $j \neq m$. If $\eta_{jm} > \beta_m$ holds, then it follows that $(\partial C / \partial b)$ and $(w_j - \hat{w}_j)$ are of opposite sign. If $\eta_{jm} < \beta_m$ holds, then it follows that $(\partial C / \partial b)$ and $(w_j - \hat{w}_j)$ share the same sign. If $\eta_{jm} = \beta_m$ holds, then we have $(\partial C / \partial b) = 0$.*

   (D) *If we have $w_i = k\hat{w}_i$ for $i = 1, \ldots, m$, where k is a positive scalar, then it follows that $(\partial C / \partial b) = 0$.*

Proof: (A)–(C) are similar to those of Theorem 7.4 of Fisher and Shell (1972, pp. 73–74; repeated above as Theorem 3.2.1) with two exceptions. First, note that b, rather than $(1/b)$ appears in (5.5.1). Second, η_{mm} is an own net elasticity of *demand* rather than supply. It is therefore neces-sarily negative rather than necessarily positive. Hence, the expression

$(\eta_{mm} + 1 - \beta_m)$ is not automatically signed. (A) of the present theorem therefore uses Lemma 7.4 of Fisher and Shell (1972, p. 69), which is also the source of (A) of Theorem 7.4 therein. The proof of (D) is similar to that of (C) of Theorem 7.2 of Fisher and Shell (1972, p. 70), but (D) is also obvious.   ■

Thus, uniform factor-augmenting technical progress in the mth factor increases the importance of the factor in the production-theoretic price index if and only if the absolute value of the own net elasticity of demand for that factor exceeds the combined share of all other factors in total costs. This change also reduces the importance of the price of any factor whose net elasticity of demand with respect to the mth factor price exceeds its share of total costs. This condition is equivalent to the property that the net elasticity of demand for the mth factor with respect to the price of the factor in question exceeds the share of the mth factor in total factor costs.[3]

These results can also be interpreted in terms of the well-known Allen–Uzawa partial elasticities of substitution. (See Allen 1938, pp. 503–9, and Uzawa 1962.) Using this interpretation quite clearly demonstrates what is involved.[4]

Let σ_{ij} denote the Allen–Uzawa partial elasticity of substitution between factors i and j *in the production of total revenue* y. Then, in terms of the cost function whose dependent variable is C as defined in (5.2.3),

$$\sigma_{ij} = \frac{CC_{ij}}{C_i C_j},\tag{5.5.4}$$

where the subscripts denote differentiation. Further, define the scalar $\overline{\sigma}_m$ by

$$\overline{\sigma}_m = \frac{\sum_{i=1}^{m} \beta_i \sigma_{im}}{1 - \beta_m},\tag{5.5.5}$$

---

3. For a direct proof that these are identical statements, see Fisher and Shell (1972, p. 110, Note 18). This proposition also follows from the interpretation in terms of the Allen–Uzawa partial elasticity of substitution, which follows in the text. Fisher and Shell (1972, Theorem 7.2, p. 70) give a result isomorphic to the one in the present context in terms of elasticities with costs rather than with money output being constant. We leave the implications of this isomorphism to the reader.

4. Note that a similar interpretation in terms of appropriately defined partial elasticities of substitution between *outputs* can be given to the results in Section 3.2 above and in Fisher and Shell (1972, pp. 63–75). Indeed, such an interpretation can be given to the results of Theorem 3.2 of Fisher and Shell (1972, p. 18) on the effects of good-augmenting taste change in the theory of the cost-of-living index (cf. Fisher (1972)).

so that $\overline{\sigma}_m$ is the weighted average of Allen–Uzawa partial elasticities of substitution for factor m, where the weights are the shares of the factors in total cost. It is easy to show that this is the elasticity of substitution between the mth factor and a composite (Hicksian) factor consisting of expenditure on all other factors with the relative prices of all other factors fixed.

To do this, consider the effect on the cost function and its derivatives of multiplying each of the first $m-1$ factor prices by a common constant t. Denoting differentiation with respect to t by subscripts yields

$$
\frac{CC_{tm}}{C_t C_m} = \frac{C\sum_{i=1}^{m-1} C_{im} w_i}{C_m \sum_{i=1}^{m-1} C_i w_i} = \frac{\sum_{i=1}^{m-1}\left(\frac{CC_{im}}{C_i C_m}\right)\left(\frac{w_i C_i}{C}\right)}{\sum_{i=1}^{m-1}\frac{w_i C_i}{C}}
$$

$$
= \frac{\sum_{i=1}^{m-1}\beta_i \sigma_{im}}{1-\beta_m} = \overline{\sigma}_m \geq 0. \tag{5.5.6}
$$

We can now restate Theorem 5.5.1 as:

Theorem 5.5.2: *Assume that the isoquant map is homothetic.*

(A) *Suppose we have $w_i = \hat{w}_i$ for $i = 1, \ldots, m-1$. If $\overline{\sigma}_m > 1$ holds, then it follows that $(\partial C/\partial b)$ and $(w_m - \hat{w}_m)$ share the same sign. If $\overline{\sigma}_m < 1$ holds, then it follows that $(\partial C/\partial b)$ and $(w_m - \hat{w}_m)$ are of opposite sign. If $\overline{\sigma}_m = 1$ holds, then we have $(\partial C/\partial b) = 0$.*

(B) *Suppose we have $w_i = \hat{w}_i$ for $i = 1, \ldots, m-1, i \neq j$, and $j \neq m$. If $\sigma_{jm} > 1$ holds, then it follows that $(\partial C/\partial b)$ and $(w_j - \hat{w}_j)$ are of opposite sign. If $\sigma_{jm} < 1$ holds, then it follows that $(\partial C/\partial b)$ and $(w_j - \hat{w}_j)$ share the same sign. If $\sigma_{jm} = 1$ holds, then we have $(\partial C/\partial b) = 0$.*

Proof: It is easy to see[5] from (5.5.4) and the fact that $C_i = v_i$ that

$$
\eta_{ij} = \beta_i \sigma_{ij} \quad \text{for } i, j = 1, \ldots, m. \tag{5.5.7}
$$

Furthermore, the first-degree homogeneity of the cost function with respect

5. This is Problem 12 of Allen (1938, p. 519).

to factor prices yields

$$\eta_{mm} = -\sum_{i=1}^{m-1} \eta_{mi} = -\sum_{i=1}^{m-1} \beta_i \sigma_{im} = (\beta_m - 1)\bar{\sigma}_m. \tag{5.5.8}$$

The parts of the theorem now all follow from Theorem 5.5.1.   ∎

Thus, a uniform factor-augmenting change in the mth factor increases the importance in the input deflator of the prices of just those factors whose Allen–Uzawa partial elasticities of substitution with the mth factor are less than one. It decreases the importance of the prices of just those factors whose Allen–Uzawa partial elasticities of substitution with the mth factor are greater than one. The change increases or decreases the importance of the price of the mth factor itself as its elasticity of substitution with the Hicksian aggregate of all other factors is greater or less than one – this is also an appropriately weighted average of the mth factor's Allen–Uzawa partial elasticities of substitution with all other factors.

It is easy to see that these results also correspond to the effects of the technical change on the weight that a Paasche index would give to the different factor prices. Applying the Envelope Theorem to (5.2.5) and using (5.5.7) yields

$$\left(\frac{\partial \beta_j}{\partial w_m}\right)\left(\frac{w_m}{\beta_j}\right) = \frac{\partial \log(w_j v_j)}{\partial \log v_m} - \frac{\partial \log C}{\partial \log v_m}$$

$$= \eta_{jm} - \beta_m = \beta_m(\sigma_{jm} - 1) \tag{5.5.9}$$

for $j = 1, \ldots, m-1$. Hence, as is well known, the sign of the elasticity of the share of factor j with respect to factor price m is the same as that of $(\sigma_{jm} - 1)$.

Similarly, we have

$$\left(\frac{\partial \beta_j}{\partial w_m}\right)\left(\frac{w_m}{m}\right) = \frac{\partial \log(w_m v_m)}{\partial \log v_m} - \frac{\partial \log C}{\partial \log v_m}$$

$$= \eta_{mm} + 1 - \beta_m = (1 - \beta_m)(1 - \bar{\sigma}_m),$$

so that the sign of the elasticity of the share of the mth factor itself with respect to its own price is that of $(1 - \bar{\sigma}_m)$.

Now, consider an increase in b with factor prices fixed. This gives a decrease in the effective price of the mth factor (the price in "efficiency units" falls). By (5.5.9), any factor whose Allen–Uzawa partial elasticity of substitution with the mth factor is greater than unity will have its share of total costs decreased (and any factor for which that elasticity is less than unity will have its share increased). Since factor prices are fixed and $\beta_j = w_j v_j / C$, the elasticity of β_j with respect to b and that of (v_j/C) with respect to b are the same. Hence, if the jth factor has an Allen–Uzawa partial elasticity of substitution with the mth factor greater (less) than unity, (v_j/C) will decrease (increase) as a result of the technical change. But (v_j/C) is the weight given to w_j in a Paasche index.

A similar argument, using (5.5.10) shows that (v_m/C) goes up with b if and only if we have $\overline{\sigma}_m > 1$. It is instructive to derive this result in a different way, however. Consider a two-factor production function in which the two factors are v_m and the Hicksian composite of all other factors. Denote that composite factor by $\overline{v}$ and its price as t (as in (5.5.6)). Then $\overline{\sigma}_m$ is the ordinary two-factor elasticity of substitution between v_m and $\overline{v}$. If $\overline{\sigma}_m$ is greater than unity, the ratio of v_m to $\overline{v}$ will increase by more than 1% with a 1% fall in v_m. Suppose this to be true. Increase b by 1%; this decreases the effective price of the mth factor by 1%. The ratio of factor usage goes up by more than 1%; however, this is the ratio of factor usage in efficiency units, $(bv_m/\overline{v})$. Since b has gone up by 1%, it must be true that $(v_m/\overline{v})$ itself has increased. Since actual factor prices have not changed, and since the mth factor is now more productive, (v_m/C) must also have increased. A similar argument shows that (v_m/C) will decrease with an increase in b if $\overline{\sigma}_m < 1$.

These results are summarized in the next theorem.

Theorem 5.5.3: *Assume that the isoquant map is homothetic. We have*

$$\text{(A)} \quad \frac{\partial (v_j/C)}{\partial b} \begin{cases} > 0 & \text{for } \sigma_{jm} > 1 \\ = 0 & \text{for } \sigma_{jm} = 1 \quad \text{for } j = 1, \ldots, m-1 \\ < 0 & \text{for } \sigma_{jm} < 1 \end{cases}$$

and

$$\text{(B)} \quad \frac{\partial (v_m/C)}{\partial b} \begin{cases} > 0 & \text{for } \overline{\sigma}_m > 1 \\ = 0 & \text{for } \overline{\sigma}_m = 1 \\ < 0 & \text{for } \overline{\sigma}_m < 1. \end{cases}$$

Corollary 5.5.1: *A uniform factor-augmenting improvement in any factor increases the importance of the jth factor price in the production-theoretic input-price index if and only if it also increases (v_j/C), the weight that would be given to the jth factor price in a Paasche index ($j = 1, \ldots, m$).*

These results are aesthetically pleasing. Their interest is somewhat limited, however, by the fact that they only apply to *uniform* factor-augmenting changes. The assumption that the mth factor has the *same* augmenting parameter b wherever it is employed is quite restrictive; it is an assumption perhaps more suited to the treatment of quality change in the mth factor than to one of change in the technology of production (see Section 4.3). The analysis of factor-augmenting technical change in a particular industry (the production of a particular good) is more interesting in this regard, and we turn to it next. Not surprisingly, we shall find results closely related to those of the present subsection. Indeed, we shall be able to obtain the new results as corollaries to the preceding theorems.

5.6. The Fully Open Case: Factor-Augmenting Change in a Single Industry

We examine the more natural case where factor-augmenting change occurs in an individual production function rather than uniformly across all production functions. Here there are no obvious isomorphisms to apply.[6] Fortunately, we do not have to obtain the results by direct analysis, since we can get them as implications of those of Section 5.5.

To see this, consider factor augmentation of the mth factor in the first industry, so that the first industry's production function can be written as

$$x_1 = g^1(v_{11}, \ldots, v_{1m-1}, bv_{1m}), \tag{5.6.1}$$

with the technical change parameter b entering in no other place. Now, it is true, of course, that v_{1m} and the units of the mth factor used in the other industries are all physically identical and are all purchased at the same price. Nothing prevents us, however, from treating v_{1m} as a *new $m+1$st* factor having zero marginal productivity except in the first industry. If we do so, then the analysis of the technical change involved becomes one of uniform factor-augmenting technical change, which we already know how to do.[7]

---

6. The failure to find an isomorphism for use here is the same as that already observed concerning the similar case of factor-augmenting change in the analysis of the production-theoretic output-price index. In both cases the isomorphic problem would be output-augmenting change in a particular factor demand with no other changes, and this is of no interest.

7. A similar trick could have been used in Sections 3.3, 3.7, and 3.11.

Defining the elasticity η^1_{mj} by

$$\eta^1_{mj} = \left(\frac{w_1}{v_1 m}\right)\left(\frac{\partial v_{1m}}{\partial w_j}\right)_{y\,const.} \tag{5.6.2}$$

for $j = 1, \ldots, m$ allows us to state the next theorem.

Theorem 5.6.1: *Assume that the isoquant map is homothetic.*

(A) *Suppose we have $w_i = \hat{w}_i$ for $i = 1, \ldots, m - 1$. If $-\eta^1_{mm} > (1 - \beta_m)$ holds, then it follows that $(\partial C/\partial b)$ and $w_m - \hat{w}_m$ share the same sign. If $-\eta^1_{mm} < (1 - \beta_m)$ holds, then it follows that $(\partial C/\partial b)$ and $(w_m - \hat{w}_m)$ are of opposite sign. If $-\eta^1_{mm} = (1 - \beta_m)$ holds, then we have $(\partial C/\partial b) = 0$.*

(B) *Suppose we have $w_i = \hat{w}_i$ for $i = 1, \ldots, m - 1, i \neq j$, and $j \neq m$. If $\eta^1_{mj} > \beta_j$ holds, then it follows that $(\partial C/\partial b)$ and $(w_j - \hat{w}_j)$ are of opposite sign. If $\eta^1_{mj} < \beta_j$ holds, then it follows that $(\partial C/\partial b)$ and $(w_j - \hat{w}_j)$ share the same sign. If $\eta^1_{mj} = \beta_j$ holds, then we have $(\partial C/\partial b) = 0$.[8]*

(C) *If we have $w_i = k\hat{w}_i$ for $i = 1, \ldots, m$, where k is a positive scalar, then we have $(\partial C/\partial b) = 0$.*

Proof: (B) and (C) of the theorem simply restate (B) and (D) of Theorem 5.5.1, respectively, in the present context. The proof of (A) is slightly more complicated than this.

To prove (A), consider again a Hicksian composite of all factors except the mth. Define the amount of this composite factor, $\bar{v}$, by

$$\bar{v} = \sum_{i=1}^{m-1} w_j v_j. \tag{5.6.3}$$

We denote the price of this composite factor by t, a scalar that multiplies each of the $w_j (j = 1, \ldots, m - 1)$.

Now, we can think of an increase in w_m as consisting of two steps. First, with the w_i all constant ($i = 1, \ldots, m$), decrease t. Next, multiply t and w_m by that scalar (greater than unity) required to restore t to unity. Since

---

8. Because we cannot increase the price of v_{1m} without increasing the price of v_m generally, there is little point in a statement parallel to (C) of Theorem 5.5.1 that would involve the elasticity of demand v_j with respect to the price of v_{1m} with the price of the remaining units of v_m held constant.

this second step multiplies all factor prices by the same amount, it cannot affect $(\partial C/\partial b)$, a fact reflected in (C) of the theorem. Thus we can study the effect of an increase in w_m with t constant by studying the effect of a decrease in t. To put it another way, w_m will become more important in the input-price index as a result of the technical change being considered if and only if that change also increases the importance of t.

Because the price of factor j is now tw_j for $j = 1, \ldots, m - 1$, we have for the elasticity

$$\eta^1_{mt} = \left(\frac{t}{v_{1m}}\right)\left(\frac{\partial v_{1m}}{\partial t}\right)_{y \, const.} = \left(\frac{t}{v_{1m}}\right)\sum_{i=1}^{m-1} w_i \left(\frac{\partial v_{1m}}{\partial (t w_i)}\right)_{y \, const.}$$

$$= \sum_{i=1}^{m-1} \eta^1_{mi} = -\eta^1_{mm}, \tag{5.6.4}$$

since factor demands are homogeneous of degree zero in t and w_m. Applying (B) of the theorem to changes in t shows that $(\partial C/\partial b)$ has the same sign as $(t - 1)$ if and only if η^1_{mt} is less than the share of the composite factor. This share, however, is just $(1 - \beta_m)$. Therefore, $(\partial C/\partial b)$ will have the same sign as $(t - 1)$ if and only if we have $-\eta^1_{mm} < (1 - \beta_m)$. However, the construction above makes the sign of $(t - 1)$ opposite to that of $(w_m - \hat{w}_m)$, and (A) is proved.   ∎

Note that it is β_m, the "share of v_m," and not the "share of v" that appears in (A) of the theorem. This is in sharp contrast to the results for the case of factor-augmenting technical change in the analysis of the production-theoretic output-price index (Sections 3.3, 3.7, and 3.11 above and Fisher and Shell (1972, pp. 89–91)).

Restatement of these results in terms of Allen–Uzawa partial elasticities of substitution is possible but does not seem to be illuminating. It is, however, plain that the parallel statement to Corollary 5.5.1 obtains. For factor prices other than the mth, what matters is whether the elasticity of demand for the mth factor employed in the first industry with respect to the jth price exceeds or falls short of the (total) share of the jth factor. For the mth price, the dividing line is the total share of the remaining $(m - 1)$ factors.

The following corollary is immediate.

Corollary 5.6.1: *Assume that the isoquant map is homothetic.*

(A) *Let industry H be the one with the largest (in absolute value) own price* elasticity *with respect to factor m; thus we have $H = \arg\max_i |\eta^i_{mm}|$. If an mth-factor-augmenting improvement in the Hth industry would decrease the importance of w_m in the production-theoretic input-price index, then so would an mth-factor-augmenting advance in any other industry.*

(B) *Let industry h be the one with the smallest (in absolute value) own price elasticity for m. Then we have $h = \arg\min_i |\eta^i_{mm}|$. If an mth-factor-augmenting improvement in the hth industry would increase the importance of w_m in the production-theoretic input-price index, then so would an mth-factor-augmenting advance in any other industry.*

(C) *Let industry $\widetilde{H}$ be the one with the largest elasticity of demand for factor m with respect to the price of factor j; thus we have $\widetilde{H} = \arg\max_i (\eta^i_{mj})$. If an mth-factor-augmenting improvement in the $\widetilde{H}$th industry would decrease the importance of w_j in the production-theoretic input-price index, then so would an mth-factor-augmenting advance in any other industry, for $j = 1, \ldots, m - 1$.*

(D) *Let industry $\widetilde{h}$ be the one with the smallest elasticity of demand for factor m with respect to the price of factor j; thus we have $\widetilde{h} = \arg\min_i (\eta^i_{mj})$. If an mth-factor-augmenting improvement in the hth industry would increase the importance of w_j in the production-theoretic input-price index, then so would an mth-factor-augmenting advance in any other industry, for $j = 1, \ldots, m - 1$.*

5.7. Monopoly

We now consider what happens to the analysis of comparative statics when some or all of the output markets are monopolized by the productive unit. We assume that this is true of the first t outputs, $1 \leq t \leq r$, so that for these outputs the effects of price on output demand are taken into account by the productive unit. (The simplest case is that in which the effects on each output demand that are taken into account consist only of the effect of the output's own price, but our results are not restricted to this case.)

To perform this analysis, we first note that some of the output prices, at least, can differ between the base period and the current period. Denote the base-period output-price vector by $\hat{p}$ and the current-period one by p. The Lagrangian for the base-period optimization problem (5.2.4) now becomes

$$\hat{\Lambda} = \hat{p}\cdot\hat{x} + \hat{\gamma} F(\hat{x}, \hat{v}) - (1/\hat{\mu})(\hat{w}\hat{v} - \hat{C}) + \sum_{i=1}^{t} \hat{p}_i (\hat{x}_i - \hat{x}^D(\hat{p})_i), \quad (5.7.1)$$

where the final summation imposes the constraint that monopolized outputs sold must be on the demand curves facing the monopolist (the base-period demand function for the ith output being denoted by $\hat{x}^D$ for $i = 1, \ldots, t$).

Similarly, the Lagrangian for the current-period optimization problem (5.2.5) becomes

$$\Lambda = w \cdot v + \gamma F(x, v) - \mu(p \cdot x - \hat{y}) - \mu \sum_{i=1}^{t} \rho_i(x_i - x^D(p)_i), \quad (5.7.2)$$

where $x^D(p)_i$ denotes the current-period demand function for the ith output for $i = 1, \ldots, t$.

In (5.7.2), the Lagrange multipliers of the additional constraints have been expressed as $\mu\rho_i (i = 1, \ldots, t)$ so that the ρ_i and the $\hat{\rho}_i$ have a symmetric interpretation. It is not difficult to use the first-order conditions to show that the ρ_i and the $\hat{\rho}_i$ are the reductions in revenue that come about because of the effects of outputs on prices; they are the difference between marginal revenue and price. We demonstrate this for the base period. First differentiate (5.7.1) with respect to $\hat{x}_i$ and with respect to $\hat{v}_j$. Then set the results equal to zero, and solve for $(-\hat{F}_j/\hat{F}_i)$. (Here the subscript i denotes differentiation with respect to $\hat{x}_i$, the subscript j denotes differentiation with respect to $\hat{v}_j$, and the hat denotes evaluation of derivatives at $(\hat{x}, \hat{v})$.) This yields

$$-\frac{\hat{F}_j}{\hat{F}_i} = \frac{(1/\hat{\mu})\hat{w}_j}{\hat{p}_i + \hat{\rho}_i}. \quad (5.7.3)$$

The left-hand side of (5.7.3) is the marginal physical product of $\hat{v}_j$ in the production of $\hat{x}_i$. Furthermore, the numerator of the right-hand side is the shadow price of factor $\hat{v}_j$, which takes into account both the money factor price $\hat{w}_j$ and the effect on the cost constraint. The standard condition that marginal revenue product equal factor price means that the denominator must be the marginal revenue of $\hat{x}_i$. A similar demonstration applies to (5.7.2).

We begin the comparative-statics analysis by examining what changes must be made in our earlier results to accommodate monopoly. The first thing to notice is that no change at all need be made unless the comparative-statics case being analyzed involves either a change in demand or a change in the first-order conditions. Thus, in particular, all the results on factor-augmenting technical change of Sections 5.5 and 5.6 carry over unaltered. It is important to note, however, that the isoquant being used for analysis is the locus of factor combinations efficiently generating a given revenue *including the effects of output on prices*. Elasticities of substitution, in particular, are to be defined with this interpretation of technology.

The case of Hicks-neutral technical change of Section 5.4 requires more attention. For the case in which the output whose production function undergoes such a change is not one of the first t outputs (the monopolized ones), no change is required. For the case however, in which one of the monopolized outputs is involved the results are somewhat altered. Letting technology be represented by

$$F(x_1/a, x_2, \ldots, x_r, v_1, \ldots, v_m) = 0, \tag{5.7.4}$$

where output 1 is monopolized, Corollary 5.4.1 (with r replaced by 1) becomes

Theorem 5.7.1:

$$\frac{\partial C}{\partial (1/a)} = a[(p_1 + \rho_1)x_1 - (\hat{p}_1 + \hat{\rho}_1)\hat{x}_1].$$

Proof: Apply the Envelope Theorem to (5.7.2) and (5.7.1) and use the first-order conditions. ∎

In the case of a competitively sold output (Corollary 5.4.1), Hicks-neutral technical progress reduces (increases) the importance of those factor prices an increase in which would increase (reduce) production of the augmented good. Equivalently, since competitively sold goods are sold at constant prices, those are the factor prices an increase in which would increase (reduce) the value of that production. In the case of Hicks-neutral progress in the production of a monopolistically supplied output, the criterion remains whether an increase in a factor price increases the value of production of the good in question but now that value is to be taken by multiplying output *not* by price but by *marginal revenue*. This is a natural extension.

The remaining results to be adapted are those of Section 5.3 concerning the effect of changes in output prices. Obviously it makes no sense to consider exogenous changes in the endogenously determined prices of the monopolized goods. The effects of a change in some other output price will be the same as before, provided that the change does not shift the demand for any monopolized good. If it does, there will be an additional effect because of this shift; we now explicitly study these demand shifts.

We first consider a general parametric change in the demand function for the first good (the monopolized one), which we write as

$$x_1^D = x_1^D(p, \sigma), \tag{5.7.5}$$

where σ is the shift parameter. (We make the appropriate changes in notation wherever needed.) Denote by hats functions or derivatives evaluated at base-period levels, saving bare-headed symbols for current-period levels. Application of the Envelope Theorem first to (5.7.2) and then to (5.7.1) immediately yields

Theorem 5.7.2:

$$\frac{\partial C}{\partial \sigma} = \left(\rho_1 \frac{\partial x_1^D}{\partial \sigma} - \hat{\rho}_1 \frac{\partial \hat{x}_1^D}{\partial \sigma} \right).$$

This theorem is rather similar to Theorem 3.13.1. It demonstrates the importance of the differences between price and marginal revenue (i.e., the monopoly profits per unit of output) multiplied by the marginal effect of σ on demand.

Theorem 5.7.2 is our direct result for general shifts in demand (we shall explore more readily interpretable special cases below). Define M_1 by

$$M_1 = \rho_1 \left(\partial x_1^D / \partial \sigma \right), \tag{5.7.6}$$

and construct a similar definition for $\hat{M}_1$. Then Theorem 5.7.2 states that if an increase in the jth factor price would make $M_1 > \hat{M}_1$, then an increase in σ will increase the importance of the jth factor price in the production-theoretic input-price index.

Clearly, how interesting these results are in particular cases depends on the values of M_1 and $\hat{M}_1$. The obvious leading cases are those of multiplicative and additive shifts in demand, and we provide the corresponding corollaries of Theorem 5.7.2 next.

Corollary 5.7.1: *The effect on the production-theoretic input-price index of a multiplicative increase in x_1^D has the sign of $(\rho_1 x_1^D - \hat{\rho}_1 \hat{x}_1^D)$. In other words, the jth factor price will become more important as a result of the shift if and only if an increase in the jth factor price would reduce monopoly profits in the first good.[9]*

Corollary 5.7.2: *The effect on the production-theoretic "input-price" index of an additive increase in x_1^D has the sign of $(\rho_1 - \hat{\rho}_1)$. In other words, the jth factor price will become more important as a result of the shift if and*

---

9. Recall that ρ_1 is negative; it is the difference between marginal revenue and price.

only if an increase in the jth factor price would reduce monopoly profits per unit *in the first good.*

These results parallel those for monopsony in Section 3.13. In both cases, the crucial feature is the difference between marginal valuation (cost or revenue) and price.[10]

This concludes our discussion of the monopoly case. It would also be possible to go on to a discussion of monopsony (parallel to that of monopoly in Section 3.14), but we leave that to the reader. In general, what will be involved are shift parameters in the cost function as seen by the monopsonized production sector with marginal factor costs replacing factor prices as the fundamental objects of analysis.

10. Although the results of Section 3.13 involve ratios of monopsony profits to total shadow valuation of factors, no corresponding ratio seems to be involved here. The apparent difference stems from the use in Section 3.13 of the hybrid rather than the fully open model as the base to which monopsony elements are added. This same issue was discussed at length in Section 3.7.

6 Aggregation

6.1. Introduction: Types of Aggregation

In this chapter, we consider a set of topics all of which involve aggregation in the production-theoretic deflators. Some of these topics have been briefly discussed in earlier chapters; others are new.

We can divide the aggregation problems to be considered into three types. It will be convenient to name the types – with a nod to the literature on industrial organization and mergers – as (i) "horizontal," (ii) "conglomerate," and (iii) "vertical."

As far as the production-theoretic output-price index is concerned, horizontal integration means aggregation over units producing the same set of outputs – in effect, firms in the same industry (e.g., shoe manufacturers). Isomorphic to this in the case of the production-theoretic input-price index is aggregation over units that use the same set of inputs (e.g., ferrous-metals users). Clearly, the latter will not generally be aggregation over firms in the same industry.

For the case of the output-price index, conglomerate aggregation means aggregation over different goods, that is, over different industries. The issue here is whether the economy-wide production-theoretic output-price index can be formed from subindexes. For example, can the overall output deflator be built up from deflators for steel, agricultural products, and so forth? The isomorphic case for the input-price index is aggregation over different input types (labor, plant, and equipment, for example).

Finally, vertical aggregation again refers to aggregation over two units, but this time the units are in a vertical relationship where one unit produces outputs that are used by the other as inputs. Here the questions involve how the production-theoretic input- and output-price indexes for the aggregated unit relate to those for the individual components.

As we shall see, all of these aggregation types present interesting problems, but the solutions are often unhappy ones.

6.2. Horizontal Aggregation

We begin with the case of horizontal aggregation and take up the case of outputs. Here a number of units ("firms") produce the same outputs. Production-theoretic output-price indexes can be constructed for each firm and for the industry as a whole (with the productive unit consisting of all the firms together). How does the industry output-price index relate to those for the individual firms?

In essence, we have already encountered this problem and found that it does not have a very satisfactory solution. Suppose, for simplicity, that there is perfect competition in the industry in question. Then each of the firms operates in a fully open world. Accordingly, the appropriate production-theoretic output-price index for each firm is the price index for the fully open economy defined in Section 2.7.

Now consider the industry-wide output-price index. This is the index studied in Section 2.11 for the general competitive case. We already know that this index has a very complicated structure. Moreover, the complexity stems precisely from the fact that the industry as a whole will typically face upward-sloping supply curves for factors and that the individual firms take no account of this when making their decisions. As a result, the firm-level production-theoretic output-price indexes will not be based on the true structure of input supply faced by the industry; it follows that the industry-wide production-theoretic output-price index cannot be built up from the firm-level indexes.

There is a special case in which this problem is absent. If the industry itself is also fully open because even in toto it is a very small buyer in its factor markets, then the problem may disappear. In that case, provided we can think of the industry as having an aggregate production function the same as that of the individual firms, then the production-theoretic output-price index for the industry and for each of its component firms will be identical.

When will that occur? Obviously, if all firms have the same constant returns-to-scale technology, then as long as we look at equilibrium positions, the industry can be thought of as a giant firm with the same technology. Note, however, that the restriction to equilibrium positions is important here. This is because efficient production for the industry as a whole requires that each firm have the same set of factor ratios and produce the same market basket of outputs as every other. In the short run, when prices change, this need not be the case.

Where individual firm technologies differ or where the common technology does not exhibit constant returns-to-scale, the problem proves more complicated. It remains true that, when considering long-run equilibrium positions, the industry can be thought of as having an aggregate production function that depends on the production functions of the individual firms, but this dependence is not simply stated in closed form.[1] Although it is probably possible to work out how the industry-level production-theoretic indexes are related to the firm-level ones, the industry-level fully open case involved seems too special to go to the trouble of doing so.

Turning to the case of production-theoretic input-price indexes, as we already know, we face a similar problem. Here the issue is one of declining demand curves for output rather than of rising supply curves for factors. Firms in a perfectly competitive industry maximize as though they faced fixed output prices. The industry as a whole, however, generally does affect output prices. Hence, the production-theoretic input-price index, which takes demand *conditions* as given, cannot be built up from firm-level indexes, which assume quite different demand conditions.[2]

That industry-level Laspeyres and Paasche price indexes can easily be built up from their firm-level counterparts is not helpful. This is because, as we have seen in earlier chapters, the same problem (rising supply curves or declining demand curves) that keeps us from aggregating firm-level production-theoretic price indexes into industry-level ones also destroys the bounding properties of industry-wide Paasche and Laspeyres price indexes.

It will be illuminating at this point to consider the parallel aggregation problem in the theory of the cost-of-living index. That problem is analyzed in Fisher and Griliches (1995), and it will be convenient to repeat some of their results and exposition here.

We adopt the following notation: Households are indicated by a superscript $h = 1, \ldots, H$. There are n goods. p denotes the vector of prices in the current period, and $\hat{p}$ the price vector in the base period. Similarly, x^h

---

1. The aggregate production function for a single output, for example, is derived by assigning factors to firms to maximize total output. See Fisher (1993), especially Chapter 1.
2. We have more to say on this in Section 6.4 below.

denotes the vector of commodities consumed by household h in the current period, and $\hat{x}^h$ the similar vector in the base period. With h's utility function represented by U^h, we denote the level of $U^h(x^h)$ by u^h and the level of $U^h(\hat{x}^h)$ by $\hat{u}^h$, that is, we have $u^h = U^h(x^h)$ and $\hat{u}_h = U^h(\hat{x}_h)$.[3]

In comparing base-period prices and current period-prices, the true cost-of-living index for household h based on an arbitrary indifference curve with utility level u is given by

$$I^h(u) = E^h(p, u)/E^h(\hat{p}, u), \tag{6.2.1}$$

where E^h is the expenditure function of household h. This is the ratio of the minimum expenditures at current- and base-period prices, respectively, needed for h to attain utility level u. As is well known, we have

$$L^h = (p \cdot \hat{x}^h / \hat{p} \cdot \hat{x}^h) \geq I^h(\hat{u}^h) \quad \text{and}$$
$$P^h = (p \cdot x^h / \hat{p} \cdot x^h) \leq I^h(u^h), \tag{6.2.2}$$

where L^h and P^h are, respectively, the Laspeyres and Paasche price indexes relevant to consumer h.

Now consider an aggregate price index – that is, one intended to apply to all consumers together.[4] It is easy enough to define an aggregate Laspeyres or Paasche index, but what are the corresponding "true" indexes that such commonly constructed indexes are approximating?

Begin with the Laspeyres index. Consider an index $\hat{I}$ defined by

$$\hat{I} = \frac{\sum_h E^h(p, \hat{u}^h)}{\sum_h E^h(\hat{p}, \hat{u}^h)}. \tag{6.2.3}$$

The index $\hat{I}$ corresponds to the index $I^h(\hat{u}^h)$ in the following sense: $I^h(\hat{u}^h)$ gives the ratio of the minimum expenditures necessary for h to achieve utility level $\hat{u}^h$ at current- and base-period prices. Similarly, $\hat{I}$ gives the ratio of the minimum *total* expenditures necessary for every household to achieve its utility level $\hat{u}^h$ at current-period prices and at base-period prices.

---

3. Although it makes no difference in the present context, we avoid the locution that $U^h(\hat{x}^h)$ and $U(x^h)$ are the levels of utility actually achieved in the base period and the current period, respectively. Those utility levels are incomparable. (See Fisher and Shell (1972, Essay I).) With unchanging tastes, however, it does no harm to ignore this and to assume that U^h is the same function in both periods (not just that the indifference map is unchanging). Since it will ease the exposition to do so, we shall implicitly adopt this approach from now on.
4. This is a "group" price index in the sense of Pollak (1980). Unlike the work of Pollak (1980, 1981), however, the analysis that follows does not involve a social welfare function.

Obviously, this construction takes as given the base-period income distribution. This becomes evident when we inquire as to how $\hat{I}$ is related to the individual cost-of-living indexes, I^h. Define $\hat{K}(w)$ by

$$\hat{K}(w) = \sum_h w^h I^h(\hat{u}^h) = \sum_h w^h [E^h(p, \hat{u}^h)/E^h(\hat{p}, \hat{u}^h)], \qquad (6.2.4)$$

for $h = 1, \ldots, H$, where we have $w_h \geq 0$ and $\sum_h w^h = 1$. Suppose that the weights w^h are given by

$$w^h = \frac{\sum_h E^h(\hat{p}, \hat{u}^h)}{\sum_h E^h(\hat{p}, \hat{u}^h)} = \hat{y}^h/\hat{Y}, \qquad (6.2.5)$$

where $\hat{Y} = \sum_h \hat{y}^h$ is total base-period income. Then we have

$$\hat{K}(\hat{w}) = \frac{\sum_h (\hat{p} \cdot \hat{x}^h) \left(\dfrac{E(p, \hat{u}^h)}{\hat{p} \cdot \hat{x}^h} \right)}{\sum_h \hat{p} \cdot \hat{x}^h} = \hat{I}. \qquad (6.2.6)$$

Thus the aggregate index $\hat{I}$ comprises a weighted average of the individual indexes, $I^h(\hat{u}^h)$, with the weights being given by the distribution of income.

This brings us to the aggregate Laspeyres index L defined by

$$L = \frac{\sum_h p \cdot \hat{x}^h}{\sum_h \hat{p} \cdot \hat{x}^h} = \frac{\sum_h (\hat{p} \cdot \hat{x}^h) \left(\dfrac{p \cdot \hat{x}^h}{\hat{p} \cdot \hat{x}^h} \right)}{\sum_h \hat{p} \cdot \hat{x}^h} = \sum_h \hat{w}^h L^h, \qquad (6.2.7)$$

where the weights $\hat{w}^h$ are defined as in (6.2.5) to be the base-period income shares. It is evident that we have

$$\hat{L} \geq K(\hat{w}) = \hat{I}. \qquad (6.2.8)$$

Hence the aggregate Laspeyres price index bounds the "true" aggregate cost-of-living index $\hat{I}$ from above, preserving the property that holds for individual consumers. Similar properties hold for an aggregate index I based on the utility levels attained in the current period, u^h, with the aggregate Paasche index bounding I from below.

We can now return to the production-theoretic price indexes. Since the theory of the cost-of-living index and that of the production-theoretic price index are isomorphic, why is it that aggregation works in this way for the cost-of-living index while it fails to do so for production-theoretic price indexes? This question seems especially appropriate for the case of the production-theoretic input-price index, and we shall answer it directly for that case.

There are two answers. First, the theory of the cost-of-living index presents no issue parallel to that of falling demand curves.[5] In the consumer case, the only "outputs" are individual utility levels. Second, and more important, the aggregate cost-of-living index $\hat{I}$ defined in (6.2.3)[6] measures the ratio of the minimum expenditures required in the current period and the base period, respectively, to allow *each* consumer to attain a particular utility level. That construction is of interest in the consumer case because we are interested in the welfare of individual consumers.

In the case of firms, however, there is no such interest. Continuing to focus on the production-theoretic input-price index, we are interested in the ratio of the minimum costs necessary to produce a given output in the current period and the base period, respectively. But these are costs at the *industry* level. In general, no special interest attaches to the requirement that each *firm* be on the same isoquant in both periods.

Note, however, that although the readily agreeable Paasche and Laspeyres indexes are of no interest at the industry level, they regain interest at the economy-wide level – at least for an economy that is fully closed, fully open, or hybrid. That is because any one of these economies operates on its PPF and thus solves an optimization problem. This raises the question of whether economy-wide production-theoretic output-price indexes or input-price indexes can be built up from component parts and thus brings us to the subject of conglomerate aggregation.

6.3. Conglomerate Aggregation: Outputs

We now outline the conglomerate aggregation problem for outputs. Suppose that each industry in the economy uses primary factors of production to produce final outputs.[7] Suppose further that we have constructed a production-theoretic output-price index for each industry. Under what

---

5. Or rising supply curves in the isomorphic case of the production-theoretic output-price deflator.
6. A parallel statement holds for I and for aggregate cost-of-living indexes based on different utility levels.
7. Problems of vertical aggregation are considered later.

circumstances can we use these industry-level deflators to construct the economy-wide production-theoretic output-price index? Such a construction would be useful, enabling us, for example, to assess the contribution of each industry to overall inflation.

Unfortunately, we should not expect that conglomerate aggregation in the production-theoretic output-price index will generally be possible. We have seen throughout this study that the production-theoretic output-price index depends on the factor supply conditions facing the economic unit being analyzed. This is most obvious in the case of rising supply curves, but it is true more generally. Thus, in the fully closed case, where factor supplies are fixed, the production-theoretic output-price index depends on the values of the fixed factor prices, and similarly for the hybrid case. Our study of comparative statics (Chapter 3) is the study of such dependence.

This dependence on supply conditions has implications for conglomerate aggregation. In general, with the possible exception of the fully closed case, the factor supply conditions faced by one economic unit will depend in part on the output-prices of *other* economic units. This comes about because different units are likely to compete for the same total factor supply. Further, factor supplies will depend on output prices because factor owners are concerned with real rather than money rewards. When considering aggregation over large sectors, this effect can be important.

The reason that such phenomena create aggregation problems for the construction of an output-price index is as follows: Suppose that there are two units, denoted by superscripts 1 and 2, with price vectors p^1 and p^2, respectively. Let the production-theoretic output-price index for the aggregate of the two units together be denoted by $I^a(p^1, p^2)$. The aggregation question is: Under what circumstances is it possible to define individual production-theoretic output-price indexes for two units, say $I^1(p^1)$ and $I^2(p^2)$, such that for some function Φ we have

$$I^a(p^1, p^2) = \Phi[I^1(p^1), I^2(p^2)], \qquad (6.3.1)$$

which thus breaks down movements in the aggregate index into movements in its component parts? This would enable us to measure the respective contributions of each of the two units to overall inflation.

If changes in p^2 affect the factor supply conditions facing unit 1 (or the reverse) such measurements will generally not be possible. Indeed, under those circumstances one will generally not even be able to construct a production-theoretic index $I^1(p^1)$ for the first unit that is independent of p^2. As is often true about exact aggregation problems, the surprising thing is that they can ever be solved, not that they usually are not solvable.

The formal problem just described above was solved for the fully closed economy in Fisher (1982), which we reprint as Appendix A to this book. Perhaps unsurprisingly, we find that aggregation is possible in only a quite restricted set of special cases. Some of these require the production functions of the outputs of the first sector to be related by Hicks-neutral technical differences, so that not much technical diversity within a sector can be accommodated.

Unfortunately, moving away from the closed economy case to the hybrid case fails to help. This is because, in the hybrid case, the cost of the purchased factors can be considered as just another factor in the closed-economy case. The exception occurs (as one might expect) when the first sector is itself fully open and a fortiori when the entire economy has this property.

Suppose that the first sector is fully open, so that dollars of cost can be considered the only factor used there. If the remainder of the economy uses no factors with horizontal supply curves, then aggregation over the prices of the first sector is always possible.[8] If there are such factors, then, assuming the production functions of the first sector to be homothetic, aggregation is possible if and only if they are all homogeneous of the same degree. Note that this case includes that of constant returns-to-scale.[9]

It is difficult to go beyond this. In the general case of a competitive economy that is neither fully open nor fully closed nor hybrid, the construction of the production-theoretic output-price index is sufficiently complex to make the aggregation problem difficult to study. Given the results for the simpler cases, however, there is no warrant for assuming that conglomerate aggregation is likely to be possible in such a case.

Related to this is the following observation: The results for the special cases based on Appendix A all depend on whether the economy *as a whole* forms one of the special cases. It does not matter at this stage whether a particular sector does. The reason for this has to do with the fact that we are asking the question of whether *any* aggregation is possible. Were aggregation to be possible over the first sector's prices, the issue of how that aggregate was related to the first sector's own production-theoretic price index would become important, and this would necessarily involve the nature of this index and hence the nature of the factor-supply curves facing this sector. Because aggregation is possible in only a few very special cases, we do not consider such questions in detail.

8. See Appendix A, Theorem A.3.1.
9. This follows from Appendix A, Theorems A.6.1–A.6.3.

In general, then, construction of separate production-theoretic output-price indexes for separate sectors of the economy is likely to be a problem if the indexes are then to be combined to form an aggregate. The construction of such an index for a particular sector takes as given the factor supply conditions facing that sector, and these in turn will depend on the output prices of other sectors. The production-theoretic output-price index for a given sector can thus be constructed *taking output prices outside that sector as given*, and the effects of changing those outside output prices studied through comparative statics.

If one attempts to combine such sectoral price indexes in conglomerate aggregation, however, one runs into trouble because one cannot then assume that outside output prices are fixed. The construction of an aggregate production-theoretic output-price index depends on the factor-supply conditions facing the aggregate economy. It will generally not be possible to break these down into the supply conditions facing each component part independent of the others. This sort of decentralization in index-number construction and interpretation becomes impossible. The sectoral price indexes will have to be constructed as functions of the "outside" output prices, so that each output price has effects not only on its own sectoral index but also on the other sectoral indexes. It is these intersectoral effects through factor supplies that the construction of individual sector price indexes will typically miss.

It may be thought that we have been too pessimistic here. After all, it is easy to see that conglomerate aggregation is *always* possible in Paasche and Laspeyres output-price indexes. Hence, in examining the contribution of the steel industry to overall inflation, for example, the answer is clear for a Paasche or Laspeyres index; one need only examine the total weight given to steel products.

This is, of course, a snare and a delusion. The correct answer to the question about the steel industry's contribution to inflation involves the extent to which an increase in the steel industry's production-theoretic output-price index leads to an increase in the economy-wide production-theoretic price index. Where conglomerate aggregation of the production-theoretic output-price indexes is possible, this question has an answer. Furthermore, in that case, if it is also true that Paasche or Laspeyres indexes bound the production-theoretic price index, then there is also some economic interest in the effect of the steel industry's Paasche price index, say, on the economy-wide Paasche price index. But if conglomerate aggregation of production-theoretic output-price indexes is not possible, then there is little but mechanical interest in the weight that the steel industry has in the overall Paasche or Laspeyres index.

There is another catch. As we have seen, Laspeyres and Paasche indexes for sectors of interest will generally not provide useful bounds on the production-theoretic output-price indexes for those sectors – even though they do provide such bounds for a large closed economy. Hence, even though conglomerate aggregation of Paasche and Laspeyres indexes can be achieved, the economic meaning of such aggregation is open to question.

Note that both the problems with Paasche and Laspeyres indexes and the difficulty of conglomerate aggregation stem from the same phenomenon: Factor-supply conditions affect production-theoretic output-price indexes, and factor-supply conditions themselves generally depend indirectly on output prices. Only in (important) special cases can such interdependence be ignored.

6.4. Conglomerate Aggregation: Inputs

Similar problems arise when we consider aggregation over inputs. Here, however, we must note a distinction. As opposed to the output case where it is natural to associate sectors or industries and outputs, such association is not particularly natural when it comes to inputs.[10] This apparently means that we must consider two types of conglomerate aggregation over inputs rather than one.

The first kind of aggregation is aggregation over several economic units. This is the question of how production-theoretic input-price indexes for different industries affect the similar index for the economy as a whole. The second kind of aggregation involves aggregation directly over groups of factor prices rather than over economic units.[11]

6.4.1. Aggregation Over Economic Units

Some reflection reveals that we have already covered the first kind of aggregation. It is isomorphic to horizontal, rather than conglomerate, aggregation in the case of outputs. Even if firms are in different industries – classified

---

10. Geographically defined sectors can be an exception. Another exception can occur for subindexes such as the set of all ferrous-metals users.
11. We continue to classify this under "conglomerate" aggregation, even though the nomenclature is a bit strained.

by their outputs – the fact that they use the same inputs makes the problem horizontal, rather than conglomerate.

Of course, this makes little difference to the conclusions to be drawn or the reasons for them. As already suggested, the problem with both horizontal and conglomerate aggregation in the case of output prices lies with the dependence of production-theoretic output-price indexes on factor-supply conditions and the dependence of those conditions in turn on output prices outside the economic unit that is to be a piece of the aggregate. In the case of the production-theoretic input-price index and aggregation over economic units, the problem lies in the dependence of the production-theoretic input-price index on demand conditions and on the dependence of those conditions in turn on factor prices outside the unit forming part of the aggregate. (Of course, factor prices may be the same across units: This is what makes aggregation directly over factor prices rather than over economic units interesting. This is the second kind of aggregation mentioned above and taken up below.)

It is illuminating to describe the problem with an example. Suppose that there are two industries comprising the entire economy. Suppose also that both industries buy only primary factors and sell only to final demand. As we have seen, the construction of the production-theoretic price index for the first industry must take into account the demand conditions that the first industry faces. This is true even when the first industry is small and open. The isoquants used for construction of the index are those corresponding to a given total revenue at fixed output prices, and those fixed output prices are the ones corresponding to equilibrium in all the industry's output markets.

In general, however, the demand conditions facing the first industry and, hence, the relevant isoquants will depend on what goes on in the second industry. In particular, they will depend on the second industry's factor prices, because the outputs of the second industry compete for consumer dollars with those of the first. A change in the factor prices confronting the second industry will alter that industry's costs. This will affect its output prices and hence, indirectly, alter the demand conditions facing the first industry. Therefore, an aggregate production-theoretic price index for the economy as a whole cannot be built up from separate indexes for the two component industries. Separate price indexes would have to ignore the interindustry effects to be truly separate.[12]

---

12. Industry interdependence is even more obvious where one industry's outputs are used as inputs by the other, the case of "vertical" aggregation considered below. For remarks on production indexes for commodity groups where some of the commodities are outputs and others inputs, see Shell (1975).

The matter does not quite end here, however, because of the strong possibility that the two industries are likely to face many of the same factor prices. That phenomenon actually makes the matter clearer (although it does not make aggregation easier).

For simplicity, suppose that the two industries face identical factor prices. Then the problem of aggregating over economic units can be thought of as follows: The production-theoretic input-price index for the first industry taken alone examines the effects of a change in input prices on that industry's input decisions. The output prices of the second industry are taken as given and the first industry's output markets are taken to be in equilibrium. Similarly, the production-theoretic input-price index for the second industry considers only the effects of input-price changes on the second industry's input decisions, keeping that industry's output markets in equilibrium with first-industry output prices held constant. But when the common factor prices change there are effects on both industries. The resulting equilibria in output markets will generally not coincide with equilibria constructed taking only one industry at a time with the other one's output prices held constant. The production-theoretic input-price index for the economy as a whole is the one that takes full account of such effects. It is evident that it cannot generally be built up from two industry-specific indexes that do not take such effects into account. This is a larger version of the same phenomenon that makes horizontal aggregation over firms difficult; here it means that this kind of conglomerate aggregation over economic units will generally be impossible.

Are there any exceptions? The answer here is in the affirmative, but, as in the case of conglomerate aggregation of the production-theoretic output-price index, the exceptions require extremely special circumstances. What is required is that the isoquants used to construct each industry's separate input-price index be shifted homothetically by changes in the output prices of the other industry. Although this can happen, it is unlikely and can safely be ignored.[13]

---

13. We do not pursue this question further. In the case of the production-theoretic output-price index for the fully closed case (and its generalizations) treated above and in Appendix A, we could further explore the parallel question for PPFs. This was because of the interesting case in which the PPF is built up from several technologies each involving the production of one output from several inputs according to a production function. The isomorphic case would involve technologies in which the technological requirements for a given factor depended only on outputs and not on the amounts of other inputs used. This case is not interesting. The interesting case is the one isomorphic to that of coproduction of several outputs. (See the remarks following Theorem A.3.1 in Appendix A and also Section A.7.)

6.4.2. Direct Aggregation Over Groups of Inputs

In a real sense, of course, the kind of aggregation considered above is not aggregation over input prices at all. For the economy as a whole, the production-theoretic input-price index is a function of the input prices it faces. The natural aggregation issue is whether those prices can somehow be grouped and inputs aggregated. The question considered above has little to do with this. The difficulties there arise not because of differences among inputs, but because the questions to be asked when constructing a production-theoretic input-price deflator are different when the economic unit being studied is different. Briefly put, input deflation for an industry is not the same problem as input deflation for the whole economy.

In the case of output deflation, the two kinds of aggregation tend to coincide. Grouping output prices together for use in an economy-wide output-price index invites a discussion of aggregation over the economic units producing the outputs whose prices are to be so grouped. Because the association of particular inputs with particular economic units is far less natural than the parallel association for outputs, it is important to consider the question of aggregation over input prices directly, without associating it with aggregation over economic units.[14]

This is easy enough to do. (Note that we are now speaking of aggregation of input prices within *any* economic unit, not just in the full economy.) The production-theoretic input-price index I for the economic unit involved can be written as a function of current-period factor prices (with base-period factor prices understood to be fixed), so we have

$$I = I(w_1, \ldots, w_r),\tag{6.4.1}$$

for some function I. Suppose that we wish to aggregate over the first t factor prices $(1 < t < r)$, and so wish to write I as

$$I = I(w_1, \ldots, w_r) = H(A(w_1, \ldots, w_t), w_{t+1}, \ldots, w_r),\tag{6.4.2}$$

where A is a scalar-valued function. Then Leontief's well-known theorem on aggregation[15] assures us that this can be done if and only if we have

$$\frac{\partial(I_i/I_j)}{\partial w_k} = 0\tag{6.4.3}$$

14. Isomorphic results apply to aggregation over output prices where such aggregation is not associated with aggregation over economic units. We do not pursue this.
15. Leontief (1947a, 1947b). A simple proof is given in Fisher (1993, pp. xiv–xvi).

for $i, j = 1, \ldots, t$ and $k = t + 1, \ldots, r$, so that the I-constant marginal rate of substitution between any pair of prices in the aggregate must be independent of any price not in the aggregate.

Consideration of the general competitive case reveals that a change in w_k has two effects. First, even if the economic unit were fully open and thus continued to face the same output prices, there would be a shift in its maximization problem. Second, with declining demand curves for output, output prices will in fact change, a different position of equilibrium will be reached, and the maximization problem the fully open economy solves will change as well.

This latter type of change is too complicated to be analyzed further. Too much information is involved. Instead, we analyze the consequences of (6.4.3) for only the fully open case. Since the conditions for aggregation are extremely restrictive even in this case, it seems a forlorn hope that they will be less so in more general circumstances.

Restricting attention to the fully open case, application of the Envelope Theorem to the optimization problem "solved" by the economy (see Section 4.4 above) shows that we have

$$I_i / I_j = v_i / v_j \qquad (6.4.4)$$

for $i, j = 1, \ldots, t$, where v_i is the quantity of the ith input employed. Thus (6.4.3) requires that changes in w_k leave unchanged the ratio in which v_i and v_j are employed. Hence that ratio can depend only on the first t factor prices, the ones to be included in the aggregate. Under constant returns-to-scale (or other appropriately homothetic technologies), such dependence will be on the ratios of the factor prices to be aggregated. Since employment of factors whose prices are left out of the aggregate will certainly depend on their own prices, it follows that the marginal rates of substitution in production among factors whose prices are to be aggregated must depend only on the ratios of such factors and not on the employment of other factors. Together with another application of Leontief's theorem, this implies that aggregation over the first t factors is possible for constant returns-to-scale and related technologies if and only if the efficient production surface for the economic unit can be written as

$$0 = F(x, v) = H(x, \phi(v_1, \ldots, v_t), v_{t+1}, \ldots, v_r), \qquad (6.4.5)$$

where x is the output vector, the function ϕ is scalar valued and homothetic, and the function H is scalar valued.

In other words, factor-price aggregation in the production-theoretic input-price index is possible for such technologies if and only if the corresponding aggregation is possible in the production surface. (Homotheticity of the function ϕ is guaranteed for the class of technologies involved.)

If the economic unit involved is a micro unit and the production relation $F(x, v) = 0$ simply describes its efficient technology, then the story ends here. If, however, the economic unit is an aggregate with its efficient technology built up from those of underlying units (say, firms) by allocating a total stock of factors and assigning outputs to achieve efficient production, then there is much more that can be said.

Indeed, one of us has already done so in a series of papers.[16] Basically, aggregation of factors as in (6.4.5) requires some very special conditions. First, such aggregation must be possible within each firm. The remaining conditions vary depending on whether or not all factors are employed and all outputs produced by every firm in the economic unit. The sort of condition involved is that either the t-factor aggregate within each firm must be the same for all firms or else the way in which that aggregate is combined with factors $t + 1, \ldots, r$ must be the same for all firms. For the leading case in which each firm produces a different output but all factors are employed by all firms, either of these conditions is sufficient, and it is necessary that at least one of them hold. Where some factors (capital types, for instance) are firm specific, one or the other of the alternative conditions (the choice depending on whether the fixed or the mobile factors are to be aggregated) is necessary and sufficient, but not both.

Obviously, such cases are very special, and we must conclude that, in general, it will not be possible to perform aggregation in the production-theoretic input-price index.

6.5. Vertical Relationships: Combining Input-Price and Output-Price Indexes

So far our discussion of aggregation over economic units has concerned units at the same level of production. In the case of the output-price index, these were units that competed for the same pool of inputs; in the case of the input-price index, they were units that competed for customer expenditures.

---

16. These are conveniently reprinted in Fisher (1993), which also gives other references. See especially Chapter 5 of that book.

In situations where units are in a vertical relationship, with one unit buying from another, a related but different set of issues arises. We can best discuss those issues by posing them in an extreme (but simple) example.

Suppose that Unit I, the "Seller," buys only primary factors and sells only to Unit II. Suppose further that Unit II, the "Buyer," buys only from Unit I. Obviously, the prices faced by consumers – those of the Buyer – are influenced by the Buyer's input prices – the output prices of the Seller – and these in turn are influenced by the prices of primary factors. A sensible set of questions to ask is how to measure the relative contributions of the Seller and of primary factors to inflation as seen by the Buyer and how to measure the relative contributions of primary factors, the Seller, and the Buyer to inflation as seen by consumers. Indeed, such questions arise even if there is only one productive unit and it buys primary factors and sells output to consumers.

It will be convenient to begin with the latter case with only one stage of production between primary factors and final outputs; we can then generalize. In this simplest case, one obvious thought is to solve the problem by calculating the single production unit's production-theoretic output-price and input-price indexes and to take the ratio of the two indexes as the contribution of the productive unit itself to inflation. The important point to understand is that this "obvious thought" is wrong.

There is more than one way to see this. We begin with the relatively formal way. For simplicity, we concentrate first on the case of competition in all markets. The production-theoretic output-price index is constructed assuming output prices to be given by demand conditions outside the productive unit and solving optimization problems within that unit given those prices and a certain set of factor-supply conditions. In contrast, the production-theoretic input-price index is constructed assuming factor prices to be given by supply conditions outside the productive unit and solving optimization problems within that unit given those prices and a certain set of output-demand conditions. To compare the production-theoretic output-price index and the production-theoretic input-price index is to take as simultaneously valid two sets of conditions that can at best hold simultaneously only if *all* prices are determined outside the productive unit – a situation in which the question of the contribution of this unit to inflation loses all interest.

The same sort of problem persists even where monopoly or monopsony problems are present. Where there is monopsony in factor markets but no monopoly power in output markets, the production-theoretic output-price index takes output prices as determined outside the productive unit. It makes no sense to ask how much of an increase in those prices is accounted for by the actions of the productive unit itself. A similar statement applies to the production-theoretic input-price index where there is monopoly in output markets but no monopsony in input markets. Where both monopoly in output markets and monopsony in factor markets are present, then this particular difficulty disappears. In this case, however, all prices are under the control of the productive unit and the question of that unit's contribution to inflation essentially vanishes.

The underlying reason for such problems is not hard to find. The method being explored is not an answer to the question of interest. This question has to do (in this example) with inflation *as seen by consumers*. But inflation as seen by consumers is properly measured by the cost-of-living index and not by the production-theoretic output-price index. The production-theoretic output-price index takes output prices as demand determined: output prices then reflect tastes; they give the trade-offs at which firms can *sell*. It is the cost-of-living index that takes prices as production determined, as reflective of costs: They then give the trade-offs at which consumers can *buy*. Each measure has its uses, but if we seek to evaluate inflation as seen by consumers, it is the cost-of-living index that must be used.

Once this distinction is realized, it is possible to see how to proceed. As observed in Fisher and Shell (1972, pp. 7–8) in discussing the difference between taste and quality changes, there is a choice as to where we place the interface between the household and its opportunity set.[17] Consumers buy goods and use them in activities within the household to maximize utility. Some of those activities can be considered as production activities within the household rather than directly as consumption (food preparation, for example).[18] Now suppose that the productive system were differently organized, with the activities now carried on in the productive unit under analysis being carried on within the household.[19] Then the household would buy primary factors and use them in its productive activities to maximize utility. The prices it would then face would be those of the primary factors. Its cost-of-living index would be computed using *those* prices. A comparison of such a cost-of-living index with the actual cost-of-living index thus measures the extent to which the production unit being analyzed contributes to inflation as seen by the household.

17. See also Shell (1975) for the options in designing production price indexes.
18. There is a large literature on the economic analysis of such household production activities. The seminal reference is Becker (1981).
19. As is usually done, we ignore the difficulties involved in aggregating over households and consider only a single household. See, e.g., Griliches (1996).

If such an approach seems somewhat forced, consider its generalization to the case of two productive units, one of whom buys from the other – the case of the Seller and the Buyer described earlier. Consider inflation from the point of view of the Buyer; this is the Buyer's production-theoretic input-price index. The relative contributions to this index of the Seller and of primary factor prices can be analyzed quite naturally by asking how different the production-theoretic input index would be for a vertically integrated unit consisting of the Buyer and Seller together. (Note that the Seller's *output-price* index plays no role in this.) This is the same procedure as that involving households; we have merely placed it in a more familiar context.

It is easy to see that the same principle applies when the Buyer also purchases primary factors directly. One divides the Buyer's production-theoretic input-price index (an index that includes the Seller's output prices) by the production-theoretic input-price index that would face a vertically integrated unit consisting of both Buyer and Seller together.[20]

Note also that a similar procedure can be used to measure the Buyer's (or consumer's) contribution to *output-price* inflation as seen by the Seller. This might be of interest in considering cases of demand-pull rather than cost-push inflation. We do not explore this matter further, however, leaving details to the reader.

Now, it is interesting to ask how such vertically integrated indexes relate to the corresponding unintegrated indexes. In particular, can the same comparison be made by using the input-price index of the Buyer and the input-price index of the Seller alone? One would hope that it could, as this would simplify matters. Returning to the case in which the Buyer buys only from the Seller, the input-price index of the Buyer reflects inflation as seen by the Buyer, while the input-price index of the Seller reflects inflation as seen by the Seller – inflation involving only changes in the prices of primary factors. It is natural to compare the two to see if the Seller is contributing anything to the Buyer's input inflation.

Any such attempt fails for much the same reasons as given earlier for the failure of the "obvious thought." The Seller's input-price index is calculated *taking as given the Seller's output prices* – the prices at which the Seller sells to the Buyer. However, it is the change in just these prices that is measured by the Buyer's input-price index. The contribution of the Seller

20. In so doing, one should assume that the same conditions of competition would apply with vertical integration as apply without it.

to inflation as seen by the Buyer cannot be assessed using a measure that assumes there is no such inflation.

The difficulty of constructing the vertically integrated price index that, as we have seen, is the proper one to use is no greater than the (already considerable) difficulty of constructing the production-theoretic input-price index for an unintegrated sector. (A similar remark applies to the construction of a "vertically integrated" cost-of-living index as earlier described.) If we had perfect information about productions sets (or utility functions), this construction would be straightforward. The construction differs from that of the nonvertically integrated index only as regards which production processes we group as belonging inside the same unit. For analytical purposes, this is not a problem.

For practical purposes, on the other hand, the problems are large, but they are the same as those encountered without the complication of considering independent units as if they were vertically integrated. In practice, we do not have the detailed information on production sets required to construct these indexes and must fall back on approximations. We have already seen the inadequacies of Paasche and Laspeyres indexes as approximations in all but special cases; next we encounter an additional failure of these indexes for many approximations.

Consider a Laspeyres input-price index for the Seller alone. (The same comments, mutatis mutandis, apply to Paasche indexes.) Ignoring other difficulties, this index will bound from above the production-theoretic input-price index both of the Seller *and* of the constructed vertically integrated entity. This is not very useful for present purposes, since we wish to compare this index with the production-theoretic input-price index of the Buyer. All we are likely to have here, however, is another Laspeyres bound on *that* index. Comparison of the bounds does not yield a reliable comparison of the indexes themselves, since the degrees of approximation can easily differ.[21] The best that can be said is that a Laspeyres bound on the Seller's production-theoretic input-price index could be used together with the true production-theoretic index of the Buyer were it available.[22]

---

21. Note that the same problem would arise even with the incorrect procedure of comparing the Seller's and Buyer's production-theoretic input-price indexes. The use of Laspeyres or Paasche bounds simply does not lead to useful conclusions here.
22. A Laspeyres bound on the production-theoretic input-price index of the Buyer could be used together with the true production-theoretic input-price index of the vertically integrated entity, but the latter number is even less likely to be available.

Appendix: On Perfect Aggregation in the National Output Deflator and Generalized Rybczynski Theorems[1,2]

A.1. Introduction

Fisher and Shell (1972) attempted to place the theory of output deflation on a production-theoretic foundation in the same way as the theory of the cost-of-living index is based on a consumer-theoretic foundation. It developed a production-theoretic output deflator to which actually computed indexes, such as the GNP deflator, serve (sometimes) as bounding approximations.

The present paper continues that work. In it, I inquire as to the possibility of building up the production-theoretic deflator from subindexes each of which is a deflator for a particular sector or industry. In what sense, if any, is it possible, for example, to talk of the steel industry's contribution to inflation? Clearly, such a statement would be well defined if the full output deflator could be expressed in terms of specific industry deflators; the question is whether this is possible.

Obviously, such questions are trivial when considering the Paasche approximation to national output deflation, the GNP deflator. Paasche or Laspeyres indices can be expressed in terms of subindexes in a simple, arithmetic way. Yet to be content with this answer is, in effect, to ignore the question. The steel industry deflator in the Paasche approximation is a bound on the production-theoretic deflator for the steel industry. The full Paasche

1. Reprinted from Fisher, F. M. (1982): "On Perfect Aggregation in the National Output Deflator and Generalized Rybczynski Theorems," *The International Economic Review*, Vol. 23, No. 1, February, with the permission of *The International Economic Review*.
2. This research was carried out under contract to the Bureau of Labor Statistics, the United States Department of Labor. I am indebted to Karl Shell for helpful conversations. I take sole responsibility, however, for the views expressed and any error.

approximation is a similar bound on the production-theoretic deflator for the economy as a whole. Yet if the economy-wide, production-theoretic deflator is not simply a function of production-theoretic deflators for separate industries, it is not at all plain that much interest should attach to the percent of Paasche-approximated deflation accounted for arithmetically by the Paasche deflator for the steel industry.

More generally, someone attempting to construct deflators for a particular sector or industry will do so without regard for prices outside that sector. If this is done for every sector of the economy, can the results then be used directly to construct the national output deflator? If not, then what can one say concerning the errors that are likely to be committed in proceeding on a sector-by-sector basis? What approximation theorems can be proved?

The present paper is only the beginning of research into such questions. It asks only whether perfect aggregation is likely to be possible. Not surprisingly, in view of what is known of similar questions in cost-of-living theory,[3] the answer turns out to be that perfect aggregation requires certain separability properties in the structure of the overall technology. However, while "*de gustibus non est disputandum*" this is not true about production-possibility sets and it is therefore possible to inquire further. While the conditions for perfect aggregation remain quite stringent, it is moderately interesting to see what they come down to in terms of individual production functions.

A second purpose of this paper appears in the course of the analysis. As we shall see below, the conditions for perfect aggregation in the national output deflator turn out to be intimately related to the well-known Rybczynski Theorem of international trade theory.[4] It turns out that some of our results can be interpreted as at least mild generalizations of that theorem in ways which do not appear to be fully covered in the literature. I discuss this in detail in a separate section below.

Interestingly enough, the results of the present paper (and therefore also of the Rybczynski Theorem) turn out also to be related mathematically to the theorem on capital aggregation which I proved some time ago.[5] Indeed, the method of proof below is often to establish an isomorphism. It is perhaps not surprising that theorems on aggregation of prices and

---

3. See Pollak (1975) and Blackorby and Russell (1978).
4. Rybczynski (1955). I am indebted to M. Machina for first calling the relationship to the Rybczynski Theorem to my attention, and to him, J. Bhagwati, E. Helpman, and A. Razin for helpful references.
5. Fisher (1965) and (1968). A nontechnical summary is given in Fisher (1969).

of factors should have the same general structure; it seems less obvious that the Rybczynski Theorem should also. The relation ceases to appear coincidental, however, when one realizes that the Rybczynski Theorem gives conditions under which a change in factor supplies makes the same relative output prices correspond to different output ratios. The condition that this should not occur is a condition that the marginal rates of substitution among different outputs depend only on the output ratios. By Leontief's well-known theorem, this is seen to be a theorem about aggregation over outputs.[6]

A.2. Formal Statement of the Problem

We begin with a formal description of the production-theoretic deflator; for present purposes, we can use a slight simplification of the description in Fisher and Shell (1972) (to which the reader is referred for extensive discussion).[7]

The economy produces outputs $x^1, \ldots, x^r$. The column vector of the x_j is denoted by x. The corresponding row vector of prices is denoted by p' and the money value of output by y. Hats are used to denote base-period magnitudes and are omitted on current-period ones.

The production possibility frontier (PPF) in the base period was:

$$\Phi(\hat{x}) = \hat{\mu}, \tag{A.2.1}$$

where $\hat{\mu}$ is a shift parameter which will simply be constant in the present analysis. To construct the deflator, we find that current output, x, which lies on the base-period PPF and which maximizes value at current prices, p. That is, we solve

$$\text{Maximize } p'x \quad \text{subject to } \Phi(x) = \Phi(\hat{x}). \tag{A.2.2}$$

Let y be the resulting value of $p'x$ and $\hat{y} \equiv \hat{p}'\hat{x}$. The deflator is then given by $y/\hat{y}$.

To study aggregation in this context, it will suffice to consider two sectors. The first of these will consist of the first r_1 outputs and associated prices and the second of the remainder. Sectoral vectors will be denoted by superscripts, so that, in particular, p^1 is the vector of the first r_1 prices, and so forth.

---

6. Leontief (1947a). It is also not surprising to find some relation here to the theorem on correcting for quality change by simple price adjustments proved in Fisher and Shell (1972, pp. 105–107).

7. Appropriate differentiability and regularity conditions are assumed throughout.

Now, consideration of the deflation problem as posed makes it plain that we can focus on the way in which y depends on p, since the dependence of $\hat{y}$ on $\hat{p}$ will be essentially the same (because a competitive economy locates the value-maximizing point on the PPF). Certainly, y is a function of p and hence of p^1 and p^2. We seek the circumstances under which the goods of the first sector can be considered together and the function in question written as:

$$y = R[r(p^1), p^2] \tag{A.2.3}$$

where $r(\cdot)$ is a scalar-valued function.

A.3. Independent Output Ratios and the Rybczynski Theorem

By Leontief's well-known aggregation theorem (Leontief, 1974a), such aggregation will be possible if and only if the ratio of the partial derivatives of y with respect to any two prices in sector 1 is independent of every price in sector 2. Consideration of the maximum problem in (A.2.2) and application of the Envelope Theorem now yields immediately:

Lemma A.3.1: *A necessary and sufficient condition for prices in the first sector to be aggregated in the deflator is that any ratio x_i^1 / x_j^1 be independent of p^2, where x_i^1 and x_j^1 are any two outputs in the first sector.*

Thus, aggregation over first-sector prices will be possible if and only if all first-sector output ratios are independent of prices not in that sector. We must now explore what such a requirement implies about the underlying technology. The first possibility is a simple one. Suppose that none of the factors of production used in the first sector are used anywhere else.[8] Then the prices of goods not in the first sector will have no effect on outputs in that sector which will be determined entirely by their own relative prices and the amounts of the first-sector-specific factors which are available. By Lemma A.3.1, aggregation will then be possible. I shall refer to this as the completely decomposable case.

Consideration of the completely decomposable case points the way towards analysis of more general cases. The prices of goods not in the first

---

8. As we are dealing with production possibility frontiers, intermediate outputs are netted out and we consider production from primary factors only.

sector can influence the relative outputs of goods in that sector only by changing the amounts of the common factors (i.e., not sector-specific factors) which it is optimal to devote to that sector. It is possible, however, that such changes leave relative outputs in the first sector unchanged.

This can happen in the following manner. Given the inputs (sector-specific and common) to be devoted to the first sector, the PPF of the first sector considered in isolation is determined. Now vary the amounts of the common factors. This will shift the PPF. Such shifts will leave relative outputs unaffected at any given set of first-sector prices if and only if the collection of PPF's so generated is homothetic.

Analytically, drop sector superscripts from now on and consider the technology of the first sector taken in isolation. Let x be the t-vector of first-sector outputs; v be the m-vector of common factors devoted to the first sector; and u be the n-vector of first-sector-specific factors. The efficient frontier is given by:

$$F(x, u, v) = 0. \tag{A.3.1}$$

Lemma A.3.2: *A necessary and sufficient condition for prices in the first sector to be aggregated in the deflator is that there exist functions $J(\cdot, \cdot)$ and $G(\cdot, \cdot, \cdot)$ such that*

$$F(x, u, v) = G[J(x, u), u, v]. \tag{A.3.2}$$

If v actually affects the value of F, then $J(x, u)$ must be homothetic in x.

Proof: By Lemma A.3.1 and the remarks following, aggregation is possible if and only if given output ratios correspond to the same marginal rates of substitution among outputs, varying v (but taking u as fixed). This means such marginal rates of substitution can depend on u but must be independent of v. A second application of Leontief's aggregation theorem yields (A.3.2). If v actually influences F, then the requirement that the same marginal rates of substitution correspond to the same output *ratios,* given u, implies that $J(x, u)$ must be homothetic in x. ∎

To see that this result is the same as that of homotheticity in generated PPF's described above, observe that if (A.3.2) holds, (A.3.1) can be solved for j, obtaining:

$$J(x, u) = M(u, v). \tag{A.3.3}$$

Parametric on u, this gives the PPF for each v. Changes in v which shift the PPF will generate a homothetic map if J is homothetic in x.

Obviously, if there are no common factors, (A.3.2) is automatically satisfied and the homotheticity requirement is vacuous, so that, as we already know:

Theorem A.3.1: *Aggregation is always possible in the completely decomposable case.*

We shall explore the other ways in which the conditions of Lemma A.3.2 can be satisfied. This means looking behind (A.3.1) to see what restrictions the conditions of Lemma A.3.2 put on individual production functions. Obviously, one possibility is that all the outputs of the first sector are jointly produced with the conditions of Lemma A.3.2 describing the technology of such joint production. If that is so, then there is no more to be said. We proceed, therefore, by examining the other extreme (and leading) case in which each element of x is produced from a separate production function with the PPF (A.3.1) derived by efficient allocation of resources in the usual way. We shall discuss the extension of our results to the intermediate case of co-production of some but not all of the first-sector outputs in a later section.

As promised, we are now dealing squarely with the Rybczynski (1955) Theorem which states that for a two-factor-two-output constant returns world in which production of the two outputs differ in factor intensities, a change in a factor supply *always* shifts the relative production of the two outputs. In terms of the underlying production functions, the absence of such Rybczynski effects would require the two production functions to differ only by a Hicks-neutral technical change so that factor intensities will *always* be the same. (Note that in this case the PPF will be a straight line and it is thus not surprising that it is easy to aggregate over the prices.)

It is not surprising that our attempt to aggregate over prices turns out to involve the Rybczynski Theorem. It was shown in Fisher and Shell (1972, p. 85) that an increase in the supply of the ith factor would increase (reduce) the importance of the kth output price in the deflator if and only if an increase in the kth output price would increase (reduce) the share of the ith factor in total factor payments. But this latter condition essentially involves the Stolper-Samuelson (1941) Theorem which is well known to be dual to the Rybczynski Theorem.[9] Hence, if we ask for conditions under which

---

9. Indeed, the duality results proved in Fisher and Shell (1972, pp. 86–87) essentially reprove this.

a change in factor supplies to the first sector leave the deflator for that sector unchanged, we should expect to encounter conditions under which the Rybczynski effect is absent.

The literature contains a number of generalizations of the Rybczynski Theorem. The two articles which come closest to accomplishing the present purpose are Ethier (1974) and Kemp and Wan (1976).[10] While the results proved in the present paper are, of course, consistent with those of Ethier and Kemp and Wan and occasionally overlap them, they are not identical to them.

In particular, the results below do not assume a non-singular factor-intensity matrix as does Ethier. Indeed, as do Kemp and Wan, I allow different numbers of goods and factors. However, whereas Kemp and Wan explore the consequences of assuming constant factor prices, I take the "other path" of assuming full employment of factors with factor prices adjusting. (See Kemp and Wan (1976, p. 56).)[11] In addition, I consider some cases of non-constant returns providing some generalization of the Rybczynski Theorem in that direction.

My concentration is on the properties of the underlying production functions required for there never to be any Rybczynski effects. The results thus turn out as already indicated to be in terms of the relations among the individual production functions rather than in terms (directly) of factor intensity conditions (although the implications are usually obvious). In what follows, I do not explicitly restate the theorems in terms of Rybczynski effects but the foregoing discussion (and Lemma A.3.2) makes it plain how to do so; except for the completely decomposable case, aggregation over first-section prices is possible if and only if there are no Rybczynski effects. In general, Rybczynski effects are the rule, rather than the exception, as we should expect. Indeed, most non-homothetic production functions have the property of leading to Rybczynski effects whether or not the different production functions are related to each other by Hicks-neutral technical changes or are even the same. It is an open question whether there are *any* non-homothetic cases which do not generate Rybczynski effects.

10. Other references are given in these papers.
11. As a matter of fact, the results below are more general than this. What matters are the assumptions on which the PPF is drawn. It can be drawn as usual with fixed factor supplies or with some (or all) factors purchased at fixed factor prices and the total expenditure on such "variable" factors fixed along with the individual amounts of the remaining factors. The results below would still apply considering expenditure on "variable" factors as a factor in an "indirect" production function. (One can show that the same conditions developed below would have to hold for the original production functions in order to hold for the desired "indirect" production functions.) Such an interpretation of the case of some or all factor prices fixed leads to a different case from that analyzed by Kemp and Wan, however.

It turns out to be useful (after a preliminary lemma) to organize the discussion by considering first the case in which there are no sector-specific factors, u, used in the first sector. Our results are easiest and most complete for this case. After that, we reintroduce such factors but divide the discussion between the very difficult case in which all such factors are used for all outputs and the easier contrary case which we shall term that of "output-specific" factors. The case in which there are only sector-specific and no common factors is the completely decomposable case already handled.

Translation of these different cases into Rybczynski-effect terms is straightforward. The case of price aggregation with no sector-specific factors is the case of no Rybczynski effects. The case of price aggregation with some sector specific and some common factors is the case in which changes in *some* factor supplies (the common factor) generate no Rybczynski effects although changes in *other* factor supplies (the sector-specific factors) may generate such effects. The interpretation of output-specific factors is immediate.

The possibility of having sector-specific factors which are also output specific raises a question which it is convenient to dispose of now. Can there be common factors which are output specific? Is it possible that some of the factors used both in and out of the first sector, the elements of v, in fact are not used everywhere in the first sector? The answer is in the negative as shown by the somewhat more general lemma:

Lemma A.3.3: *If at some point on the first sector PPF (A.3.1) optimal allocation results in a corner solution with a particular common factor, v_j, not employed in the production of some output, x_i, then aggregation over the prices of the first sector is impossible.*

Proof: Add a little more v_j to the first sector. Because of the corner solution, at the same output prices as before it must be optimal to assign the extra input entirely to outputs other than x_i. Evidently the resulting shift in the PPF cannot leave output ratios unchanged, i.e., it is not a homothetic outward shift.   ■

For the remainder of the paper we shall assume that common factors are always employed in the production of all first-sector outputs. (Actually, tangency conditions at zero employment would make no difference, as the lemma suggests.)

A.4. Homotheticity and Additivity

It will be useful to proceed by stating the following lemma.

Lemma A.4.1: *Suppose that, for some $n > 1$,*

$$J(x) \equiv \sum_{i=1}^{t} H^i(x_i) \tag{A.4.1}$$

is homothetic and that, for all i, $H^i(0) = 0$, and for $x_i \geq 0$, $H^i(\cdot)$ is twice differentiable with $H^{i'}(x_i) > 0$. Then for all $x_i \geq 0$,

$$H^i(x_i) = C_i x_i \tag{A.4.2}$$

with the same $\alpha > 0$ for all i.

Proof: This follows from Lau (1969, Lemma II, p. 383), the logarithmic case being ruled out by $H^i(0) = 0$.   ∎

A.5. No Sector-Specific Factors

We now consider the case of no sector-specific factors. Here the production functions of the first sector can be written as:

$$x_i = g^i[v(i)] \quad i = 1, \ldots, t, \tag{A.5.1}$$

where $v(i)$ is the vector of common factors devoted to the production of x_i and

$$\sum_{i=1}^{t} v(i) = v. \tag{A.5.2}$$

We assume $g^i(\cdot)$ monotonic in all arguments and $g^i(0) = 0$. In addition, save where separable cases are specifically considered, we assume that the factor demand functions generated by production functions here and below all have positive definite Hessians in their factor arguments (outputs held constant).

It is convenient to begin by considering the very special case of $m = 1$.

Theorem A.5.1: *If the only factor employed in the first sector is a single common factor, then a necessary and sufficient condition for aggregation*

*over the prices of the first sector is that every production function (A.5.1)
be in the form:*

$$g^i[v(i)] = b_i v(i)^\beta \tag{A.5.3}$$

where β is the same for all i.

Proof:[12]   Solve (A.5.1) for $v(i)$ to obtain the factor demand functions

$$f^i(x_i) = v(i) \tag{A.5.4}$$

where $f^i(\cdot)$ is the inverse function of $g^i(\cdot)$. Summing (A.5.4) over i, the
first-sector PPF is given by

$$\sum_{i=1}^{t} f^i(x_i) = v, \tag{A.5.5}$$

recalling that some factor is employed in the production of every output.
Lemma A.3.2 now shows that a necessary and sufficient condition for the
aggregation in question is that the left-hand side of (A.5.5) be homothetic
in the x_i. This makes Lemma A.4.1 applicable with $H^i(\cdot) = f^i(\cdot)$ and the
theorem follows from (A.4.2) with $b_i = 1/C_i$ and $\beta = 1/\alpha$.   ∎

Thus aggregation will be possible in this case if and only if every production function is homogeneous of the same degree and differs from the others
by at most a multiplicative parameter (Hicks-neutral) shift. In particular,
under constant returns, this makes the PPF linear, and relative prices in the
first sector will never change so long as the corresponding outputs are produced making aggregation trivial. As the Rybczynski Theorem suggests,
these results will recur in more interesting and complicated cases.

We now go on to consider the case of more than one common factor,
$m > 1$. As in the proof of Theorem A.5.1, it will be convenient to solve
(A.5.1) for a particular element of $v(i)$, say $v(i)_m$, and obtain the factor-
demand functions:

$$f^i[x_i, \tilde{v}(i)] = v(i)_m, \tag{A.5.6}$$

where $\tilde{v}(i)$ is the subvector of $v(i)$ obtained by deleting $v(i)_m$.

Now, we can consider the derivation of the aggregate technological frontier (A.3.1) as follows. Let the x_i be fixed and minimize v_m given (A.5.6)

---

12. I am indebted to A. Dixit for suggesting the first part of the proof.

and the first $m - 1$ of the factor constraints in (A.5.2). We then wish to aggregate over the x_i (homotheticity comes later). This problem, however, is precisely isomorphic to the standard capital aggregation problem studied in Fisher (1965)[13] with the x_i playing the role of capital, the $\tilde{v}(i)$ the role of labor, and $v(i)_m$ the role of output. We can therefore proceed by adapting the capital-aggregation results to the present case.

There are two possibilities. The first of these, which we shall refer to as the "Nataf case,"[14] is that, for every choice of m, and every i, the factor demand functions (A.5.6) are all additively separable in x_i and $\tilde{v}(i)$, being written as

$$f^i[x_i, \tilde{v}(i)] = H^i(x_i) - M^i[\tilde{v}(i)], \tag{A.5.7}$$

where the form of $H^i(\cdot)$ and $M^i(\cdot)$ depend on the choice of m. The other possibility is that for some i, this cannot be done for at least one choice of m. We begin with the Nataf case and prove:

Theorem A.5.2: *In the Nataf case, aggregation is possible over first-sector prices if and only if every first-sector production function (A.5.1) is in the form:*

$$g^i[v(i)] = b_i \left[\sum_{j=1}^{m} a_j v(i)_j \right]^\beta \tag{A.5.8}$$

where β and the a_j are independent of i.

Proof: It is obvious[15] that since separability (A.5.7) of the factor demand functions must hold for every choice of m, (A.5.6) can be rewritten as

$$H^i(x_i) = \sum_{j=1}^{m} a_j^i v(i)_j. \tag{A.5.9}$$

Then, letting $G^i(\cdot)$ be the inverse function of $H^i(\cdot)$, the production functions (A.5.1) are all in the form

$$g^i[v(i)] = G^i \left[\sum_{j=1}^{m} a_j^i v(i)_j \right]. \tag{A.5.10}$$

13. See Fisher (1969) for an expository discussion of this and related works.
14. See Nataf (1948) and Fisher (1969).
15. A similar proposition occurs in the course of the proof of Theorem A.6.1 below.

Examining marginal rates of substitution between pairs of factors, it is evident that the absence of corner solutions (Lemma A.3.3) implies that the ratios a_j^i/a_k^i ($j, k = 1, \ldots, m$) must be independent of i. It is then a matter of notation to absorb any common multiplicative difference into the definition of $H^i(\cdot)$ and to take the a_j^i as themselves independent of i, dropping the superscript.

Now sum (A.5.9) over i, obtaining the first-sector PPF as:

$$\sum_{i=1}^{t} H^i(x_i) = \sum_{j=1}^{m} a_j v_j. \tag{A.5.11}$$

Lemma A.3.2 now shows that a necessary and sufficient condition for the desired aggregation is that the left-hand side of (A.5.11) be homothetic in the x_i. This makes Lemma A.4.1 applicable (the remaining properties of the $H^i(\cdot)$ present no difficulty) and the theorem follows from (A.5.9) and (A.4.2) with $b_t = 1/C_i$ and $\beta = 1/\alpha$. ∎

One again, aggregation requires all production functions homogeneous of the same degree and with only Hicks-neutral differences. Under constant returns this makes the PPF linear and relative prices unchanging so long as the corresponding outputs are produced. These results carry over to what is perhaps our most straightforward generalization of the Rybczynski Theorem:

Theorem A.5.3: *Suppose that all first-sector production functions (A.5.1) are homothetic. Then aggregation over first-sector prices will be possible if and only if all such production functions are homogeneous of the same degree and differ by at most Hicks-neutral shifts.*

Proof: For the single-factor case, this holds by Theorem A.5.1 and for the Nataf case by Theorem A.5.2. We must therefore take $m > 1$ and consider the non-Nataf case.

Consider the factor demand functions (A.5.6) for that choice of i and m for which separability does not hold. We know from Fisher (1965, p. 267) that aggregation over the x_i will require that for the same choice of m, separability not hold *for any* i. Since a homothetic function is a monotonic transformation of a function homogeneous of degree one, it is easy to see that the factor demand functions (A.5.6) can be written as:

$$f^i[x_i, \tilde{v}(i)] = F^i[H^i(x_i), \tilde{v}(i)] \tag{A.5.12}$$

where the $H^i(\cdot)$ are monotonic with $H^i(0) = 0$ and the $F^i(\cdot, \cdot)$ are all homogeneous of degree one.

This means, however, that all the factor demand functions are in a class isomorphic to the class of capital-generalized, constant-returns (CGCR) production functions introduced in Fisher (1965, pp. 270–272) and Theorem A.4.2 therein applies to the present problem. That theorem, however, which is a generalization of the standard capital aggregation theorem for constant returns,[16] states that aggregation over the x_i will be possible if and only if the $F^i(\cdot, \cdot)$ can all be taken to be the same, differences being absorbed in the $H^i(\cdot)$. Moreover, it is not hard to see[17] that, in that case, the aggregate is the sum of the $H^i(x_i)$ so that Lemma A.4.2 becomes applicable. Putting all this together and solving (A.5.12) for x_i, routine calculations show that aggregation over prices will be possible if and only if we can write:

$$g^i[v(i)] = b_i[N[v(i)]]^\beta \tag{A.5.13}$$

where $N(\cdot)$ and β are independent of i and $N(\cdot)$ is homogeneous of degree one. This proves the theorem.[18] ∎

Theorem A.5.3 covers the leading case of homothetic production functions. It includes, in effect, the earlier two theorems, since in both the scalar and Nataf cases it turns out that aggregation requires homotheticity (indeed, homogeneity). It seems quite possible that the homotheticity requirement of Lemma A.3.2 can only be satisfied if all production functions (A.5.1) are themselves homothetic, but I have been unable to prove this.

This is about as far as it seems possible to go, largely because complete closed-form results for the isomorphic capital aggregation problem are not known. It is an open question whether there exist any non-homothetic cases which fail to generate Rybczynski effects and thus permit aggregation. Most non-homothetic production functions will create such effects regardless of how they are related to each other. This is the equivalent statement to that of capital aggregation theory that most production functions do not permit capital aggregation over any set which contains them (see Fisher (1965), and (1969)).[19]

---

16. Fisher (1965, Theorem A.3.2, p. 268).
17. See Fisher (1969, pp. 559–560).
18. Note that, concerning sufficiency, the form of (A.5.13) eliminates the asymmetry between $\bar{v}(i)$ and $v(i)_m$ and thus presents no problem as far as aggregation in factor demands other than (A.5.12) is concerned.
19. The class of examples given (misprinted) in Fisher (1965, p. 273) appears to lead back to the Nataf case here if it is to apply for every choice of m in the factor demand functions (A.5.6). In

A.6. Sector-Specific But No Output-Specific Factors

These results can be used to study the case in which there are sector-specific factors present. In this section I do so, assuming that such factors are not also output specific; that is, I assume that such factors, u, are allocated across outputs so that marginal revenue products are equalized. The case of corner solutions where such factors are productive only in some but not all of the outputs of the first sector is taken up later. Note that since aggregation will require the ability to aggregate over sub-groups of outputs and prices within the first sector there is no loss of generality in assuming each sector-specific factor used in all outputs and each output-specific factor used in only one.

Obviously, any condition which is sufficient for pure aggregation when there are no sector-specific factors remains so when such factors are present. To see this, observe that the preceding section found necessary and sufficient conditions for the absence of Rybczynski effects when any factor supply changes. Such conditions are certainly sufficient to ensure the absence of such effects when only certain factor supplies (the common factors) change. What is new about the present case is that such strong conditions may not be necessary if we are only interested in ruling out Rybczynski effects from changes in the supply of some but not all factors. Unfortunately, the problem considered in the present section turns out to be very difficult and, except for the case of a single sector-specific factor, I can only give partial answers. Lengthy proofs are omitted. Some readers may wish to skip to the next section.

Write the production functions of the first sector as:

$$x_i = g^i[v(i), u(i)] \tag{A.6.1}$$

where the $g^i(\cdot, \cdot)$ are monotonic in all arguments and $g^i(0, 0) = 0$. Consider solving (A.6.1) for the demand for a particular sector-specific factor, $u(i)_n$, obtaining

$$k^i[x_i, v(i), \tilde{u}(i)] = u(i)_n \tag{A.6.2}$$

---

the present notation that class would involve two factors, v_1 and v_2, with every factor demand function in the from

$$v(i)_2 = f^i[x_i, v(i)_1] = \psi^i[H^i(x_i) + d_i v(i)_1]$$

where $\psi^i(\cdot)$, $H^i(\cdot)$, and d_i can vary with i. It is known (R. Feenstra has shown me some results on this point) that this does not exhaust the set of cases permitting aggregation, although the conditions are very restrictive.

where $\widetilde{u}(i)$ is $u(i)$ with its nth element deleted. Similarly, I shall write the factor demand functions for a particular common factor, $v(i)_m$, as

$$f^i[x_i, \widetilde{v}(i), u(i)] = v(i)_m. \tag{A.6.3}$$

As before, I begin by considering special cases. The case of $m = 1$ turns out to be no longer special unless, in addition, it turns out that every one of the factor demand functions for the sector-specific factors (A.6.2) for every choice of n is separable into the sum of a function of x_i and a function of $\widetilde{u}(i)$ and $v(i)$. I shall refer to this as the "sector-specific Nataf case." It is not hard to show that the factor demands must be linear in $u(i)$ and then to generalize Theorem A.5.1 as:

Theorem A.6.1: *If there is only a single common factor employed in the first sector and the sector-specific Nataf case is present, then a necessary and sufficient condition for aggregation over the prices of the first sector is that every production function (A.6.1) be in the form*

$$g^i[v(i), u(i)] = b_i \left[v(i) + \sum_{k=1}^{n} d_k u(i)_k \right]^{\beta} \tag{A.6.4}$$

where β and the d_k are the same for all i.

The Nataf case considered in the previous section similarly generalizes. Now it becomes the case in which, for every i and every choice of m and n, each of the factor demand functions (A.6.2) and (A.6.3) are additively separable in a function of output and a function of the remaining factors. We shall call this the "general Nataf case." A proof substantially identical to that of Theorem A.5.2 then shows:

Theorem A.6.2: *In the general Nataf case, aggregation is possible over first-sector prices if and only if every first-sector production function is in the form:*

$$g^i[v(i), u(i)] = b_i \left[\sum_{j=1}^{m} a_j v(i)_j + \sum_{k=1}^{n} d_k u(i)_k \right]^{\beta} \tag{A.6.5}$$

where β, the a_j, and the d_k are independent of i.

Suppose then that neither of the special cases so far considered is applicable. Then for some i, there is some factor demand (A.6.2) or (A.6.3), with an element of $v(i)$ on the left-hand side, which cannot be written as the sum of a function of x_i and a function of the factors on the left-hand side. We shall refer to this as the "absence of Nataf-separability" for the particular factor demand. In this case, it is not hard to show that aggregation will only be possible if the corresponding factor demand function is also not Nataf-separable for all i. We may therefore suppose that such Nataf-separability does not hold for any i for the factor demand in question. In what follows, it does not matter whether that factor demand is for a common or a sector-specific factor, and, we shall suppose that it is the latter,[20] in the form (A.6.2), leaving the other case to the reader.

This leads us to consider the generalization of Theorem A.5.3 to the present case. As it turns out, this is not so straightforward, and there are a number of cases to consider.

In the first place, Theorem A.5.3 implies:

Corollary A.6.1: *Suppose that all first-sector production functions, $g^i[v(i), u(i)]$, are homothetic in the $v(i)$ when $u(i) = 0$. Then a necessary condition for aggregation over first-sector prices is that the $g^i[v(i), 0]$ all be homogeneous of the same degree and differ by at most Hicks-neutral shifts.*

Corollary A.6.2: *Suppose that all first-sector production functions, $g^i[v(i), u(i)]$, are homothetic. Then a necessary condition for aggregation over first-sector prices is that the $g^i[v(i), 0]$ all be homogeneous of the same degree and differ by at most Hicks-neutral shifts.*

Now consider the special case in which, for every i, the factor demand function for the particular choice of n under consideration can be written as

$$k^i[x_i, v(i), \widetilde{u}(i)] = K^i(J^i[x_i, \widetilde{u}(i)], v(i)). \qquad (A.6.6)$$

We shall refer to this as the "weakly separable case." Note that it is automatically present if there is only one sector-specific factor.

Now, Lemma A.3.2 can be regarded as stating two requirements for price aggregation. The first of these, the "existence requirement" is given by (A.3.2). The second, the "homotheticity requirement" involves homotheticity of the function $J(x, u)$. It is easiest to consider these requirements separately.

---

20. It *would* matter if no element of $v(i)$ appeared on the left-hand side. This possibility was taken care of in Theorem A.6.1.

Lemma A.6.1: *In the weakly separable case, suppose that every produc-tion function (A.6.1) is homothetic. If the existence requirement of Lemma A.3.2 is satisfied and if aggregate factor demand for u_n can be written as $K[J(x, \tilde{u}), v]$ (the aggregate equivalent of (A.6.11)), then the $K^i(\cdot, \cdot)$ of (A.6.6) can be taken to be independent of i.*

Proof: The aggregation problem involved here is isomorphic to that of ag-gregation over fixed and movable capital goods considered in Fisher (1968). See especially Corollary A.5.2, p. 425.

It is important to realize that the condition of Lemma A.6.1 is not suf-ficient for aggregation. Apart from homotheticity, the existence require-ment involves marginal rates of substitution among the x_i independent of v for *every* factor demand optimum problem. This was not a problem with Theorem A.5.3 above.

We now consider homotheticity in these cases. It is not hard to show.   ∎

Lemma A.6.2: *In the weakly separable case, suppose that all production functions are homothetic. Suppose that aggregation over first-sector prices is possible and that aggregate factor demand for u_n can be written as $K[J(x, \tilde{u}), v]$. Then all production functions (A.6.1) must be in the form*

$$g^i[v(i), u(i)] = Q^i(N[v(i), u(i)_n], \tilde{u}(i)) \tag{A.6.7}$$

where $N(\cdot, \cdot)$ is homogeneous of degree one and independent of i, and

$$Q^i(N[v(i), u(i)_n], 0) = b_i\{N[v(i), u(i)_n]\}^{\beta}. \tag{A.6.8}$$

Unfortunately, Lemma A.6.2 is not directly very interesting because it requires the aggregate equivalent of (A.6.6), that $\tilde{u}$ not enter the factor demand for u_n directly. This would be satisfied if $\tilde{u}$ (or even stronger, u) entered the function $G[J(x, u), u, v]$ of (A.3.2) only through $J(x, u)$ and not directly, but it seems likely that this is not required for aggrega-tion.

We can state, however:

Theorem A.6.3: *Suppose that all production functions (A.6.1) are homo-thetic and that there is only one sector-specific factor. Suppose further that for some i the demand for that factor is not Nataf-separable. Then a neces-sary condition for aggregation over first-sector prices is that all production* *functions (A.6.1) be in the form*

$$g^i[v(i), u(i)] = b_i\{N[v(i), u(i)]\}^\beta \tag{A.6.9}$$

where $N(\cdot, \cdot)$ is homogeneous of degree one and, like β, does not vary over i. That is, all production functions must be homogeneous of the same degree and differ by at most Hicks-neutral shifts.

Proof: In this case $\tilde{u}$ does not exist and Lemma A.6.2 is immediately applicable. Further $Q^i[\cdot, \tilde{u}(i)] = Q^i(\cdot, 0)$. ∎

It is easy to see from Theorem A.5.3:

Corollary A.6.3: *A sufficient condition for aggregation over first-sector prices is that all production functions be in the form (A.6.9).*

Corollary A.6.4: *Suppose that all production functions (A.6.1) are homothetic and that there is only one sector-specific factor. Suppose further that for some i the demand for that factor is not Nataf-separable. Then a necessary and sufficient condition for aggregation over first-sector prices is that all production functions (A.6.1) be homogeneous of the same degree and differ by at most Hicks-neutral shifts.*

There are a number of problems in going beyond these results. First, the aggregate will be the sum of the $J^i[x_i, \tilde{u}(i)]$. The $\tilde{u}(i)$, however, are functions of the elements of u and of all the elements of x (but not of v in this case). This makes each of the $J^i(\cdot, \cdot)$ a function of all the x_i and of u. Even with u held constant, therefore, Lemma A.4.1 does not apply so that further restrictions on the form of the functions $Q^i(\cdot, \cdot)$ are not readily available.

Moreover, one cannot be sure, in general, even if (A.6.7) and (A.6.8) hold, that the solution of (A.6.7) for one of the common factors or for one of the sector-specific factors other than $u(i)_n$ will result in a weakly separable factor demand function. This makes most of our results necessary but not sufficient conditions. Further, even necessary conditions in the weakly separable case, however, are not directly of great interest because of the requirement that separability hold not only for factor demands in the ith production process (A.6.6) but also for aggregate factor demand.

In the non-weakly separable case, closed form conditions for aggregation are not known, even under homotheticity. Some idea of the problems involved may be obtained from the following discussion.

Consider the demand for a sector-specific factor (A.6.2). The Leontief conditions for aggregation require that the marginal rates of substitution between any pair of the x_i with optimized demand for u_n constant must be independent of v when the $v(i)$ *and* the $\tilde{u}(i)$ are adjusted optimally. This is certainly a weaker requirement than the requirement that such independence hold when the $v(i)$ are optimally adjusted and the $\tilde{u}(i)$ arbitrary *and* that such marginal rates of substitution be independent of the $\tilde{u}(i)$. Imposing that requirement, however, produces a problem isomorphic to that of capital aggregation with some capitals (the x_i) in the aggregate and some [the $\tilde{u}(i)$] left out. This problem was considered in Fisher (1965, pp. 274–277) and complete closed form results are not known for it. *A fortiori*, we shall not be able to obtain complete closed form results for our problem.

An example may help here. Suppose that there are only two sector-specific factors and a single common factor. Suppose further that every production function (A.6.1) is in the form:

$$g^i[v(i), u(i)] = D^i(S^i[u(i)] + c_i v(i)), \qquad \text{(A.6.10)}$$

where the $D^i(\cdot)$, $S^i(\cdot)$, and c_i can all vary with i. Then the factor-demand functions for either sector-specific factor are in the form:

$$u(i)_n = L^i[H^i(x_i) - c_i v(i), \tilde{u}(i)]. \qquad \text{(A.6.11)}$$

It can be verified by direct computation that the conditions of Theorem A.5.1 of Fisher (1965) are satisfied[21] so that at least the existence requirements of Lemma A.3.2 are met. Whether or not the homotheticity requirement is also met depends on the nature of the aggregate, and this is not known. Note that (A.6.10) can be homothetic or even constant returns, although it would then be further restricted by Corollary A.6.2. Note further that common factor indispensability would rule it out. I have not found it possible to go further along these lines.[22]

---

21. The statement of the theorem there should have "(5.8)" in place of (A.5.10), although it makes no substantive difference. Note that (A.6.11) with $\tilde{u}(i)$ constant involves the same class of examples as that given in footnote 19 above.
22. Nor have I found it profitable to drop weak separability at the aggregate level while retaining (A.6.6).

A.7. Output-Specific Factors and Co-Production

I now take up the two matters which have been postponed, the introduction of output-specific factors and the case in which a single production function produces more than one output.

Begin with the case of output-specific factors. The amounts of such factors can be arbitrary; there are no Leontief conditions involved in their factor demands; and aggregation must hold for all such amounts. Hence, such factors act as parameters of the production functions. For given amounts of such factors, all of our earlier results must apply.

Unfortunately, this is not so simple a matter as it appears. If a production function is homothetic in all the factors, it will generally (not always) fail to be so in the remaining factors when one or more are held constant. We have nice closed-form results only for homothetic cases, however. It follows that simply holding output-specific factors constant and applying earlier results only leads to definite answers in a rather restricted class of cases, even given homotheticity. Although Corollaries A.6.1 and A.6.2 above obviously apply here also.

The nicest of the new results is a generalization of Theorem A.5.3 when all sector-specific factors are also output-specific.

Corollary A.7.1: *Suppose that all sector-specific factors are also output specific. Suppose further that every production function (A.6.1) is homothetic in the elements of $u(i)$ for every value of $v(i)$. Then a necessary and sufficient condition for aggregation over the prices of the first sector is that all such production functions be in the form*

$$g^i[v(i), u(i)] = b_i[u(i)]\{N[v(i)]\}^\beta \qquad (A.7.1)$$

where $N(\cdot)$ and β are independent of i and $N(\cdot)$ is homogeneous of degree one.[23]

Note that for given amounts of the sector-specific factors this reduces to Theorem A.5.3. In particular, for constant returns it will again be the case that relative first-sector prices do not vary.[24] Unfortunately, the conditions

---

23. Note that for the $u(i)$ to be output specific in (A.7.1), they must be non-zero in different components for each i.
24. For constant returns, the $b_i(\cdot)$ of (A.7.1) must be homogeneous of degree $1 - \beta$. This means that if the ith production function has a single output-specific factor it cannot be in this class.

of Corollary A.7.1 are much stronger than simple homotheticity, so it is of
interest to look further.

There is another class of special cases which can be generated in a different way. Suppose that in (A.3.2), the output-specific components of u
only entered through $J(x, u)$ and not directly as arguments of $G(\cdot, \cdot, \cdot)$.
Then we could think of (A.3.2) as involving aggregation over outputs *and*
output-specific factors. Exploring this possibility, however, is obviously
equivalent to supposing that there are no output-specific factors but that
certain production functions involve more than one output. I now turn to
that problem and shall not give the interpretation of the results in terms of
output-specific factors explicitly.[25]

Denote the vector of outputs produced by the ith production process by
x^i, using the superscript instead of the subscript. For simplicity, we assume
no sector-specific factors, although not all results depend on this. We begin
by writing the production frontiers for this case as:

$$F^i[x^i, v(i)] = 0, \qquad\qquad (A.7.2)$$

with $F^i(\cdot, \cdot)$ monotonic in $v(i)$ and $F^i(0, 0) = 0$.

We prove:

Theorem A.7.1: *A necessary condition for aggregation over the prices of
the first sector is that the production frontiers (A.7.2) can be rewritten
as:*

$$H^i(x^i) = g^i[v(i)], \qquad\qquad (A.7.3)$$

where $H^i(\cdot)$ is homothetic.

Proof: If there is a single factor this is trivial. If there is more than one
factor, solve (A.7.2) for the factor demand for $v(i)_m$. Aggregation in the
resulting optimum problem in which v_m is to be minimized is isomorphic
to the capital aggregation problem in which each production function has
more than one capital and these are all to be included in the aggregate. The
existence of (A.7.3) follows from Fisher (1965, p. 280).   ∎

Moreover, observe that aggregation must remain possible when some
outputs are zero. Then (A.7.3) is the equivalent of (A.3.2) when only the

---

25. Much of this development is similar to that of the weakly separable case of Section 6, however.

ith production process is active. Homotheticity of the $H^i(\cdot)$ follows by similar reasoning.

This result makes it relatively easy to proceed since we can treat each production process (A.7.3) as having a single output, $H^i(x^i)$, and aggregate over such outputs. Further, since the $H^i(\cdot)$ will have to remain homothetic when all elements of x_i save one are set equal to zero, our results derived from Lemma A.4.1 will stand as well.

I shall not spell out all those results in formal detail. In general, for the cases considered in Theorems, A.5.1–A.5.3, which include homotheticity of the $g^i(\cdot)$ and thus constant returns, it turns out to be necessary and sufficient that the $g^i(\cdot)$ all be homogeneous of the same degree with only Hicks-neutral differences. For constant returns this will make the relative prices of the $H^i(\cdot)$ constant, so to speak, but it will no longer invariably follow that relative prices of actual outputs in the first sector should be so.

In terms of the Rybczynski Theorem this last result implies that even when production functions involve more than one output Rybczynski effects are to be expected under constant returns (unless *all* outputs are jointly produced).

References

Adelman, I. and Z. Griliches. (1961): "On an Index of Quality Change," *Journal of the American Statistical Association*, 56:535–548.

Afriat, S. N. (1977): *The Price Index*. Cambridge: Cambridge University Press.

Allais, M. (1943): *A la Recherche d'une Discipline Économique*, vol. 1. Paris: Ateliers Industria.

Allen, R. C. and W. E. Diewert. (1981): "Direct Versus Implicit Superlative Index Number Formulae," *Review of Economics and Statistics*, 63:430–435.

Allen, R. G. D. (1935): "Some Observations on the Theory and Practice of Price Index Numbers," *Review of Economic Studies*, 3:57–66.

Allen, R. G. D. (1938): *Mathematical Analysis for Economists*. London: Macmillan.

Allen, R. G. D. (1949): "The Economic Theory of Index Numbers," *Economica, New Series*, 16:197–203.

Allen, R. G. D. (1963): "Price Index Numbers," *Review of the International Statistical Institute*, 31:281–297.

Allen, R. G. D. (1975): *Index Numbers in Theory and Practice*. London: Macmillan.

Antonelli, G. B. (1886): *Sulla Teoria Matematica della Economia Pura*. Reprinted (1951) in *Giornali delli Economisti*, 10:233–263.

Archibald, R. (1975): "On the Theory of Industrial Price Measurement: Input Price Indexes," Working Paper No. 48, Bureau of Labor Statistics, Washington, D.C.

Archibald, R. (1977): "On the Theory of Industrial Price Measurement: Output Price Indexes," *Annals of Economic and Social Measurement*, 6:57–72.

Arrow, K. J. (1958): "The Measurement of Price Changes," in *The Relationship of Prices to Economic Stability and Growth*, U.S. Congress, Joint Economic Committee, pp. 77–88. Washington, D.C: Government Printing Office.

Arrow, K. J. (1974): "The Measurement of Real Value Added," in *Nations and Households in Economic Growth*, P. A. David and M. Reder (eds.), pp. 3–19. New York: Academic Press.

Balk, B.M. (1995): "Axiomatic Price Index Theory: A Survey," *International Statistical Review*, 63:69–93.

Banerjee, K. S. (1975): *Cost of Living Index Numbers: Practice, Precision and Theory.* New York: Marcel Dekker.

Becker, G. S. (1981): *A Treatise on the Family.* Cambridge, MA: Harvard University Press.

Bergson, A. (1961): *National Income of the Soviet Union Since 1928.* Cambridge, MA: Harvard University Press.

Berndt, E. R. and L. R. Christensen. (1974): "Testing for the Existence of a Consistent Aggregate Index of Labor Inputs," *American Economic Review*, 64:391–404.

Berndt, E. R. and L. R. Christensen. (1983): "Quality Adjustment, Hedonics, and Modern Empirical Demand Analysis," in *Price Level Measurement: Proceedings from a Conference Sponsored by Minister of Supply and Services Canada*, W. E. Diewert and C. Montmarquette (eds.), pp. 817–863. Ottawa: Minister of Supply and Services Canada.

Berndt, E. R., Z. Griliches, and J. G. Rosett. (1983): "Auditing the Producer Price Index: Micro Evidence from Prescription Pharmaceutical Preparations," *Journal of Business & Economic Statistics*, 11:251–264.

Blackorby, C. and D. Donaldson. (1983): "Preference Diversity and Aggregate Economic Cost-of-Living Indexes," in *Price Level Measurement: Proceedings From a Conference Sponsored by Minister of Supply and Services Canada*, W. E. Diewert and C. Montmarquette (eds.), pp. 373–409. Ottawa: Minister of Supply and Services Canada. Reprinted (1990) in *Price Level Measurement*, W. E. Diewert (ed.), pp. 285–320. Amsterdam: North-Holland.

Blackorby, C. and D. Primont. (1980): "Index Numbers and Consistency in Aggregation," *Journal of Economic Theory*, 22:87–98.

Blackorby, C., D. Primont, and R. R. Russell. (1975): "Budgeting, Decentralization, and Aggregation," *Annals of Economic and Social Measurement*, 4:23–44.

Blackorby, C., D. Primont, and R. R. Russell. (1977): "Dual Price and Quantity Aggregation," *Journal of Economic Theory*, 14:130–148.

Blackorby, C., D. Primont, and R. R. Russell. (1978): *Duality, Separability and Functional Structure: Theory and Economic Applications.* New York: American Elsevier.

Blackorby, C. and R. R. Russell. (1978): "Indices and Subindices of the Cost of Living and the Standard of Living," *International Economic Review*, 19:229–240.

Blackorby, C. and W. Schworm. (1984a): "Consistent Aggregation in Competitive Economies," Discussion Paper No. 8446, Center for Operations Research and Econometrics, Université Catholique de Louvain, Louvain-la-Neuve, Belgium.

Blackorby, C. and W. Schworm. (1984b): "The Structure of Economies with Aggregate Measures of Capital: A Complete Characterization," *Review of Economic Studies*, 51:633–650.

Bowley, A. L. (1908): "Wages, Nominal and Real," in *Dictionary of Political Economy*, vol. 3, R. H. I. Palgrave (ed.), pp. 638–641. London: Macmillan.

Bowley, A. L. (1901): *Elements of Statistics.* London: P. S. King.

Bowley, A. L. (1919): "The Measurement of Changes in the Cost of Living," *Journal of the Royal Statistical Society*, 82:343–372.

Bowley, A. L. (1921): "An Index of the Physical Volume of Production," *Economic Journal*, 31:196–205.

Bowley, A. L. (1923): "Review of *The Making of Index Numbers* by Irving Fisher," *Economic Journal*, 33:90–94.

Bowley, A. L. (1928): "Notes on Index Numbers," *Economic Journal*, 38:216–237.

Bureau of Labor Statistics. (1983): *Trends in Multifactor Productivity 1948–1981.* Bulletin 2178, Washington, D.C.

Burmeister, E. and R. Dobell (1970): *Mathematical Theories of Economic Growth.* London: Macmillan.

Buscheguennce, S. S. (1925): "Sur une Classe des Hypersurfaces. A Propos de 'l'Index Idéal' de M. Irving Fisher," *Recueil Mathématique* XXXII, 4, Moscow, USSR.

Carli, G. R. (1764): "Del Valore e della Proporzione de' Metalli Monetati con i Generi in Italia Prima delle Scoperte dell' Indie col Confronto del Valore e della Proporzione de' Tempi Nostri," in *Opere scelte di Carli*, vol. 1, pp. 299–366. Milano.

Caves, D. W., L. R. Christensen, and W. E. Diewert. (1982a): "The Economic Theory of Index Numbers and the Measurement of Input, Output and Productivity," *Econometrica*, 50:1393–1414.

Caves, D. W., L. R. Christensen, and W. E. Diewert. (1982b): "Multilateral Comparisons of Output, Input and Productivity using Superlative Index Numbers," *The Economic Journal*, 92:73–86.

Christensen, L. R. and D. W. Jorgenson. (1970): "U.S. Real Product and Real Factor Input, 1929–1967," *Review of Income and Wealth*, 16:19–50.

Copeland, M. A. (1937): "Concepts of National Income," in *Studies in Income and Wealth*, pp. 3–63. vol. 1. New York: National Bureau of Economic Research.

Court, A. T. (1939): "Hedonic Price indexes with Automobile Examples," in *The Dynamics of Automobile Demand*, pp. 95–117. New York: General Motors Corporation.

Court, A. T. (1942–1943): "Production Cost Indices," *Review of Economic Studies*, 10:28–42.

Crowe, W. R. (1965): *Index Numbers – Theory and Applications*. London: MacDonald & Evans.

David, P. A. (1966): "Measuring Real Net Output: A Proposed Index," *Review of Economics and Statistics*, 48:419–425.

Davies, G. R. (1924): "The Problem of a Standard Index Number Formula," *Journal of the American Statistical Association*, 19:180–188.

Deaton, A. and J. Muellbauer. (1983): *Economics and Consumer Behavior*. Cambridge: Cambridge University Press.

Debreu, G. (1951): "The Coefficient of Resource Utilization," *Econometrica*, 19:273–292. Reprinted (1983) in *Mathematical Economics: Twenty Papers of Gerard Debreu*, G. Debreu, pp. 30–49. Cambridge: Cambridge University Press.

Debreu, G. (1954): "Numerical Representations of Technical Change," *Metroeconomica*, 6:45–54.

Denny, M. (1980): Comment on Diewert's "Aggregation Problems in the Measurement of Capital," in *The Measurement of Capital*, D. Usher. (ed.), pp. 528–538. D. Usher. Chicago: The University of Chicago Press.

de Scitovsky, T. (1941): "A Note on Welfare Propositions in Economics," *Review of Economic Studies*, 9:77–88.

Diewert, W. E. (1976): "Exact and Superlative Index Numbers," *Journal of Econometrics*, 4:114–145. Reprinted (1993) in *Essays in Index Number Theory*, W. E. Diewert and A. O. Nakamura (eds.), pp. 223–252. Amsterdam: North-Holland.

Diewert, W. E. (1978a): "Hicks' Aggregation Theorem and the Existence of a Real Value Added Function," in *Production Economics: A Dual Approach to Theory and Applications*, vol. 2, M. Fuss and D. McFadded (eds.), pp. 17–51. Amsterdam: North-Holland. Reprinted (1993) in *Essays in Index Number Theory*, W. E. Diewert and A. O. Nakamura (eds.), pp. 435–470. Amsterdam: North-Holland.

Diewert, W. E. (1978b): "Superlative Index Numbers and Consistency in Aggregation," *Econometrica*, 46: 883–900. Reprinted (1993) in *Essays in Index Number Theory*, W. E. Diewert and A. O. Nakamura (eds.), pp. 253–273. Amsterdam: North-Holland.

Diewert, W. E. (1980): "Aggregation Problems in the Measurement of Capital," in *The Measurement of Capital*, D. Usher (ed.), pp. 433–528. Chicago: University of Chicago Press.

Diewert, W. E. (1981a): "The Economic Theory of Index Numbers: A Survey," in *Essays in the Theory and Measurement of Consumer Behavior in Honour of Sir Richard Stone*, A. Deaton (ed.), pp. 163–208. London: Cambridge University Press. Reprinted (1993) in *Essays in Index Number Theory*, W. E. Diewert and A. O. Nakamura (eds.), pp. 163–208. Amsterdam: North-Holland.

Diewert, W. E. (1981b): "The Measurement of Deadweight Loss Revisited," *Econometrica*, 49:1225–1244.

Diewert, W. E. (1982): "Duality Approaches to Microeconomic Theory," in *Handbook of Mathematical Economics*, vol. II, K. J. Arrow and M. D. Intriligator (eds.), pp. 535–599. Amsterdam: North Holland. Reprinted (1993) in *Essays in Index Number Theory*, vol. I, W. E. Diewert and A. O. Nakamura (eds.), pp. 105–175. Amsterdam: North-Holland.

Diewert, W. E. (1983a): "The Theory of the Cost-of-Living Index and the Measurement of Welfare Change," in *Price Level Measurement*, W. E. Diewert and C. Montmarquetee (eds.), pp. 163–233. Ottawa: Minister of Supply and Services Canada. Reprinted (1990) in *Price Level Measurement*, W. E. Diewert (ed.), pp. 79–148. Amsterdam: North-Holland.

Diewert, W. E. (1983b): "The Theory of the Output Price Index and the Measurement of Real Output Change," in *Price Level Measurement*, W. E. Diewert and C. Montmarquette (eds.), pp. 1049–1113. Ottawa: Minister of Supply and Services Canada.

Diewert, W. E. (1987): "Index Numbers," in *The New Palgrave: A Dictionary of Economics*, vol. 2, J. Eatwell, M. Milgate, and P. Newman (eds.), pp. 767–780. London: Macmillan. Reprinted (1993) in *Essays in Index Number Theory*, W. E. Diewert and A. O. Nakamura (eds.), pp. 71–104. Amsterdam: North-Holland.

Diewert, W. E. (ed). (1990): *Price Level Measurement*. Amsterdam: North-Holland.

Diewert, W. E. (1992a): "Fisher Ideal Output, Input and Productivity Indexes Revisited," *Journal of Productivity Analysis*, 3:211–248.

Diewert, W. E. (1992b): "The Measurement of Productivity," *Bulletin of Economic Research*, 44:163–198.

Diewert, W. E. (1993a): "Essays in Index Number Theory: An Overview of Volume I," in *Essays in Index Number Theory*, W. E. Diewert and A. O. Nakamura (eds.), pp. 1–31. Amsterdam: North-Holland.

Diewert, W. E. (1993b): "The Early History of Price Index Research," in *Essays in Index Number Theory*, W. E. Diewert and A. O. Nakamura (eds.), pp. 33–65. Amsterdam: North-Holland.

Diewert, W. E. and C. Montmarquette (eds.). (1983): *Price Level Measurement: Proceedings from a Conference Sponsored by Minister of Supply and Services Canada*. Ottawa: Minister of Supply and Services Canada.

Diewert, W. E. and C. J. Morrison. (1986): "Adjusting Output and Productivity Indexes for Changes in the Terms of Trade," *The Economic Journal*, 96:657–679.

Diewert, W. E. and A. O. Nakamura (eds.). (1993): *Essays in Index Number Theory*, Amsterdam: North-Holland.

Divisia, F. (1925): "l'Indice Monétaire et la Théorie de la Monnaie," *Revue d'Économie Politique*, 39:842–861, 980–1008, 1121–1151.

Divisia, F. (1926): *l'Indice Monétaire et la Théorie de la Monnaie*. Paris: Société anonyme du Recueil Sirey. Published as Divisia (1925).

Divisia, F. (1928): *Économique Rationelle*. Paris: G. Doin.

Edgeworth, F. Y. (1888): "Some New Methods of Measuring Variation in General Prices," *Journal of the Royal Statistical Society*, 51:346–368.

Edgeworth, F. Y. (1896): "A Defence of Index-Numbers," *Economic Journal*, 6:132–142.

Edgeworth, F. Y. (1925a): *Papers Relating to Political Economy*, vol. 1. New York: Burt Franklin.

Edgeworth, F. Y. (1925b): "The Plurality of Index Numbers," *Economic Journal*, 35:379–388.

Eichhorn, W. (1973): "Zur axiomatischen Theorie des Preisindex," *Demonstratio Mathematica*, 6:561–573.

Eichhorn, W. (1976): "Fisher's Tests Revisited," *Econometrica*, 44:247–256.

Eichhorn, W. (1978): "What is an Economic Index? An Attempt of an Answer," in *Theory and Applications of Economic Indices*, Proceedings of an International Symposium held at the University of Karlsruhe April–June 1976, W. Eichhorn, R. Henn, O. Opitz, and R. W. Shephard (eds.), pp. 3–42. Würzburg: Physica-Verlag.

Eichhorn, W., R. Henn, O. Opitz, and R. W. Shephard (eds.). (1978): *Theory and Applications of Economic Indices*, Proceedings of an International Symposium held at the University of Karlsruhe April–June 1976. Würzburg: Physica-Verlag.

Eichhorn, W. and J. Voeller. (1976): *Theory of the Price Index: Fisher's Test Approach and Generalizations*. Lecture Notes in Economics and Mathematical Systems, vol. 140. Berlin: Springer-Verlag.

Eichhorn, W. and J. Voeller. (1983): "Axiomatic Foundation of Price Indexes and Purchasing Power Parities," in *Price Level Measurement: Proceedings from a Conference Sponsored by Minister of Supply and Services Canada*, W. E. Diewert and C. Montmarquette (eds.), pp. 411–450. Ottawa: Minister of Supply and Services Canada.

Epstein, L. G. (1981): "Generalized Duality and Integrability," *Econometrica*, 49:655–678.

Ethier, W. (1974): "Some of the Theorems of International Trade with Many Goods and Factors," *Journal of International Economics*, 4:199–206.

Färe, R. (1975): "A Note on Ray-Homogeneous and Ray-Homothetic Production Functions," *Swedish Journal of Economics*, 77:366–372.

Färe, R. (1978a): "Production Theory Dualities for Optimally Realized Values, " in *Theory and Applications of Economic Indices*, Proceedings of an International Symposium held at the University of Karlsruhe April–June 1976, W. Eichhorn, R. Henn, O. Opitz, and R. W. Shephard (eds.), pp. 657–666. Würzburg: Physica-Verlag.

Färe, R. (1978b): "Separability and Index Properties of Ray-Homothetic Dynamic Production Structures," in *Theory and Applications of Economic Indices*, Proceedings of an International Symposium held at the University of Karlsruhe April–June 1976, W. Eichhorn, R. Henn, O. Opitz, and R. W. Shephard (eds.), pp. 357–380. Würzburg: Physica-Verlag.

Färe, R. and S. Grosskopf. (1983): "Measuring Congestion in Production," *Zeitschrift für Nationalökonomie*, 43:257–271.

Färe, R. and S. Grosskopf. (1990): "A Distance Function Approach to Price Efficiency," *Journal of Public Economics*, 43:123–126.

Färe, R., S. Grosskopf, and C. A. K. Lovell. (1985): *The Measurement of Efficiency of Production*. Boston: Kluwer-Nijhoff.

Färe, R., S. Grosskopf, and C. A. K. Lovell. (1994): *Production Frontiers*. Cambridge: Cambridge University Press.

Färe, R., S. Grosskopf, and J. Nelson. (1990): "On Price Efficiency," *International Economic Review*, 31:709–720.

Färe, R. and C. A. K. Lovell. (1978): "Measuring the Technical Efficiency of Production," *Journal of Economic Theory*, 19:150–162.

Färe, R. and T. Mitchell (1993): "Multiple Outputs and 'Homotheticity'," Southern Economic Journal, 60:287–296.

Färe, R. and D. Primont (1995a): Multi-Output Production and Duality: Theory and Applications, Dordrecht: Kluwer Academic Publishers.

Färe, R. and D. Primont (1995b): "On Inverse Homotheticity," Bulletin of Economic Research 47:161–166.

Färe, R. and R. W. Shephard (1977): "Ray-Homothetic Production Functions," *Econometrica*, 45:133–146.

Farrell, M. J. (1957): "The Measurement of Production Efficiency," *Journal of the Royal Statistical Society*, 120 (Series A):253–281.

Feenstra, R. C., J. R. Markusen, and W. Zeile (1992): "Accounting for Growth with New Inputs: Theory and Evidence," *American Economic Review*, 82:415–421.

Fisher, F. M. (1965): "Embodied Technical Change and the Existence of an Aggregate Capital Stock," *Review of Economic Studies*, 32:263–288.

Fisher, F. M. (1968): "Embodied Technology and the Aggregation of Fixed and Movable Capital Goods," *Review of Economic Studies*, 35:417–428.

Fisher, F. M. (1969): "The Existence of Aggregate Production Functions," *Econometrica*, 37:553–577.

Fisher, F. M. (1982): "Aggregate Production Functions Revisited: The Mobility of Capital and the Rigidity of Thought," *Review of Economic Studies*, 49:615–626.

Fisher, F. M. (1985): "Production-Theoretic Input Price Indices and the Measurement of Real Aggregate Input Use," Working Paper No. 384, Department of Economics, M.I.T., Cambridge, MA.

Fisher, F. M. (1988): "Production-Theoretic Input Price Indices and the Measurement of Real Aggregate Input Use," in *Measurement in Economics*, W. Eichhorn (ed.), pp. 87–98. Heidelberg: Physica-Verlag.

Fisher, F. M. (1993): *Aggregation: Aggregate Production Functions and Related Topics*, Cambridge, MA: M.I.T. Press.

Fisher, F. M. (1995): "The Production-Theoretic Measurement of Input Price and Quantity Indices," *Journal of Econometrics*, 65:155–174.

Fisher, F. M. and Z. Griliches. (1995): "Aggregate Price Indices, New Goods, and Generics," *Quarterly Journal of Economics*, 110:229–244.

Fisher, F. M. and K. Shell. (1968): "Taste and Quality Change in the Pure Theory of the True Cost-of-Living Index," in *Value, Capital and Growth: Papers in Honour of Sir John Hicks*, J. N. Wolfe (ed.), pp. 97–139. Edinburgh: Edinburgh University Press. Reprinted (1971) in *Price Indexes and Quality Change*, Z. Griliches (ed.), pp. 16–54. Cambridge, MA: Harvard University Press. Also appears (1972) as Essay I in *Economic Theory of Price Indices: Two Essays on the Effects of Taste, Quality and Technological Change*, F. M. Fisher and K. Shell, pp. 1–48. New York: Academic Press.

Fisher, F. M. and K. Shell. (1970): "The Pure Theory of the National Output Deflator," Working Paper No. 59, M.I.T., Department of Economics, Cambridge, MA. Reprinted (1972) in *The Economic Theory of Price Indices*, F. M. Fisher and K. Shell, pp. 49–113. New York: Academic Press.

Fisher, F. M. and K. Shell. (1972): *The Economic Theory of Price Indices: Two Essays on the Effects of Taste, Quality, and Technological Change*, New York: Academic Press.

Fisher, F. M. and K. Shell. (1979): "The Theory of Price Indices and Subindices for Output and Input Deflation: Progress Report," Working Paper No. 79-02, Center for Analytic Research in Economics and the Social Sciences, University of Pennsylvania, PA.

Fisher, F. M. and K. Shell. (1981): "Output Price Indices," Working Paper No. 81-05, Center for Analytic Research in Economics and the Social Sciences, University of Pennsylvania, PA.

Fisher, I. (1911): *The Purchasing Power of Money*. New York: Macmillan.

Fisher, I. (1921): "The Best Form of Index Number," *Journal of the American Statistical Association*, 17:533–537.

Fisher, I. (1922): *The Making of Index Numbers*. Boston: Houghton Mifflin.

Fisher, I. (1923): "Professor Bowley on Index Numbers," *Economic Journal*, 33:246–251.

Fixler, D. and K.D. Zieschang (1992): "Incorporating Ancillary Measures of Process and Quality Change into a Superlative Productivity Index," *Journal of Productivity Analysis*, 2: 245–267.

Fourgeaud, C. and A. Nataf. (1959): "Consommation en Prix et Revenue Réels et Théorie des Choix," *Econometrica*, 27:329–354.

Frisch, R. (1930): "Necessary and Sufficient Conditions Regarding the Form on an Index Number Which Shall Meet Certain of Fisher's Tests," *Journal of the American Statistical Association*, 25:397–406.

Frisch, R. (1936): "Annual Survey of General Economic Theory: The Problem of Index Numbers," *Econometrica*, 4:1–38.

Gillingham, R. (1974): "A Conceptual Framework for the Consumer Price Index," *Proceedings of the Business and Economic Statistics Section, American Statistical Association*, pp. 246–252.

Gillingham, R. (1975): "A Conceptual Framework for the Consumer Price Index," Mimeogr. Bureau of Labor Statistics, Washington, D.C.

Gorman, W. M. (1968): "Measuring the Quantities of Fixed Factors," in *Value, Capital and Growth: Papers in Honour of Sir John Hicks*, J. N. Wolfe (ed.), pp. 141–172. Chicago: Aldine Publishing Co.

Green, J. A. J. (1964): *Aggregation in Economic Analysis*. Princeton, N. J.: Princeton University Press.

Griliches, Z. (1964): "Notes on the Measurement of Price and Quality Changes," in *Models of Income Determination*, Studies in Income and Wealth, vol. 28, pp. 301–404. Princeton, NJ: National Bureau of Economic Research.

Griliches, Z. (1967): "Hedonic Price Indexes Revisited: Some Notes on the State of the Art," in *Proceedings of the Business and Economic Statistics Section*, pp. 324–332, American Statistical Association, Business and Economics Section, Washington, D.C.

Griliches, Z. (1971a): "Introduction: Hedonic Prices Revisited," in *Price Indexes and Quality Change: Studies in New Methods of Measurement*, Z. Griliches, (ed.), pp. 3–15. Cambridge, MA: Harvard University Press.

Griliches, Z. (1971b): "Hedonic Price Indexes for Automobiles: An Econometric Analysis of Quality Change," in *Price Indexes and Quality Change: Studies in New Methods of Measurement*, Z. Griliches (ed.), pp. 55–77. Cambridge, MA: Harvard University Press.

Griliches, Z. (ed.). (1971c): *Price Indexes and Quality Change: Studies in New Methods of Measurement*, Cambridge, MA: Harvard University Press.

Griliches, Z. (1988): "Hedonic Price Indexes and the Measurement of Capital and Productivity: Some Historical Reflections," Paper Presented at the 50th Anniversary Meeting of the Conference on Income and Wealth, Washington, D.C., May 12.

Griliches, Z. (1990): "Hedonic Price Indexes and the Measurement of Capital and Productivity: Some Historical Reflections," in *Fifty Years in Economic Measurement 54*, E. R. Berndt and J. E. Triplett (eds.), pp. 185–202. Chicago: University of Chicago Press.

Griliches, Z. (1996): "The Discovery of the Residual: A Historical Note," *Journal of Economic Literature*, 34:1324–1330.

Haberler, G. (1927): *Der Sinn der Indexzahlen*. Tübingen: J. C. B. Mohr.

Hicks, J. R. (1932): *The Theory of Wages*. London: Macmillan.

Hicks, J. R. (1939): "The Foundations of Welfare Economics," *Economic Journal*, 49:696–712.

Hicks, J. R. (1940): "The Valuation of the Social Income," *Economica*, 7:105–124.

Hicks, J. R. (1941–1942): "Consumers' Surplus and Index-Numbers," *Review of Economic Studies*, 9:126–137.

Hicks, J. R. (1945–1946): "The Generalised Theory of Consumers' Surplus," *Review of Economic Studies*, 13:68–74.

Hicks, J. R. (1946): *Value and Capital. An Inquiry into Some Fundamental Principles of Economic Theory*. Oxford: Clarendon Press.

Hicks, J. R. (1958): "The Measurement of Real Income," *Oxford Economic Papers*, 10:125–162.

Hicks, J. R. (1961): "Measurement of Capital in Relation to the Measurement of Other Economic Aggregates," in *The Theory of Capital*, F. A. Lutz and D. C. Hague (eds.). London: Macmillan.

Hicks, J. R. (1975): "The Scope and Status of Welfare Economics," *Oxford Economic Papers*, 27: 307–326.

Hicks, J. R. (1981): *Wealth and Welfare*. Cambridge, MA: Harvard University Press.

Hulten, C. R. (1973): "Divisia Index Numbers," *Econometrica*, 41:1017–1025.

Jevons, W. S. (1865): "Variations of Prices and the Value of Currency since 1792," *Journal of the Royal Statistical Society*, 28:294–325.

Jorgenson, D. W. and Z. Griliches. (1967): "The Explanation of Productivity Change," *Review of Economic Studies*, 34:249–283.

Jorgenson, D. W., L. J. Lau, and T. M. Stoker. (1980): "Welfare Comparison Under Exact Aggregation," *American Economic Review*, 70:268–272.

Jorgenson, D. W. and D. T. Slesnick. (1983): "Individual and Social Cost-of-Living Indexes," in *Price Level Management*, W. E. Diewert and C. Montmarquette (eds.), pp. 241–323. Ottawa: Minister of Supply and Services Canada.

Kemp, M. and H. Wan. (1976): "Relatively Simple Generalizations of the Stopler–Samuelson and Samuelson–Rybczynski Theorems," in *Three Topics in the Theory of International Trade*, pp. 49–59. New York: M. Kemp. American Elsevier.

Klein, L. R. and H. Rubin. (1947–1948): "A Constant-Utility Index of the Cost of Living," *Review of Economic Studies*, 15:84–87.

Klock, T. and G. M. de Wit. (1961): "Best Linear Unbiased Index Numbers," *Econometrica*, 29:602–616.

Konüs, A. A. (1924): "The Problem of the True Index of the Cost-of-Living" (1939 translation), *Econometrica*, 7:10–29.

Konüs, A. A. (1968): "The Theory of the Consumer Price Indexes and the Problem of the Comparison of the Cost of Living in Time and Space," in *The Social Sciences: Problems and Orientations*, pp. 93–107. Paris: UNESCO.

Konüs, A. A. and S. S. Byushgens. (1926): "K Probleme Pokumatelnoi cili Deneg" (English translation of Russian title: "On the Problem of the Purchasing Power of Money"), *Voprosi Konyunkturi* (supplement to the *Economical Bulletin of the Conjuncture Institute*), 2:151–172.

Koopmans, T. C. (1951): "An Analysis of Production as an Efficient Combination of

Activities," in *Activity Analysis of Production and Allocations*, T. C. Koopmans (ed.). Cowles Commission for Research in Economics Monograph No. 13. New York: Wiley.

Koopmans, T. C. (1957): *Three Essays on the State of Economic Science*. New York: McGraw Hill.

Laspeyres, E. (1863): *Geschichte der Volkswirtschaftlichen Anschauungen der Niederländer und ihrer Literatur zur Zeit der Republik*. Leipzig: S. Hirzel.

Laspeyres, E. (1871): "Die Berechnung einer mittleren Waarenpreissteigerung," *Jahrbücher für Nationalükonomie und Statistik*, 16:296–314.

Lau, L. J. (1969): "Duality and the Structure of Utility Functions," *Journal of Economic Theory*, 1:374–396.

Lau, L. J. (1974): "Applications of Duality Theory: Comments," in *Frontiers of Quantitative Economics*, vol. II, M. D. Intriligator and D. A. Kendrick (eds.), pp. 176–199. Amsterdam: North Holland.

Lau, L. J. (1979): "On Exact Index Numbers," *Review of Economics and Statistics*, 61:73–82.

Lau, L. J. (1982): "A Note on the Fundamental Theorem of Exact Aggregation," *Economics Letters*, 9:119–126.

Lehr, J. (1885): *Beitrëge zur Statistik der Preise*. Frankfurt: J. D. Sauerländer.

Leontief, W. (1936): "Composite Commodities and the Problem of Index Numbers," *Econometrica*, 4:39–59.

Leontief, W. (1947a): "Introduction to a Theory of the Internal Structure of Functional Relationships," *Econometrica*, 15:361–373.

Leontief, W. (1947b): "A Note on the Interrelation of Subsets of Independent Variables of a Continuous Function with Continuous First Derivatives," *Bulletin of the American Mathematical Society*, 53:343–350.

Lerner, A. P. (1935): "A Note on the Theory of Price Index Numbers," *Review of Economic Studies*, vol. III, No. 1, pp. 50–56.

Liviatan, N. and D. Patinkin. (1961): "On the Economic Theory of Price Indices," *Economic Development and Cultural Change*, 9:501–536.

Lloyd, P. J. (1975): "Substitution Effects and Biases in Nontrue Price Indices," *American Economic Review*, 65:301–313.

Malmquist, S. (1953): "Index Numbers and Indifference Surfaces," *Trabajos de Estadistica*, 4:209–242.

Mankiw, N. G. and D. Romer (eds.). (1991): *New Keynesian Economics*, vol. 1: *Imperfect Competition and Sticky Prices*. Cambridge, MA: MIT Press.

Marris, R. (1958): *Economic Arithmetic*. London: Macmillan.

Maunder, W. F. (ed.). (1970): *Bibliography of Index Numbers*. University of London: The Athlone Press.

Mitchell, W. C. (1921): *The Making and Using of Index Numbers*, Bulletin 284, Bureau of Labor Statistics, Washington, D.C.

Montgomery, J. K. (1929): *Is There a Theoretically Correct Price Index of a Group of Commodities?* Rome: L'Universale Tipografica Poliglotta.

Montgomery, J. K. (1937): *The Mathematical Problem of the Price Index*. London: P. S. King.

Moorsteen, R. (1961): "On Measuring Productive Potential and Relative Efficiency," *Quarterly Journal of Economics*, 75:451–461.

Morgenstern, O. (1983): *On the Accuracy of Economic Observations*. Princeton, N.J.: Princeton University Press.

Mudget, B. D. (1951): *Index Numbers*. New York: Wiley.

Muellbauer, J. (1971): "The 'Pure Theory of the National Output Deflator' Revisited," Warwick Economic Research Paper 16, University of Warwick, Coventry, England.

Muellbauer, J. (1972): "The Theory of True Input Price Indices," revision of University of Warwick Economic Research Paper 17, University of Warwick, Coventry, England.

Muellbauer, J. (1973): "The 'Pure Theory of the True Cost-of-Living Index' Revisited," Warwick Economic Research Paper 15, University of Warwick, Coventry, England.

Muellbauer, J. (1974a): "Household Production Theory, Quality and the 'Hedonic Technique'," *American Economic Review*, 64:977–994.

Muellbauer, J. (1974b): "The Political Economy of Price Indices," Birkbeck Discussion Paper No. 22, March. London: Birkbeck College.

Muellbauer, J. (1975a): "Aggregation, Income Distribution and Consumer Demand," *Review of Economic Studies*, 42:525–543.

Muellbauer, J. (1975b): "The Cost of Living and Taste and Quality Change," *Journal of Economic Theory*, 10:269–283.

Muellbauer, J. (1976): "Community Preferences and the Representative Consumer," *Econometrica*, 44:979–999.

Nataf, A. (1948): "Sur la Possibilité de Construction de Certains Macromodèles," *Econometrica*, 16:232–244.

Newman, P. (1987): "Duality," in *The New Palgrave: A Dictionary of Economics*, vol. 1, J. Eatwell, M. Milgate, and P. Newman, pp. 924–934. London: Macmillan.

Nordhaus, W. and J. Shoven. (1974): "Inflation 1973: The Year of Infamy," *Challenge*, May–June. 17(2):14–22.

Paasche, H. (1874): "Über die Preisentwicklung der letzten Jahre nach den Hamburger Börsennotierungen," *Jahrbècher für Nationalökonomie und Statistik*, 23:168–178.

Pencavel, J. H. (1977): "Constant-Utility Index Numbers of Real Wages," *American Economic Review*, 67:91–100.

Phlips, L. (1983): *Applied Consumption Analysis*, 2nd ed. Amsterdam: North-Holland.

Phlips, L. and R. Sanz-Ferrer. (1975): "A Taste-Dependent True Index of the Cost of Living," *Review of Economics and Statistics*, 42:495–501.

Pierson, N. G. (1895): "Index Numbers and Appreciation of Gold," *Economic Journal*, 5:329–335.

Pierson, N. G. (1896): "Further Considerations on Index-Numbers," *Economic Journal*, 6:127–131.

Pigou, A. C. (1912): *Wealth and Welfare*. London: Macmillan.

Pigou, A. C. (1932): *The Economics of Welfare*, 4th ed. London: Macmillan.

Pollak, R. A. (1970): "Habit Formation and Dynamic Demand Functions," *Journal of Political Economy*, 78:745–763.

Pollak, R. A. (1971): "The Theory of the Cost-of-Living Index," Research Discussion Paper 11, Office of Prices and Living Conditions, Bureau of Labor Statistics,

Washington, D.C. Reprinted (1983) in *Price Level Measurement; Proceedings from a Conference Sponsored by Minister of Supply and Services Canada*, W. E. Diewert and C. Montmarquette (eds.), pp. 87–161. Ottowa: Minister of Supply and Services Canada. Also reprinted (1989) in *The Theory of the Cost-of-Living Index*, R. A. Pollack, pp. 3–52. New York: Oxford University Press. Also reprinted (1990) in *Price Level Measurement*, W. E. Diewert (ed.), pp. 5–77. Amsterdam: North-Holland.

Pollak, R. A. (1975): "Subindexes of the Cost-of-Living Index," *International Economic Review*, 16:135–150. Reprinted in Pollak (1989), pp. 53–69.

Pollak, R. A. (1978): "Welfare Evaluation and the Cost-of-Living Index in the Household Production Model," *American Economic Review*, 68:285–299.

Pollak, R. A. (1980): "Group Cost-of-Living Indexes," *American Economic Review*, 70:273–278.

Pollak, R. A. (1981): "The Social Cost of Living Index," *Journal of Public Economics*, 15:311–336. Reprinted in Pollak (1989), pp. 128–152.

Pollak, R. A. (1983): "The Treatment of 'Quality' in the Cost-of-Living Index," *Journal of Public Economics*, 20:25–53.

Pollak, R. A. (1989): *The Theory of the Cost-of-Living Index*. New York: Oxford University Press.

Richter, M. (1966): "Invariance Axioms and Economic Indexes," *Econometrica*, 34:739–755.

Ruggles, R. (1967): "Price Indexes and International Price Comparisons," in *Ten Economic Studies in the Tradition of Irving Fisher*, W. Fellner, et al. (eds.), pp. 171–205 New York: John Wiley.

Russell, R. R. (1985): "Measures of Technical Efficiency," *Journal of Economic Theory*, 35:109–126.

Russell, R. R. (1990): "Continuity of Measures of Technical Efficiency," *Journal of Economic Theory*, 51:255–267.

Rybczynski, T. M. (1956): "Factor Endowment and Relative Commodity Prices," *Economica*, 22:336–341.

Samuelson, P. A. (1947): *Foundations of Economic Analysis*. Cambridge, MA: Harvard University Press.

Samuelson, P. A. (1950): "Evaluation of Real National Income," *Oxford Economic Papers*, New Series, 2:1–29. Reprinted in *The Collected Scientific Papers of Paul A. Samuelson*, vol. 2, J. E. Stiglitz (ed.), pp. 1044–1072. Cambridge, MA: M.I.T. Press.

Samuelson, P.A. (1961): "The Evaluation of 'Social Income': Capital Formation and Wealth," in *The Theory of Capital*, F.A. Lutz and D.C. Hague (eds.), pp. 32–57. London: Macmillan.

Samuelson, P. A. (1974): "Analytical Notes on International Real-Income Measures," *The Economic Journal*, 84:595–608.

Samuelson, P. A. and S. Swamy. (1974): "Invariant Economic Index Numbers and Canonical Duality: Survey and Synthesis," *American Economic Review*, 64:566–593.

Sato, K. (1976a): "The Ideal Log-Change Index Number," *Review of Economics and Statistics*, 58:223–228.

Sato, K. (1976b): "The Meaning and Measurement of the Real Value Added Index," *Review of Economics and Statistics*, 58:434–442.

Sato, K. (1980): "The Price Reversal Test and Economic Indexes," *Satistische Hefte*, 21:127–130.

Schultz, H. (1939): "A Misunderstanding in Index-Number Theory: The True Konüs Condition on Cost-of-Living Index Numbers and Its Limitations," *Econometrica*, 7:1–9.

Sen, A. K. (1970): "Real National Income," *Review of Economic Studies*, 43:19–40.

Sen, A. K. (1973): *On Economic Inequality*. Oxford: Clarendon Press.

Sen, A. K. (1979): "The Welfare Basis of Real Income Comparisons: A Survey," *Journal of Economic Literature*, 17:1–45.

Shell, K. (1966): "Comparative Statics for the Two-Sector Model," *Metroeconomica*, 18:117–124.

Shell, K. (1967): "A Model of Inventive Activity and Capital Accumulation," in *Eassays on the Theory of Economic Growth*, K. Shell (ed.), pp. 67–85. Cambridge: MIT Press.

Shell, K. (1973): "Inventive Activity, Industrial Organization and Economic Growth," in *Models of Economic Growth*, J. Mirrless and N. Stern (eds.), pp. 77–100. New York: MacMillan and Halsted.

Shell, K. (1975): "Some Reflections on the Theoretical Underpinnings of Indexes of the WPI-Type," Prepared for the BLS Round-Table Discussion of the Industrial Price Program, Washington, D. C., October 17.

Solow, R. M. (1957): "Technical Change and the Aggregate Production Function," *Review of Economics and Statistics*, 39:312–320.

Staehle, H. (1935): "A Development of the Economic Theory of Price Index Numbers," *Review of Economic Studies*, 2:163–188.

Staehle, H. (1936): "A Note on Index Numbers," *Review of Economic Studies*, 3:153–155.

Staehle, H. (1937): "A General Method for the Comparison of the Price of Living," *Review of Economic Papers*, 4:205–214.

Stolper, W. F. and P. A. Samuelson. (1941): "Protection and Real Wages," *Review of Economic Studies*, 9:58–73.

Stone, R. (1956): *Quantity and Price Indexes in National Accounts*. Paris: The Organization for European Cooperation.

Stone, R. (1951): *The Role of Measurement in Economics*. Cambridge, MA: Harvard University Press.

Theil, H. (1960): "Best Linear Index Numbers of Prices and Quantities," *Econometrica*, 28:464–480.

Theil, H. (1968): "On the Geometry and the Numerical Approximation of Cost-of-Living and Real Income Indices," *De Economist*, 116, pp. 677–689.

Theil, H. (1973): "A New Index Number-Formula," *Review of Economics and Statistics*, 55:498–502.

Triplett, J. E. (1971): "Quality Bias in Price Indexes and New Methods of Quality Measurement," in *Price Indexes and Quality Change*, Z. Griliches (ed.), pp. 180–214. Cambridge, MA: Harvard University Press.

Triplett, J. E. (1975a): "Consumer Demand and Characteristics of Consumption Goods," in *Household Production and Consumption, Studies in Income and Wealth*, No. 40, E. Terleckyj (ed.), pp. 305–323. National Bureau of Economic Research, Conference on Research in Income and Wealth. New York: Columbia University Press.

Triplett, J. E. (1975b): "The Measurement of Inflation: A Survey of Research on the Accuracy of Price Indexes," in *Analysis of Inflation*, P. H. Earl (ed.), pp. 19–82. Lexington, MA: D. C. Health and Company Lexington Books.

Triplett, J. E. (1983a): "Concepts of Quality in Input and Output Price Measures: A Resolution of the User-Value Resource-Cost Debate," in *The U. S. National Income and Product Accounts: Selected Topics*, Murray F. Foss. (ed.), pp. 269–311. Chicago: The University of Chicago Press.

Triplett, J. E. (ed.). (1983b): *The Measurement of Labor Cost*, NBER Studies in Income and Wealth, vol. 44. Chicago: University of Chicago Press.

Triplett, J. E. (1988): "Price Index Research and its Influence on Data: A Historical Review," Paper Presented at the 50th Anniversary of the Conference on Income and Wealth, Washington, D.C., May 12.

Triplett, J. E. (1992): "Economic Theory and BEA's Alternative Quantity and Price Indexes," *Survey of Current Business*, 72(4):49–52.

Uzawa, H. (1962): "Production Functions with Constant Elasticities of Substitution," *Review of Economic Studies*, 29:291–299.

Vartia, Y. O. (1976): "Ideal Log-Change Index Numbers," *Scandinavian Journal of Statistics*, 3:121–126.

von Hofsten, E. (1952): *Price Indexes and Quality Change*. London: Allen and Unwin.

von Hoftsten, E. (1952): *Price Indexes and Quality Change*. Stockholm: Bokförlaget Forum.

Wald, A. (1937): "Zur Theorie der Preisindexziffern," *Zeitschrift für Nationalökonomie*, 8:179–219.

Wald, A. (1939): "A New Formula for the Index of Cost of Living," *Econometrica*, 7:319–335.

Walsh, C. M. (1921): "The Best Form of Index Number: Discussion," *Quarterly Publication of the American Statistical Association*, 17:537–544.

Wald, A. (1924): "Professor Edgeworth's Views on Index-Numbers," *Quarterly Journal of Economics*, 38:500–519.

Weinberg, J. (1980): "A Note on Debreu's Coefficient of Resource Utilization," Discussion Paper 71, University of Bonn.

Wicksell, K. (1958): *Selected Papers on Economic Theory*. Cambridge, MA: Harvard University Press.

Zieschang, K. D. (1984): "An Extended Farrell Technical Efficiency Measure," *Journal of Economic Theory*, 33:387–396.

Index